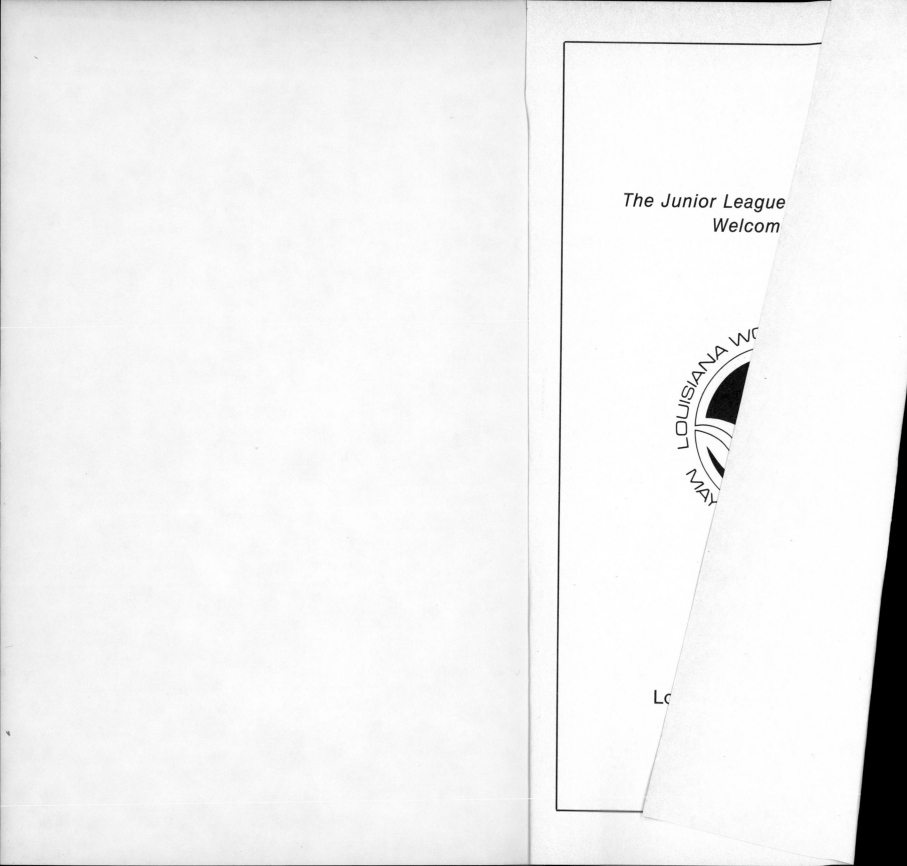

The Junior League
Welcom

LOUISIANA WO

MAY

Lo

Jambalaya

The official cookbook of the
Louisiana World Exposition

Published by
THE JUNIOR LEAGUE
OF NEW ORLEANS, INC.

For additional copies of *Jambalaya,* send $11.95 each, plus $2.00 shipping.

To order *The Plantation Cookbook,* send $17.95 each, plus $2.00 shipping.

(Louisiana residents add 3% tax.)

The Junior League of New Orleans Publications
4319 Carondelet St.
New Orleans, La. 70115

1st Printing   August 1980   20,000
2nd Printing   December 1980   20,000
Revised Edition   October 1981   20,000
World's Fair Edition   July 1983   20,000
World's Fair Edition   March 1984   100,000

ISBN 0-9604774-2-X
Library of Congress Catalog #81-82780

Printed in USA by
Hart Graphics, Inc.
8000 Shoal Creek
Austin, Texas 78758

CONTENTS

INTRODUCTION

Welcome to the 1984 Louisiana World Exposition and its 82 acres of sights designed to stimulate the senses and educate the mind while you have a carefree vacation.

We hope that while you are here, you will also take time to see the sights of the city - the French Quarter, the Garden District, the Irish Channel, the lakefront, Algiers - each of which offers its own flavor to New Orleans, where you are likely to hear French, Spanish, Southern drawls and a way of speaking that sounds remarkably like the Brooklyn brogue. The food offered here is as varied as the accents, and **JAMBALAYA** presents a sampling of the best of what is labeled New Orleans cooking.

The Junior League of New Orleans, which prepared this cookbook, is another vital part of this community. Since its founding here in 1923, this women's volunteer organization has contributed to and has been a force behind many projects working to improve life in New Orleans. The Junior League has helped support Big Brothers, the Audubon Zoo Education Program, Charity Hospital endeavors, children's art and theater, the Louisiana Nature Center, the Parenting Center, the Volunteer and Information Agency, Children's Hospital, educational television, the Holman Vocational Center for retarded teen-agers, the Preservation Resource Center and a score of other programs. Proceeds from the sale of **JAMBALAYA** will provide further funds to continue the civic endeavors of the Junior League of New Orleans. It is to these endeavors that we dedicate this book.

Artist: Ed Biggs
Photographer: Paul Rico
Sketches: Ann Strub

Hors d'Oeuvres & Appetizers

SPICY STUFFED MUSHROOMS JAMBALAYA

Preheat oven to 325°   **Serves 12**

1	pound large fresh mushrooms	3	tablespoons grated Parmesan cheese
2	tablespoons butter	1	tablespoon chopped parsley
½	cup finely chopped yellow onion	½	teaspoon seasoned salt
½	cup finely diced pepperoni	¼	teaspoon oregano
¼	cup finely chopped green pepper	⅛	teaspoon pepper
¼	teaspoon pressed garlic	1	cup chicken broth
2	cups finely crushed Ritz cracker crumbs		

Wash mushrooms and drain on paper towels. Remove mushroom stems and finely chop. Melt butter in a skillet; add onion and sauté 5 minutes. Add pepperoni, green pepper, garlic, and mushroom stems. Cook vegetables and meat 10 minutes, until tender but not brown. Add cracker crumbs, cheese, parsley, salt, oregano, and pepper. Mix well; stir in broth. Spoon stuffing into mushroom caps, rounding the tops. Place mushrooms in a shallow pan with about ¼ inch water. Bake 25 minutes. Serve immediately.

SHRIMP DIP DELIGHT

Serves 6

- 1 pound raw shrimp
- 1 8-ounce package cream cheese, softened
- ½ cup finely chopped green onions
- ½ cup chopped celery
- 3 tablespoons lemon juice
- 2 tablespoons chopped fresh parsley
- ½ teaspoon salt
- ⅛ teaspoon cayenne pepper
- ½ cup mayonnaise

Boil, peel, devein, and chop shrimp. In a bowl, blend cream cheese with onions, celery, lemon juice, parsley, salt, cayenne, and mayonnaise. Fold in shrimp. Cover and refrigerate. Serve with crackers or fresh celery and carrot sticks.

SHRIMP MEUNIÈRE

Serves 6 to 8

- 1 stick butter
- 1 cup finely chopped green onions
- ½ cup finely chopped celery (use inside stalks)
- ¼ cup finely chopped fresh parsley
- ⅓ cup finely chopped green pepper
- 1 tablespoon garlic purée
- 1 teaspoon salt
- 1 teaspoon pepper
- 1 tablespoon Worcestershire sauce
- 1 tablespoon corn starch
- ¼ cup dry white wine
- 3 pounds raw shrimp, peeled and deveined
- Toast points or saffron rice

In a large, covered skillet, slowly melt butter. Add vegetables, garlic purée, salt, pepper, and Worcestershire sauce. Blend thoroughly, cover, and simmer 30 minutes, stirring occasionally. Dissolve corn starch in wine. Blend mixture into vegetables. Add shrimp, cover, and simmer 5 to 10 minutes. Serve immediately over toast points as an appetizer or over saffron rice as an entrée. To reheat, place in top of double boiler and heat slowly. Serves 8 as an appetizer, 6 as an entrée.

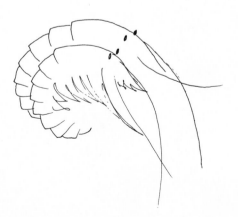

SEAFOOD GLACÉ

Makes 2 to 3 dozen

Make ahead

2	envelopes gelatin	¼	teaspoon Tabasco
½	cup cold water	3	dozen boiled shrimp or
2	10-ounce cans consommé		crawfish, *or* ½ pound fresh
1	tablespoon lemon juice		crabmeat
2	tablespoons finely	2-3	dozen crackers
	chopped green onions		Mayonnaise
2	tablespoons finely		
	chopped fresh parsley		

Pour gelatin in water and stir. Heat consommé until hot, but not boiling. Add lemon juice, onions, parsley, Tabasco, and gelatin to consommé; stir. Grease 3 egg holders or small muffin tins. Divide seafood in bottom of each holder or tin. Pour consommé mixture over seafood, cover, and refrigerate 6 to 8 hours. Unmold and serve on plain crackers spread thinly with mayonnaise.

SHRIMP APPETIZER

Serves 12 to 14

Make a day ahead

6	pounds raw shrimp in shells	1	tablespoon Worcestershire sauce
2	bay leaves	1	5-ounce jar fresh horseradish
1	tablespoon celery seed		
¾	cup salt	1	5-ounce jar hot creole mustard
1	teaspoon cayenne pepper		
2	cups oil	1	cup thinly sliced yellow onion
½	cup catsup		
3	tablespoons lemon juice		Salt to taste
¼	cup apple cider vinegar		Pepper to taste

In a large pot, place shrimp; cover with water. Add bay leaves, celery seed, salt, and cayenne. Bring to a boil and cook 5 minutes, until shrimp are pink. Drain and peel.

Combine remaining ingredients. Add shrimp. Cover and refrigerate. Serve with toothpicks or on crackers.

CAPONATA

Make 4 days ahead

2	pounds eggplant, peeled and cut into ½ inch cubes	½	cup vodka
1½	tablespoons salt	2	teaspoons sugar, dissolved in ½ cup wine vinegar
½	cup olive oil		
1	cup chopped yellow onion	3	cups canned Italian plum tomatoes, partially drained and chopped
1½	cups finely chopped celery		
¾	teaspoon minced garlic		
1	cup sliced pimiento stuffed olives	4	tablespoons tomato paste
		6	finely chopped anchovies
1	cup sliced pitted black olives	1	teaspoon black pepper
		½	teaspoon Tabasco
¼	cup capers		

Sprinkle eggplant with salt and let stand in a colander 1 hour. Drain well on paper towels. Heat oil in a large, heavy saucepan; sauté onion, celery, and garlic 10 minutes. Remove vegetables. Place eggplant in pan and cook, stirring until lightly browned, about 15 minutes. Add more oil if necessary. Return vegetable mixture to pan along with remaining ingredients and bring to a boil. Reduce heat and simmer 45 minutes, stirring frequently. Refrigerate at least 4 days before serving. Serve with crackers or melba toast. Caponata will keep several months under refrigeration, but does not freeze well.

CRABMEAT STUFFED MUSHROOMS

Preheat oven to 350°

12	large, fresh mushrooms, stems removed and reserved	½	cup crabmeat
		2	tablespoons sherry
		1	tablespoon chopped fresh parsley
6	tablespoons butter		
1	cup finely chopped yellow onion	½	teaspoon salt
		¼	teaspoon pepper
1	tablespoon flour	½	cup cornflake crumbs

Wash mushrooms and dry on paper towels. Place mushrooms caps, top side down, on a well-greased baking pan. Finely chop mushroom stems. In 3 tablespoons butter, sauté onion until golden, about 5 minutes. Add stems and cook 5 minutes. Stir in flour, crabmeat, sherry, parsley, salt, and pepper. Sauté 2 to 3 minutes, stirring gently. Remove from heat and stuff mushroom caps with crabmeat mixture. Sprinkle with corn flake crumbs and dot each cap with a pat of remaining butter. Bake 20 minutes. Serve immediately.

MARINATED CRAB CLAWS

Serves 6 to 8

Make a day ahead

1   1-pound can fresh crab
    claws

Marinade

1   0.6-ounce package dry
    Italian salad dressing mix,
    prepared with ¾ cup olive
    oil and ¼ cup champagne
    vinegar
½   teaspoon oregano
1   tablespoon lemon juice
½   teaspoon finely minced
    garlic

¼   cup dried parsley flakes
¼   teaspoon salt
½   teaspoon pepper
¼   cup grated Parmesan
    cheese
1   tablespoon white wine
1   tablespoon
    Worcestershire sauce

Place crab claws in a heavy plastic bag with marinade, leaving enough
room for ingredients to mix. Place bag in a flat dish and refrigerate,
turning several times.

MOLDED CRABMEAT OR SHRIMP RING

Serves 12

Make a day ahead

1   10-ounce can cream of
    mushroom soup
6   ounces cream cheese,
    softened
2   tablespoons gelatin
6   tablespoons white wine
1   cup finely chopped green
    onions
1   cup finely chopped celery
1   pound white crabmeat *or* 4
    pounds raw shrimp,
    cooked, peeled, and
    deveined

1   cup mayonnaise
½   teaspoon Tabasco
2   teaspoons salt
2   tablespoons lemon juice
2   tablespoons
    Worcestershire sauce
½   teaspoon pepper
1   2-ounce jar pimiento, *or* ¼
    cup sliced stuffed olives

In top of a double boiler, warm soup. Add cream cheese and whisk
until well blended. Dissolve gelatin in wine; add to cheese mixture.
Blend and remove from heat. Add remaining ingredients and pour
into a well-greased 8 inch mold. Cover and refrigerate overnight.
Unmold and garnish with pimientos or stuffed olives. Serve with melba
toast or crackers.

HOT CRABMEAT

1½ sticks butter
1 cup finely chopped yellow onion
½ cup finely chopped green onions
¾ teaspoon pressed garlic
½ cup finely chopped fresh parsley

4 tablespoons flour
1 cup milk
1 cup white wine
1 pound lump crabmeat
1½ cups croutons
½ cup French dressing

In a small skillet, sauté vegetables in one stick butter until tender. Drain vegetables on paper towel. In the top of a double boiler, melt remaining butter and gradually stir in flour. Slowly add milk and cook until mixture thickens, about 15 minutes. Slowly add wine, folding with a wire whisk. Add sautéed vegetables. Gently fold in crabmeat and keep hot over double boiler until ready to transfer to a chafing dish. Soak croutons in French dressing 20 minutes. Fold saturated croutons into crabmeat just prior to serving.

CRAWFISH OR SHRIMP MOUSSE   Serves 12

Make a day ahead

2 10-ounce cans tomato soup
1 8-ounce package cream cheese
3 tablespoons gelatin
⅔ cup cold water
1 pound crawfish tails, coarsley chopped, or 2 cups cooked, peeled, and chopped shrimp
1 cup mayonnaise

1½ cups finely chopped celery
½ cup finely chopped green onions
½ cup finely chopped green pepper
1 teaspoon Worcestershire sauce
¾ teaspoon Tabasco
½ teaspoon salt
1 tablespoon lemon juice

In a large saucepan, heat soup. Add cream cheese, melt, and whisk until smooth. Dissolve gelatin in water. Add to saucepan; mix well. Remove from heat and cool. Add crawfish tails, mayonnaise, celery, onions, green pepper, and seasonings. Pour into a well-greased 1-quart fish mold, or a 9 inch spring mold. Cover and refrigerate overnight. Unmold and serve with melba toast or crackers. Will serve 8 as a salad.

CAVIAR MOLD

Serves 12 to 16

Make a day ahead

1	cup finely chopped green onions	¼	teaspoon cayenne pepper
1	stick and 2 tablespoons butter, softened	¼	teaspoon white pepper
		2	tablespoons mayonnaise
5	hard-boiled eggs, finely grated		Lettuce or parsley
½	teaspoon salt		

Topping

½	cup sour cream
1	2-ounce jar black caviar

In a skillet, sauté onions with 2 tablespoons butter until soft, about 5 minutes. Drain on paper towel; cool 15 minutes. Mix onions with eggs, remaining butter, seasonings, and mayonnaise. Lightly grease a 2-cup mold and fill with egg and onion mixture. Cover and refrigerate overnight.

Unmold and spread sour cream over top and sides. Top with caviar. Serve with crackers or melba toast.

OYSTERS DUNBAR

Serves 6

Preheat oven to 350°

2	artichokes, boiled	⅛	teaspoon pepper
3½	dozen oysters	½	teaspoon thyme
1½	cups oyster liquid	¼	teaspoon Tabasco
1	stick butter	1	teaspoon Worcestershire sauce
2	tablespoons flour		
½	cup finely chopped green onions	½	cup bread crumbs
		¼	cup grated Parmesan cheese
½	teaspoon minced garlic		
¼	teaspoon salt	6-8	thin lemon slices

Separate artichoke leaves from heart. Reserve 24 leaves. Scrape remaining leaves and mash pulp with a fork. Coarsely chop artichoke hearts.

Boil oysters in their liquid until edges curl, 3 to 5 minutes. Drain, reserving 2 cups liquid. In a heavy saucepan, melt butter and add flour. Stir until brown. Add onions and garlic and cook 3 minutes. Add liquid and simmer 15 minutes. Add salt, pepper, thyme, Tabasco, and Worcestershire sauce. Add scrapings, oysters, and hearts; simmer 10 minutes. Spoon oyster mixture into individual ramekins and sprinkle with bread crumbs and cheese. Recipe can be made ahead up to this point. Bake 15 minutes. Broil 3 to 5 minutes. Garnish each ramekin with a lemon slice and surround with artichoke leaves for dipping.

OYSTERS ESPAGÑOLE

Serves 4 to 6

2	cups Sauce Espagñole	4	dozen oysters, well drained
1	cup Blender Hollandaise		Toast points
2	tablespoons butter	¼	cup finely chopped fresh parsley
2½	cups sliced fresh mushrooms		
6	tablespoons chopped green onions		

Prepare sauces. In a heavy Dutch oven, sauté mushrooms in butter. Add onions and simmer 10 minutes. Add oysters, stirring constantly. Before adding sauces, spoon out and discard excess liquid. When edges of oysters have curled, slowly add sauces. Blend and heat thoroughly. Serve immediately over toast points and garnish with parsley.

For a different dish, serve recipe over prepared tournedos.

Sauce Espagñole

2	tablespoons flour	2	tablespoons lemon juice
2	tablespoons butter	2	tablespoons sherry
1	cup beef stock, heated	2	tablespoons Kitchen Bouquet
3	tablespoons tomato paste	¼	teaspoon Tabasco

In a heavy saucepan, brown flour in butter until dark brown, about 10 minutes. Add stock, tomato paste, lemon juice, sherry, Kitchen Bouquet, and Tabasco. Stir until thick and smooth. Makes 2 cups.

Blender Hollandaise

2	sticks butter	¼	teaspoon salt
2	eggs yolks	¼	teaspoon Tabasco
2	tablespoons lemon juice		

Heat butter; remove from heat. Place yolks, lemon juice, salt, and Tabasco into blender. Turn blender on and off several times. Add butter in a slow, steady stream, turning switch on and off until all butter has been absorbed. Makes 1 cup.

OYSTERS ELLIS

Serves 6

6	tablespoons butter	¾	teaspoon Tabasco
3	tablespoons flour	¼	teaspoon pepper
1	cup beef stock, heated	¼	pound mushrooms, sliced
3	tablespoons tomato paste	6	tablespoons minced green onions
2	tablespoons sherry		
2	tablespoons lemon juice	¼	cup finely chopped fresh parsley
2	tablespoons Kitchen Bouquet, or 1 tablespoon Kitchen Bouquet plus 1 tablespoon Pickapeppa Sauce	4	dozen oysters, well drained
			Toast points

In a heavy skillet, heat 3 tablespoons butter; gradually add flour, stirring constantly until roux is brown, about 10 minutes. Add stock, tomato paste, sherry, lemon juice, Kitchen Bouquet, Tabasco, and pepper. Blend until smooth.

In a large saucepan, sauté mushrooms in remaining 3 tablespoons butter. Add onions and parsley. Cook 5 minutes. Add oysters, stirring constantly. Spoon off and reserve excess liquid. Slowly add sauce to oyster mixture, blending until well heated. If sauce is too thick, add a little oyster liquid. Serve immediately with toast points.

BOURSIN CHEESE

Serves 6 to 8

Make ahead

2	tablespoons butter, softened	1	tablespoon frozen or freeze-dried chives
½	teaspoon minced garlic		Salt to taste
¼	teaspoon dry dill	8	ounces cream cheese, softened
⅛	teaspoon thyme		
2	tablespoons finely chopped fresh parsley		Freshly ground pepper

In a small bowl, using a wooden spoon, blend butter with garlic, dill, thyme, parsley, chives, and salt. When well mixed, work in cream cheese until smooth. Chill. Mold into desired shape. Sprinkle all sides with pepper. Cover and refrigerate.

BRANDY CHEESE

Serves 8

Make a day ahead

8   ounces sharp cheddar
    cheese, grated
8   ounces cream cheese,
    softened
3   tablespoons grated yellow
    onion
1   teaspoon Worcestershire
    sauce

4   dashes Tabasco
¼   teaspoon salt
⅛   teaspoon white pepper
⅓   cup brandy
½   cup finely chopped pecans
¼   cup chopped fresh parsley

In a bowl cream cheeses together. Fold in onion, Worcestershire sauce, Tabasco, salt, pepper, and brandy. Blend. Add pecans and parsley. Spoon into a 2-cup crock or bowl and refrigerate overnight. This keeps up to 2 weeks, but does not freeze well. Serve with crackers.

CHEESE DROPS

Makes 5 dozen

Freezes well

Preheat oven to 350°

2   cups flour
1   teaspoon cayenne pepper
½   teaspoon salt
2   sticks butter, softened

½   pound grated sharp
    cheddar cheese, room
    temperature
1   cup chopped pecans
2   teaspoons caraway seeds

Sift dry ingredients. In a large bowl, cream butter and cheese. Add dry ingredients. By hand, fold in pecans and caraway seeds. Drop by half teaspoons onto an ungreased baking sheet. Bake 15 to 18 minutes.

CHEESE STRAWS

Makes 50 to 75

Preheat oven to 325°

6-8	tablespoons butter, melted	2	teaspoons baking powder
2	cups grated extra sharp cheddar cheese, room temperature	1	teaspoon salt
1	cup sifted flour	½-1	teaspoon cayenne pepper
			Pecan halves, optional

Cream 6 tablespoons butter and cheese. Add flour, baking powder, salt, and cayenne. If dough is too dry, add more butter. Use a cookie gun to make straws or roll into small balls using 1 teaspoonful dough. Press a pecan half into center of each. Bake on a greased baking sheet until crisp, dried out, and beginning to turn brown.

CURRIED CHEESE PÂTÉ

Serves 24

Can be made ahead

2	8-ounce packages cream cheese, softened	2	tablespoons Worcestershire sauce
2	cups grated sharp cheddar cheese, room temperature	1	teaspoon curry
6	tablespoons sherry	½	teaspoon salt

Topping

1	8-ounce jar chutney	½	cup chopped green onions
½	cup chopped peanuts	½	cup grated coconut

Cream cheeses with sherry, Worcestershire sauce, curry, and salt. Line an 8-inch cake pan with plastic wrap, or lightly grease an 8-inch spring mold. Fill pan or mold with cheese mixture. Cover with plastic wrap and chill 4 hours. Mold can be frozen at this point. (If frozen, defrost at room temperature before garnishing with condiments.)

Unmold pâté on a large platter. Garnish in layers with chutney, peanuts, onions, and coconut. Serve with crackers. May be refrigerated up to 3 days.

LIVER PÂTÉ

Can be made ahead

1	pound chicken livers	1	teaspoon ground nutmeg
½	teaspoon salt	1	teaspoon white or black pepper
2	sticks butter, cut into pieces	¼	teaspoon cayenne pepper
2	tablespoons grated yellow onion	3-4	tablespoons brandy
½	teaspoon ground cloves	½	cup sour cream
		1	2-ounce jar caviar

In a heavy saucepan, barely cover livers with water; add salt and bring to a boil. Simmer 15 minutes. Drain and partially cool.

Place livers in a food processor fitted with metal blade. Add butter, onion, cloves, nutmeg, pepper, cayenne, and brandy; blend. Spoon pâté into a 2-cup crock, cover, and refrigerate. If frozen, pâté may be a little dry when thawed. If dry, add a little brandy and mash with a fork. Serve with melba toast. Crocks of pâté may be spread with sour cream and topped with caviar.

MARBLEHEAD PÂTÉ

Serves 12

Make ahead

2½	sticks salted butter	½	teaspoon thyme
1½	cups coarsely chopped green onions	1	teaspoon basil
1	pound chicken livers	1	teaspoon garlic salt
½	cup brandy	1	teaspoon pepper
1½	teaspoons salt	1	teaspoon nutmeg
		10	black olives, sliced

In a heavy skillet, melt 1 stick butter; sauté onions 5 minutes. Add livers and cook 5 minutes until lightly browned. Add remaining 1½ sticks butter, brandy, salt, thyme, basil, garlic salt, pepper, and nutmeg. Cook 2 minutes. Blend all ingredients in a food processor or blender. Mixture will be liquid. Line a 4-cup mold with waxed paper or foil. Place black olive slices on bottom of mold. Add liquid and refrigerate until set. Unmold and serve with melba toast or crackers.

HOT ASPARAGUS ROLL-UPS

Makes 20

Freezes well

Preheat oven to 400°

20	slices thin white bread	⅛	teaspoon cayenne pepper
3	ounces blue cheese, softened	½	cup finely chopped green onions
8	ounces cream cheese, softened	20	canned asparagus spears
1	egg, beaten	¾	cup melted butter
¼	teaspoon garlic salt	½	cup finely chopped fresh parsley

Trim crust from bread and flatten slices with a rolling pin. Mix cheeses, egg, garlic salt, and cayenne. Fold in onions. Spread bread slices generously and evenly with cheese mixture. Roll an asparagus spear in each slice of bread, sealing well by using a little cheese mixture to bind edge to roll. At this point, these can be frozen and thawed as needed. Roll each canapé in butter and place on an ungreased baking sheet. Bake 15 to 20 minutes until lightly browned. Garnish with parsley.

ARTICHOKE BALLS

Makes 60 to 80

Make a day ahead

1	6-ounce jar marinated artichoke hearts, drained (reserve marinade), finely chopped	1	tablespoon Worcestershire sauce
1	14-ounce can artichoke hearts, packed in water, drained, finely chopped	½-1	teaspoon liquid smoke
		½	teaspoon Tabasco
		1½	cups Italian seasoned bread crumbs
2	eggs	1	3-ounce can grated Parmesan, *or* Romano cheese
1	tablespoon garlic juice		

In a large bowl, beat eggs with reserved marinade and blend with garlic juice, Worcestershire sauce, liquid smoke, and Tabasco. Add artichokes and bread crumbs. Form little balls and roll each ball in grated cheese. Refrigerate. Serve at room temperature, or place on a lightly-greased baking sheet and bake in a 300° preheated oven 7 to 10 minutes. Serve immediately. Can be refrigerated up to 1 week.

MUSHROOM STRUDEL

Makes 4 dozen

Preheat oven to 350°

1	pound mushrooms, minced	½	teaspoon salt
1½	sticks butter	¼	teaspoon pepper
1	tablespoon oil	6-8	filo leaves (a Greek pastry
½	cup minced yellow onion		dough packaged in paper-
1	cup minced green onions		thin leaves)
¼	teaspoon Tabasco		
½	cup sour cream		
2	tablespoons minced fresh dill, *or* 1 tablespoon dried dill		

Place mushrooms, a handful at a time, in a tea towel and squeeze out moisture. In a skillet, heat 3 tablespoons butter and oil; sauté mushrooms with onions until moisture has evaporated, about 15 minutes. Remove skillet from heat and stir in Tabasco, sour cream, dill, salt, and pepper; cool.

Keep filo leaves moist by placing them under a damp tea towel. Melt remaining butter. On a sheet of waxed paper, place one filo leaf and brush gently with butter. Place a second filo leaf directly over the first and brush with butter. Spread a 1 inch wide strip of mushroom mixture along one of the long sides of the leaves to contain filling and roll up leaves jelly-roll fashion. Place roll, seam-side down, on a buttered baking sheet. Make remaining rolls and brush them with butter. Bake 45 minutes until crisp and golden. Allow rolls to cool 5 minutes. Cut on an angle in 1 inch slices.

BACON STUFFED MUSHROOMS

Makes 2 dozen

Preheat oven to 375°

24	fresh mushrooms	1	tablespoon soy sauce
1	8-ounce package cream cheese, softened	¼	pound bacon, cooked and crumbled
½	teaspoon salt	¼	cup finely chopped fresh parsley
¼	teaspoon pressed garlic		
⅓	cup finely chopped yellow onion		

Wash mushrooms and drain on paper towels. Remove stems and chop. Blend cream cheese, salt, garlic, onion, soy sauce, half of the bacon, and mushrooms stems until creamy. Stuff mushrooms caps with mixture and place in shallow pan. Bake 8 to 10 minutes. Remove from oven and sprinkle with remaining bacon and parsley. Serve immediately. (The cream cheese mixture can be made ahead several hours, but mushrooms must be stuffed and baked just prior to serving.)

GREEN CHILI SQUARES

Makes 4 dozen

Preheat oven to 425°

2	9-inch pastry shells	1	4-ounce can chopped
6	large eggs		green chili peppers,
2	cups hot milk		drained
¼	cup flour	½	teaspoon salt
3	cups grated Swiss cheese	¼	teaspoon pepper
1	cup grated Parmesan cheese	½	cup chopped onion

Press pastry shells into 12 × 15 jelly-roll pan, cutting to fit top edges of pan. Bake 15 minutes; remove and reduce temperature to 325°. In a large bowl, beat eggs and milk; add flour, cheeses, chili peppers, salt, pepper, and onion. Pour into crust and bake 30 to 40 minutes, or until a knife inserted in center comes out clean. Cut into small squares.

SAUSAGE HORS D'OEUVRES

Makes 6 dozen

Can be made ahead

Freezes well

1	pound ground hot sausage	1	cup sour cream
1	pound ground mild sausage	1	8-ounce jar chutney, finely chopped
¼	cup dry sherry		

In a bowl, blend sausages. Roll sausage into 1-inch balls. In a heavy skillet, cook balls until brown. With a slotted spoon, remove balls. Pour off grease, reserving crusty bits in pan. Reduce heat and add sherry, sour cream, and chutney, stirring constantly. Add balls and cook until hot. Transfer to a chafing dish and serve with toothpicks.

SPINACH DIP

Makes 2 cups

1	10-ounce package frozen chopped spinach, thawed and drained	⅛	teaspoon Tabasco
		1	cup sour cream
1	teaspoon salt	½	cup mayonnaise
¼	teaspoon pepper	½	cup finely chopped fresh parsley
½	teaspoon celery salt		
⅛	teaspoon nutmeg	½	cup minced yellow onion
¼	teaspoon garlic salt	1	teaspoon lemon juice

Mix spinach with remaining ingredients; cover and refrigerate overnight. Serve with fresh vegetables.

Soups &
Gumbos

JAMBALAYA SEAFOOD GUMBO   Serves 10

Freezes well

6	tablespoons oil	½	teaspoon black pepper
2	pounds okra, thinly sliced	1	tablespoon Worcestershire sauce
1	tablespoon flour		
2	cups finely chopped onions	1	16-ounce can whole tomatoes, cut up (reserve liquid)
½	cup finely chopped celery		
⅔	cup finely chopped green pepper	7	cups water
1	cup finely chopped green onions	2½	pounds raw shrimp, washed, peeled, and deveined
2	cloves garlic, pressed	1	pound claw crabmeat
1	6-ounce can tomato paste	2	dozen oysters and their liquid
3	large bay leaves		
¼	teaspoon thyme	2	tablespoons chopped fresh parsley
1	tablespoon salt		
½	teaspoon Tabasco	4-5	cups steamed rice
¼	teaspoon cayenne pepper		

In a large, heavy skillet, not black iron, heat 4 tablespoons oil. Add okra and cook, stirring often until stringing stops, about 40 to 50 minutes. If necessary, add more oil to prevent burning.

In a 5-quart soup pot, heat remaining 2 tablespoons oil and gradually add flour, stirring constantly until roux is dark brown. Add onions and celery and cook until tender. Add green pepper, green onions, and garlic; cook 3 minutes. Stir in tomato paste, bay leaves, thyme, salt, Tabasco, cayenne, black pepper, and Worcestershire sauce. Add tomatoes with liquid and stir until smooth. Add cooked okra. Gradually stir in water. Bring to boil, cover and simmer 30 minutes. Add shrimp and crabmeat; continue to simmer, covered, 10 minutes. Add oysters with liquid and parsley, and cook 10 minutes. If too thick, thin with water. Serve over rice.

CREAM OF ARTICHOKE SOUP

Serves 6

Best made ahead

6 small or 4 large artichokes, steamed, leaves scraped and hearts chopped to equal 3 cups (reserve ½ cup sliced hearts for garnish)	4 cups chicken stock
	1 teaspoon salt
	¼ teaspoon thyme
	¼ teaspoon pepper
	2 tablespoons lemon juice
	¼ teaspoon Tabasco
1⅓ cups chopped onions	1 cup light cream
1 tablespoon butter	1 cup heavy cream

In a heavy saucepan, sauté chopped onions in butter 5 minutes. Add artichoke scrapings, stock, salt, thyme, and pepper. Cover and simmer 15 minutes. Cool slightly; purée. Season with lemon juice and Tabasco. Stir in creams. Refrigerate several hours, or overnight. Serve cold or heat just to boiling point and garnish with sliced artichoke hearts.

CURRIED TOMATO BISQUE

Serves 10 to 12

2 tablespoons butter	½ bay leaf
1½ cups chopped onions	½ teaspoon thyme
1½ cloves garlic, pressed	½ cup rice
1-2 tablespoons curry powder	2 cups chicken stock
5 cups cored, quartered, ripe tomatoes (about 2½ pounds) (canned Italian plum tomatoes may be substituted)	⅛ teaspoon Tabasco
	1½ teaspoons salt
	2 cups milk
	1 cup heavy cream

In a large pot, melt butter and sauté onions and garlic until wilted. Sprinkle with curry and cook 3 minutes, stirring often. Add tomatoes, bay leaf, thyme, rice, stock, Tabasco, and salt. Cover and simmer 45 minutes, stirring occasionally. Remove bay leaf and purée. Add milk and cream; blend well. May be served hot or cold.

CREAM OF CARROT SOUP

Serves 6

1	pound of carrots, scraped and sliced	⅛	teaspoon thyme
1	cup chopped onion	½	teaspoon salt
4	cups chicken stock	⅛	teaspoon pepper
1	bay leaf	⅛	teaspoon Tabasco
		1	cup heavy cream

In a 2-quart saucepan, place carrots, onion, stock, bay leaf, and thyme; cover and cook until carrots are tender, about 20 minutes. Remove bay leaf; purée. Season with salt, pepper, and Tabasco. Stir in cream. May be served hot or cold.

GOLDEN CAULIFLOWER SOUP

Serves 6

1	large cauliflower, broken into florets, measuring 5 to 6 cups	8	ounces cheddar cheese, grated
1	teaspoon salt	3	cups chicken stock
3	cups water	1	teaspoon salt
1	cup finely chopped green onions	⅛	teaspoon white pepper
1	stick butter	⅛	teaspoon Tabasco
2	tablespoons flour	1	tablespoon Worcestershire sauce
2	cups whole milk, *or* 1 cup milk and 1 cup half and half cream, warmed	2	tablespoons lemon juice
			Grated cheese
			Chopped green onions
			Paprika

In a saucepan, cover and cook cauliflower in salted water until tender. Drain. In a skillet, sauté onions in butter 7 minutes; add flour and cook 2 minutes, stirring often. Slowly add milk, stirring constantly. Stir in cheese and cook until melted. Purée cauliflower and return to pot. Add stock. Stir in cheese mixture. Add salt, pepper, Tabasco, Worcestershire sauce and lemon juice. May be served hot or cold. (If chilled soup is too thick, thin with cold water or stock.) Garnish with cheese, onions, and a dash of paprika.

PECAN SOUP

Can be made ahead

2 cups pecan halves
6 cups beef stock
1 stick butter
2 tablespoons finely chopped green onions
1 clove garlic, pressed
2 tablespoons tomato paste
1 tablespoon cornstarch, dissolved in ¼ cup water

1 egg yolk
¼ cup heavy cream, room temperature
½ teaspoon salt
¼ teaspoon white pepper
⅛ teaspoon nutmeg

In a blender, grind pecans with stock. Melt butter in a 3-quart saucepan; add onions and cook 5 minutes until soft, but not brown. Add garlic and cook 1 minute. Slowly add nut mixture, tomato paste, and cornstarch. Cook 30 minutes. Beat egg yolk into cream and slowly whisk into soup. Do not boil. Season with salt, pepper, and nutmeg. May be served cold or hot.

HARVEST PUMPKIN SOUP

6 cups puréed pumpkin
3 cups chicken stock
2 cups mashed, cooked potatoes
1 cup finely chopped onion
1 cup finely chopped celery

½ teaspoon ground nutmeg
1 teaspoon salt
⅛ teaspoon white pepper
2 cups heavy cream
Grated nutmeg, chopped parsley, or snipped chives

In a large saucepan, combine pumpkin, stock, potatoes, onion, celery, and seasonings. Simmer 15 minutes. Remove from heat; cool slightly; purée. Stir in cream. Serve hot or cold. Garnish with nutmeg, parsley, or chives.

GARDEN PATCH CHOWDER

Serves 4

Best made ahead

2	cups water	¼	cup flour
1½	cups peeled, diced potatoes	1	cup milk, warmed
1	cup thinly sliced carrots	½	cup chicken broth, warmed
1	cup thinly sliced celery	8	ounces shredded cheddar cheese
⅓	cup chopped onion	⅛-¼	teaspoon dill weed
½	teaspoon salt	12-16	ounces Polish sausage, sliced ¼ inch thick, cooked and drained
1½	teaspoons pepper		
1	stick butter		

In a 2-quart saucepan, bring water to a boil; add potatoes, carrots, celery, onion, salt, and pepper. Cover and simmer 15 minutes or until vegetables are tender. In a separate 4-quart pot, melt butter, stir in flour, and cook until smooth, stirring constantly. Remove from heat and gradually stir in milk and broth. Return to heat; bring to a boil, stirring constantly. Boil 1 minute, stirring. Add cheese, stirring until melted. Add vegetables and water, dill, and sausage. Heat.

LENTIL SOUP

Serves 8

Freezes well

1	pound lentils	1	clove garlic, pressed
6	cups beef stock	1	bay leaf
2	cups water	½	teaspoon thyme
1	pound smoked sausage or ham, cut in bite-size pieces	2	cups water, if needed for desired consistency
1	cup chopped celery	¼	cup dry sherry
1	cup chopped green onions		Salt to taste
⅔	cup chopped onion		Pepper to taste
1	cup chopped carrots		Tabasco to taste
2	tablespoons chopped fresh parsley		

Rinse lentils. In a large pot, place lentils, stock, and water. Cover and simmer 1 hour. In a skillet, sauté sausage. Remove with a slotted spoon and add to lentils. In drippings, sauté vegetables until tender; add to lentils. Add bay leaf and thyme. Simmer, covered, 1 hour, stirring occasionally and adding water as necessary. Remove from heat; add sherry, salt, pepper, and Tabasco.

CREAM OF EGGPLANT SOUP
Serves 8

2	small eggplants (approximately 2 pounds)
4	tablespoons butter
1½	cups finely chopped onions
1½	cups finely chopped celery
1½	cups peeled and diced potatoes
1	teaspoon curry powder
¼	teaspoon thyme
¼-½	teaspoon basil
1	teaspoon salt
4	cups chicken stock
1½	cups half and half cream
¼	teaspoon pepper
	Tabasco to taste

Peel and slice eggplant; soak in cold salted water to cover 10 minutes. Rinse, drain, and dice. In a large, heavy saucepan, melt butter, and sauté onions, celery, potatoes, and eggplant 20 minutes, stirring often. Cover tightly and cook 40 minutes, until vegetables are tender, stirring often. Add curry, thyme, basil, and salt; stir well and cook 10 minutes. Stir in stock; cover and cook 40 minutes, stirring occasionally. Remove from heat; cool slightly; purée. Stir in half and half. Add pepper and Tabasco. If too thick, thin with milk or water. This may be made in advance and refrigerated up to 4 days.

BROCCOLI AND CHEESE SOUP
Serves 6

2	10-ounce packages frozen chopped broccoli
3½	cups chicken stock
10	large fresh mushrooms, sliced
⅔	cup finely chopped celery
⅓	cup chopped green onions
1	tablespoon finely chopped fresh parsley
2	tablespoons butter
2	teaspoons garlic salt
1½	cups grated mild cheddar cheese
½	cup sour cream
½	teaspoon Tabasco

Cook broccoli according to package directions. Drain and purée with 1½ cups stock. In a saucepan, simmer broccoli with remaining 1½ cups stock.

In a skillet, sauté vegetables in butter until tender. Season with garlic salt; add to broccoli. Cover and cook 30 minutes. Stir in cheese and sour cream. Season with Tabasco and serve hot.

BROCCOLI BISQUE

Serves 6

2	10-ounce packages frozen chopped broccoli, thawed	¾	teaspoon basil
		1	teaspoon salt
½	cup chopped onion	¼	teaspoon pepper
1	stick butter	1	tablespoon lemon juice
2	cups chicken stock	1	cup light cream

In a saucepan, sauté onion in butter 5 minutes. Add broccoli, stock, basil, salt, and pepper. Cover and simmer 15 minutes. Purée until smooth. Add lemon juice and cream. May be served hot or cold.

COLD ZUCCHINI SOUP

Serves 6

1½	pounds zucchini, peeled and sliced	1	cup heavy cream
		½	teaspoon dill weed
⅔	cup chopped yellow onion		Salt to taste
¼	cup chopped green pepper		Tabasco to taste
2½	cups chicken stock		

In a 3-quart saucepan, place zucchini, onion, green pepper, and stock. Cover and simmer 30 minutes. Cool and purée. Add cream and dill; blend well. Season with salt and Tabasco. Chill.

COLD SQUASH SOUP

Serves 4

1	pound yellow squash, thinly sliced	⅛	teaspoon white pepper
		¼	teaspoon Worcestershire sauce
⅔	cup chopped onion		
1½	cups chicken stock	3	drops Tabasco
½	cup sour cream		Bacon bits, *or* dill weed, *or* caraway seeds to garnish
¼	teaspoon salt		

In a saucepan, combine squash, onion, and 1 cup stock. Simmer, covered, 30 minutes. Purée; transfer to a bowl. Stir in remaining ½ cup stock, sour cream, salt, pepper, Worcestershire sauce, and Tabasco. Chill. Garnish with bacon bits, or dill weed, or caraway seeds.

SPINACH SOUP

Serves 6

3	10-ounce packages frozen spinach	2	8-ounce packages cream cheese, cubed
5	tablespoons butter		Tabasco to taste
⅔	cup chopped yellow onion		
3	10½-ounce cans chicken broth		

In a large saucepan, cook spinach according to package directions. Drain well. In a small skillet, melt butter and sauté onion until tender. Add onion, broth, and cheese to spinach. Purée. Season with Tabasco. May be served hot or cold.

TURNIP SOUP

Serves 6

1	tablespoon butter	2½	teaspoons sugar
½	cup chopped onion	2	tablespoons chopped fresh parsley
3½	cups chicken stock	1	bay leaf
1	cup water	1	tablespoon lemon juice
2	pounds turnips, pared and cubed	1	cup half and half cream (for a richer soup, use 1 cup heavy cream instead)
1	teaspoon basil		Chopped fresh parsley
2½	teaspoons salt		
⅛	teaspoon pepper		

In a large saucepan, melt butter; add onion and cook until soft. Add stock, water, turnips, basil, salt, pepper, sugar, parsley, bay leaf, and lemon juice. Cover and simmer 1 hour. Remove bay leaf. Purée. Return to saucepan; add cream; heat. Garnish with parsley.

CHILLED AVOCADO CUCUMBER SOUP

Serves 4

2   cups peeled, seeded, and
    coarsely chopped
    cucumbers
1   large avocado, coarsely
    chopped
2   small green onions, bulb
    only, chopped
2   cups chicken stock

1   cup sour cream
1   tablespoon lemon juice
    Salt to taste
    Tabasco to taste
    Thinly sliced cucumber, *or*
    avocado, *or* chopped
    chives

Purée cucumber, avocado, and onions. Continue blending and add stock, sour cream, and lemon juice. Season with salt and Tabasco. Chill. Garnish with cucumber, or avocado, or chives.

OYSTER AND ARTICHOKE SOUP   Serves 10

Can be made ahead

4   artichokes
1   stick butter
½   cup finely chopped green
    onions
1   outer rib celery, with
    leaves, finely chopped
1   medium carrot, scraped
    and chopped
1   tablespoon finely chopped
    fresh parsley
2   cloves garlic, pressed
½   teaspoon thyme
1   bay leaf
3   tablespoons flour

1   quart chicken stock,
    warmed
¼   teaspoon anise seeds
¼   teaspoon cayenne pepper
1   teaspoon salt
1   teaspoon Worcestershire
    sauce
1   quart oysters and their
    liquid
½   cup vermouth
¼   cup dry white wine
¼   cup half and half cream
1   teaspoon lemon juice
    Grated rind of one lemon

Cook artichokes. Scrape leaves, chop hearts, and reserve. In a 4-quart heavy pot, melt butter; sauté onions, celery, carrot, parsley, garlic, thyme, and bay leaf until celery and carrot are tender. Add scrapings and hearts; stir well. Slowly stir in flour, but do not brown. Slowly stir in stock. Add anise, cayenne, salt, and Worcestershire sauce. Simmer 15 minutes. Drain oysters, reserving liquid. Chop oysters and add with liquid to artichoke mixture. Cook over low heat 10 minutes. Add vermouth, white wine, half and half, lemon juice, and lemon rind. Remove bay leaf. Blend until smooth. Heat.

OYSTER SOUP

Serves 4

3 tablespoons butter
¼ cup finely chopped celery
¼ cup finely chopped green onions
2 tablespoons flour

1 pint oysters, with liquid
1 teaspoon salt
¼ teaspoon white pepper
2 cups milk, warmed

In the top of double boiler, melt butter. Sauté celery and onions. Add flour and cook 2 minutes. Add oysters and liquid; cook just until edges curl. Add salt, pepper, and milk; heat.

CREAM OF CRAWFISH SOUP

Serves 8

1½ sticks butter
2 tablespoons finely chopped green onions
1 pound cooked crawfish tails with fat, minced
¼ teaspoon tarragon
½ teaspoon salt
¼ teaspoon cayenne pepper
¾ cup dry sherry
¼ cup brandy
1 cup finely chopped white onion

½ cup flour
6 cups fish stock, heated (may use 3 cups clam juice and 3 cups water)
4 cups milk
1 cup heavy cream
3 egg yolks
4 tablespoons chives, fresh or frozen

In a heavy skillet, melt 4 tablespoons butter. Stir in green onions and crawfish. Season with tarragon, salt, and cayenne. Cook, stirring 5 minutes. Add sherry and boil to reduce by half. Heat brandy, flame, and add to crawfish mixture. Stir and cook 3 minutes.

In a Dutch oven, sauté onion in remaining stick butter until tender. Stir in flour and cook 3 minutes. Remove from heat and stir in stock and milk. Add crawfish mixture and simmer 30 minutes. Can be frozen at this point.

In a small bowl, whisk cream into yolks; add a little hot soup; slowly stir mixture into soup. Heat thoroughly. Garnish with chives. Additional sherry may be added to each serving.

CREOLE CRAB BISQUE

Serves 8

Freezes well

¾	cup butter	2	quarts chicken stock
¾	cup flour	1	tablespoon
3	tablespoons tomato paste		Worcestershire sauce
1½	cups finely chopped	1	bay leaf
	yellow onions	1	teaspoon thyme
1	cup finely chopped celery	1	teaspoon salt
½	cup finely chopped green	⅛	teaspoon white pepper
	onions	⅛	teaspoon cayenne pepper
4	cloves garlic, pressed	½	teaspoon catsup
⅔	cup finely chopped green	1	pound crabmeat
	pepper		
3	tablespoons finely		
	chopped fresh parsley		

In a large heavy pot, melt butter and gradually add flour, stirring constantly until roux is golden brown, 20 to 30 minutes. Add tomato paste, onions, celery, green onions, garlic, and green pepper; cook until tender. Add parsley. Slowly stir in stock. Add Worcestershire sauce, bay leaf, thyme, salt, white pepper, cayenne, and catsup. Add crabmeat. Cover and simmer 40 minutes, stirring occasionally.

CRABMEAT BISQUE CARDINALE

Serves 8

Make a day ahead

6	tablespoons butter	2	teaspoons chopped fresh
3	tablespoons grated onion		parsley
6	tablespoons flour	1	pound lump crabmeat
½	teaspoon dry mustard	2	tablespoons dry sherry
4	cups half and half cream,	2	teaspoons Worcestershire
	warmed		sauce
2	cups whole milk, warmed	¼	teaspoon Tabasco
2	tablespoon catsup	2	teaspoons salt
1½	teaspoons tomato paste		White pepper to taste

In a heavy pot, melt butter. Add onion and sauté 5 minutes. Stir in flour and cook 2 minutes. Add mustard and stir well. Lower heat and whisk in milk, cream, and catsup. In a small bowl, add ¼ cup cream mixture to tomato paste; stir until smooth. Return this mixture to pot and stir in parsley, crabmeat, sherry, Worcestershire sauce, Tabasco, salt, and pepper. When cool, refrigerate. May be served hot or cold.

SHRIMP BISQUE

Serves 8

2   pounds raw shrimp

Stock

8	cups water	1	sprig parsley
1	carrot, cut in thirds	½	lemon
1	onion, quartered	1	teaspoon salt
2	cloves	¼	teaspoon cayenne pepper
1	outer rib celery with leaves	½	cup dry white wine

Wash, peel, and devein shrimp, reserving heads and shells. Place heads and shells in pot with water and remaining ingredients. Cook 1 hour, skimming foam from top. Strain and measure 6 cups stock.

Bisque

3	tablespoons butter	½	teaspoon tarragon
½	cup finely chopped carrots	2	tablespoons tomato paste
⅔	cup finely chopped onion	1	cup dry white wine
½	cup finely chopped celery	½	cup rice
1	tablespoon finely chopped fresh parsley	6	cups shrimp stock
		½	cup heavy cream
½	bay leaf	¾	teaspoon salt
¼	teaspoon thyme	¼	cup Madeira

In a skillet, melt butter; add carrots, onion, celery, parsley, bay leaf, thyme, and tarragon. Cover and cook 10 minutes. Stir in shrimp, tomato paste, and wine. Cover and cook 5 minutes. For garnish, remove 10 to 12 shrimp and chop coarsely.

In a 3-quart saucepan, place rice and stock. Cover and cook 20 minutes. Add shrimp mixture, cover, and cook 10 minutes. Remove bay leaf. Purée. Add cream, salt, and Madeira. Heat and garnish with shrimp.

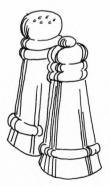

CRAWFISH GUMBO

Serves 6

Best made ahead   Freezes well

½	cup oil	1	tablespoon salt
½	cup flour	¾	teaspoon cayenne pepper
1½	cups chopped onions	2	pounds peeled crawfish,
1	8-ounce can tomato sauce		tails and fat
6	cups hot water	¼	cup chopped green onion
¾	cup chopped green pepper		tops
2	large cloves garlic,	¼	cup chopped fresh parsley
	pressed	3	cups steamed rice

In a Dutch oven, heat oil and gradually add flour, stirring constantly until roux is dark brown, about 40 minutes. Add onions and cook until tender. Add tomato sauce and cook over low heat 15 minutes. Slowly add water, stirring until smooth. Add green pepper, garlic, salt, and cayenne; bring to a boil. Reduce heat and simmer 40 minutes. Add crawfish and onion tops; simmer 15 minutes. Add parsley and serve over rice.

DUCK GUMBO

Serves 8 to 10

4	ducks, cleaned and	1	teaspoon pepper
	washed	3	onions, quartered
	Water to cover	3	celery ribs
2	tablespoons salt	2	bay leaves

Place ducks in a large pot and cover with water. Season with salt, pepper, onions, celery, and bay leaves. Bring to a boil and simmer 1 hour, until tender. Skin, debone, and cube. Reserve stock.

⅔	cup oil	3	quarts duck stock
⅔	cup flour	1	teaspoon Tabasco
2	cups chopped onions	½	cup chopped fresh parsley
1	cup chopped green pepper	½	cup chopped green onion
1½	cups chopped celery		tops
½	teaspoon salt	2	dozen oysters, well
¼	teaspoon black pepper		drained
¼	teaspoon white pepper	1	tablespoon filé powder
1½	pounds smoked sausage,	3	cups steamed rice
	sliced		

In a Dutch oven, heat oil and gradually add flour, stirring constantly until roux is dark brown. Add onions, green pepper, and celery; cook until vegetables are tender, about 10 to 15 minutes. Add salt, peppers, and duck meat. Cook 10 minutes, stirring often. In a separate skillet, cook sausage 5 minutes; drain. Add to duck mixture. Slowly add stock, mixing well. Bring to a boil. Reduce heat and simmer 1 hour. Add Tabasco, parsley, onion tops, and cook 5 minutes. Stir in oysters and cook 10 minutes. Skim off fat and thicken with filé powder. Serve over rice.

TURKEY CORN CHOWDER

Serves 10

1	turkey carcass	⅛	teaspoon rosemary
2	onions, halved	12	cups water
3	ribs celery with tops, cut in thirds	1	tablespoon salt
		1	teaspoon pepper
2	carrots, cut in thirds	1	teaspoon Worcestershire sauce
5	ears fresh corn, kernels cut from cob (3 cups)	¼	teaspoon Tabasco
1	bay leaf	¼	teaspoon curry powder
⅛	teaspoon thyme	¼	cup dry sherry
⅛	teaspoon basil	1	cup heavy cream

In an 8-quart pot, place turkey carcass, onions, celery, carrots, corn cobs, bay leaf, thyme, basil, and rosemary. Add water and bring to a boil. Cover and simmer 1½ hours, stirring occasionally. Strain and return stock to pot. Purée onions, celery, carrots, 1 cup raw corn and 2 cups stock. Return to pot with remaining 2 cups corn and cook ½ hour. Add salt, pepper, Worcestershire sauce, Tabasco, curry, sherry, and cream.

CHICKEN, SAUSAGE, AND OYSTER GUMBO

Serves 6

1	3-pound chicken, cut in pieces	1	bay leaf
		½	teaspoon thyme
4	cups water	¾	pound sausage, sliced (preferably andouille)
¼	cup flour		Salt
¼	cup oil		Pepper
1½	cups chopped yellow onions		Cayenne pepper
1½	cups chopped celery		Worcestershire sauce
½	cup chopped green pepper	1	cup oysters, with liquid
½	cup chopped green onions	3	cups steamed rice
3	cloves garlic, pressed	3	teaspoons filé powder
¼	cup chopped fresh parsley		

Cook chicken in water until tender, skimming top for fat and foam. Reserve stock and remove meat from bones.

In a Dutch oven, heat oil and gradually add flour, stirring constantly until roux is dark brown. Add onions, celery, green pepper, green onions, garlic, parsley, bay leaf, and thyme. Cook until tender, stirring often. Slowly add stock, stirring constantly. Add chicken meat. In a skillet, fry sausage; drain; add to gumbo. Cover and simmer 1 hour, stirring occasionally. Add salt, pepper, cayenne, and Worcestershire sauce. Add oysters with liquid and heat just until edges curl. Serve over rice and sprinkle ½ teaspoon filé powder over each serving.

CREOLE CHICKEN GUMBO   Serves 8

Freezes well

Stock

3½-4 pounds chicken pieces	1 carrot, cut in thirds
3 quarts water	1 medium onion, quartered
2 outer ribs celery, with leaves	1 bay leaf
	1 teaspoon salt

In a pot, place chicken, water, celery, carrot, onion, bay leaf, and salt. Bring to a boil and simmer 25 minutes, skimming top for foam and fat. Remove meat from bones and reserve. Return bones to stock and continue to simmer.

Gumbo

⅓ cup oil	½ teaspoon basil
½ cup flour	1 16-ounce can whole tomatoes, with juice
1 pound okra, washed and cut in ¼ inch pieces	½ pound ham, cubed
1 cup chopped onion	1 pound hot smoked sausage, sliced
¾ cup chopped celery	1 teaspoon Worcestershire sauce
½ cup chopped green pepper	Salt to taste
½ cup chopped green onions	Black pepper to taste
2 cloves garlic, pressed	Cayenne pepper to taste
¼ cup chopped fresh parsley	Tabasco to taste
1 bay leaf	4 cups steamed rice
¾ teaspoon thyme	
½ teaspoon marjoram	

In a large heavy pot, not black iron, heat oil and gradually add flour, stirring constantly until roux is medium brown. Add okra, onion, celery, and green pepper; cook, stirring until okra is no longer stringy. Add green onions, garlic, parsley, bay leaf, thyme, marjoram, basil, tomatoes with juice, ham, and chicken meat. Strain stock and slowly stir into gumbo. Cook sausage, drain well, and add to gumbo. Simmer 1½ hours, stirring occasionally. Season with Worcestershire sauce, salt, pepper, cayenne, and Tabasco. Serve over rice.

Salads, Dressings & Sauces

JAMBALAYA RICE SALAD

Serves 8 to 10

Make ahead

2	cups rice	1	clove garlic, pressed
4	cups salted water	1	cup diced celery
1	cup mayonnaise	2½	cups diced tomatoes
2	tablespoons prepared yellow mustard	½	cup chopped green pepper
3	tablespoons French dressing		

Cook rice in water. Cool. In a small bowl, combine mayonnaise, mustard, dressing and garlic. Place rice in salad bowl, add mayonnaise mixture and vegetables. Refrigerate.

LAYER SALAD SUPREME

Serves 10 to 12

Make a day ahead

1	10-ounce package fresh spinach, washed and stemmed
	Salt
	Pepper
1	tablespoon sugar
6	strips bacon, cooked and crumbled
3	hard-boiled eggs, sliced
	Shredded lettuce to cover
	Salt
	Pepper

1	teaspoon sugar
1	cup sliced raw mushrooms
½	cup chopped green onions
1	10-ounce box frozen uncooked peas, thawed
	Salt
	Pepper
1	teaspoon sugar
½	cup chopped pecans
1	cup mayonnaise
1	cup grated Swiss cheese
1	teaspoon paprika

In a 11 × 13 casserole dish, layer ingredients in order given. Refrigerate. May be prepared up to 48 hours in advance.

SPINACH AND BACON SALAD

Serves 8

Salad

2	10-ounce packages fresh spinach, washed and stemmed

½	pound bacon, cooked and crumbled
½	cup sliced Bermuda onions

Break spinach into bite-size pieces. Add bacon and onions.

Dressing

2	tablespoons sugar
1	teaspoon salt
1	teaspoon dry mustard
⅓	cup cider vinegar

1	cup oil
1	tablespoon poppy seeds
1½	cups cottage cheese

Combine sugar, salt, mustard, vinegar, and oil. Shake well. Add poppy seeds and shake again. Add cottage cheese and shake well. Toss into salad and serve immediately.

KOREAN SPINACH SALAD

Serves 6

Dressing

¼	cup oil
¼	cup sugar
3	tablespoons catsup
¼	cup red wine vinegar

½	teaspoon Worcestershire sauce
1	tablespoon grated onion
	Salt to taste

Mix ingredients and chill. Can be refrigerated up to two weeks.

Salad

1	10-ounce package fresh spinach, washed and stemmed
½	cup alfalfa sprouts
1	can sliced water chestnuts, drained

3	hard-boiled eggs, diced
3	slices bacon, cooked and crumbled

Combine all ingredients and toss with dressing.

WILTED SALAD

Serves 8 to 10

Salad

2	heads lettuce, broken into bite-size pieces
2	tomatoes, cut into bite-size pieces
1¼	cups chopped green onions

¾	cup shredded carrots
¾	cup chopped celery
8	slices bacon, cooked and crumbled
4	hard-boiled eggs, sliced

In a salad bowl, toss all ingredients except bacon and eggs. Let salad stand 1 hour at room temperature before adding dressing.

Dressing

½	cup sugar
½	cup vinegar

½	cup water
½	cup bacon drippings

In saucepan, mix all ingredients and let simmer 10 minutes. Pour over salad; top with bacon and eggs; serve immediately.

CRANBERRY APPLE SALAD

Serves 10 to 12

Make a day ahead

2	1-pound cans whole berry cranberry sauce	2	tablespoons lemon juice
2	cups boiling water	½	teaspoon salt
2	3-ounce packages raspberry flavored gelatin	1	cup mayonnaise
		2	cups peeled, diced apple
		½	cup chopped walnuts

In a saucepan, melt cranberry sauce. Drain, reserving liquid and berries. Mix cranberry liquid, boiling water, and gelatin; stir until gelatin is dissolved. Add lemon juice and salt. Chill until mixture mounds slightly on a spoon. Add mayonnaise and beat until smooth. Fold in cranberries, apples, and nuts. Pour into a greased 2-quart mold. Refrigerate.

FROZEN FRUIT SALAD

Serves 8

Salad

1	cup sugar	1	cup crushed pineapple, drained, reserve juice
½	cup lemon juice		
½	cup Royal Anne pitted cherries, drained	1½	cups sliced bananas
½	cup Mandarin orange sections, drained	1	cup mayonnaise
		1	cup whipping cream, whipped
1½	cups sliced canned peaches, drained	½	cup pecans

In a large bowl, combine sugar and lemon juice mixing well. Add fruits. Blend mayonnaise and whipped cream. Add with pecans to fruit mixture. Pour into greased 2½ to 3-quart mold. Freeze. May be frozen 2 weeks in advance.

Dressing

1	cup sugar	½	cup lemon juice
2	tablespoons flour	½	cup pineapple juice
2	eggs	½	cup orange juice

In saucepan, mix sugar and flour. Add eggs and whisk. Add juices and cook slowly until thick, stirring often. Refrigerate. Serve with unmolded salad.

CHICKEN SALAD

Serves 6

Can be made ahead

3	cups diced cooked chicken	2	tablespoons minced fresh parsley
1	cup finely chopped celery	1	teaspoon salt
1	cup sliced white seedless grapes	1	cup mayonnaise
½	cup slivered almonds, toasted	½	cup whipping cream, whipped

Toss ingredients and serve on lettuce.

CURRIED CHICKEN SALAD

Serves 4 to 6

Make ahead

Salad

2	cups diced cooked chicken
¼	cup sliced water chestnuts
½	pound green grapes, halved
½	cup coarsely chopped celery
½	cup toasted slivered almonds
1	8-ounce can pineapple chunks, drained

Dressing

¾	cup mayonnaise
1	teaspoon curry powder
2	teaspoons soy sauce
2	teaspoons lemon juice

In a bowl, mix chicken with water chestnuts, grapes, celery, almonds, and pineapple. Combine dressing ingredients and add to chicken mixture. Refrigerate. Serve on lettuce or in half of a scooped-out pineapple.

SOUR CREAM POTATO SALAD

Serves 8 to 10

4	hard-boiled eggs	⅓	cup chopped green onions
⅔	cup mayonnaise	1	cup chopped celery
¾	cup sour cream	7	cups cooked, cubed potatoes
1½	teaspoons prepared mustard with horseradish	⅓	cup Italian salad dressing
½	pound bacon, cooked and crumbled		Salt to taste

Cut eggs in half and remove yolks. In a small bowl, mash yolks and blend with mayonnaise, sour cream, and mustard. In a separate bowl, chop egg whites. Combine with bacon, onion, celery, potatoes, and salad dressing. Fold in mayonnaise mixture and season with salt.

SEAFOOD SALAD

Serves 6 to 8

Best made ahead

2	pounds cooked seafood (shrimp, crawfish, crabmeat, tuna, or a combination)	½	cup finely grated celery
		1	teaspoon salt
		½	teaspoon pepper
½	cup French dressing	1	teaspoon Tabasco
1½	tablespoons finely grated onion	1	teaspoon Worcestershire sauce
½	cup finely grated green pepper	1	cup mayonnaise
		2	hard-boiled eggs, chopped

In a large bowl, combine seafood with all ingredients except mayonnaise and eggs. Mix well and refrigerate 30 minutes. Fold in mayonnaise and eggs.

TUNA FISH SALAD

Serves 4

Dressing

¾	cup mayonnaise	⅛	teaspoon curry powder
½	teaspoon lemon juice	⅛	teaspoon nutmeg
1	teaspoon soy sauce		

Combine ingredients and mix well.

Salad

1	9½-ounce water-packed tuna, drained	⅓	cup sliced water chestnuts, drained
5	ounces frozen peas, thawed	1	2-ounce bag slivered almonds, toasted
1	6-ounce jar cocktail onions, drained and halved	½	teaspoon salt
⅔	cup chopped celery	1	cup Chinese noodles

In a bowl, combine tuna, peas, onions, celery, water chestnuts, and almonds. Season with salt and add dressing. Mix well and serve topped with Chinese noodles.

HAITIAN AVOCADO AND SHRIMP   Serves 8

Make ahead

1	14-ounce can hearts of palm	¼	cup minced onion
1	teaspoon prepared yellow mustard	⅓	cup olive oil
1½	teaspoons salt	1	tablespoon lemon juice
¼	teaspoon pepper	1½	cups cooked shrimp
½	teaspoon garlic salt	4	avocados, peeled and halved
3	tablespoons red wine vinegar		

Cut hearts of palm in ¼-inch rounds. In bowl, combine mustard, salt, pepper, garlic salt, vinegar, onion, oil, and lemon juice. Add hearts of palm and shrimp. Fill each avocado half with mixture. Chill. Will serve 4 as a main course.

WALNUT SHRIMP SALAD   Serves 4 to 6

Can be made ahead

1	tablespoon butter	1	11-ounce can Mandarin orange sections, drained
1	tablespoon soy sauce	3	cups cooked shrimp
1	cup walnut halves	½	cup bottled sweet and spicy salad dressing
1	cup diagonally-sliced celery		Crisp salad greens
½	cup sliced green onions		
1	5-ounce can sliced water chestnuts, drained		

Melt butter. Add soy sauce and walnuts. Stir over low heat until walnuts are lightly toasted, about 10 minutes. Remove from heat and cool. In a salad bowl, mix all ingredients and toss.

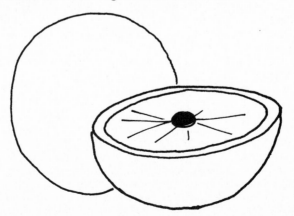

AVOCADO STUFFED WITH CRABMEAT

Make dressing a day ahead   **Serves 8**

Dressing

1½	cups mayonnaise
3	teaspoons lemon juice
2	tablespoons capers, drained
1	tablespoon chopped fresh parsley

3	tablespoons catsup
2	tablespoons chopped green onions
2	teaspoons dill weed
⅛	teaspoon pepper
⅛	teaspoon salt

Mix ingredients and refrigerate.

Salad

3	cups lump crabmeat	4	avocados, peeled and halved

Fill avocado half with crabmeat. Top with dressing.

COLD CRABMEAT SALAD   **Serves 6**

1	pound lump crabmeat

Dressing

4	tablespoons mayonnaise
1	tablespoon lemon juice
½	teaspoon dry mustard
1	teaspoon Worcestershire sauce
½	teaspoon Tabasco
⅛	teaspoon garlic salt
1½	cups coarsely chopped celery

2	green onions, finely chopped
2	tablespoons chopped fresh parsley
6	pimiento stuffed olives, chopped

Mix dressing ingredients and pour over crabmeat. Refrigerate until ready to serve.

CRABMEAT MOUSSE

Serves 8

Make ahead

1	8-ounce package cream cheese, softened	1	teaspoon garlic salt
1½	cups mayonnaise	½	teaspoon paprika
1½	pounds white crabmeat	¼	teaspoon Tabasco
1	2-ounce bottle capers, drained	1	teaspoon Worchestershire sauce
½	cup finely chopped celery	2	teaspoons gelatin
¼	cup minced fresh parsley	1	cup water

In a bowl, blend cream cheese and mayonnaise. Add crabmeat, capers, celery, parsley, garlic salt, paprika, Tabasco, and Worcestershire sauce. Soften gelatin in water, heating until dissolved. Cool and add to other ingredients. Pour into a 6-cup mold. Refrigerate.

GAZPACHO MOLD

Serves 8 to 10

4	cups spicy tomato juice	1	hard-boiled egg, finely chopped
2	tablespoons gelatin		
1	tablespoon lemon juice	½	teaspoon salt
½	cup finely chopped celery	¼	teaspoon pepper
½	cup finely chopped onion		
¼	cup finely chopped green pepper		

In a large bowl, dissolve gelatin in 2 cups tomato juice. In a saucepan, heat remaining 2 cups tomato juice and add to gelatin mixture. Add remaining ingredients and pour into a greased 5-cup mold. Refrigerate.

COLD ARTICHOKES

Serves 5

5	artichokes	2	cloves garlic, sliced
2	lemons, sliced	1	teaspoon salt

Cook artichokes in water with lemons, garlic, and salt until 1 leaf pulls free with ease, about 45 minutes. Refrigerate.

Dressing

½	cup oil	2	cloves garlic
2	tablespoons lemon juice	2	green onions
2	tablespoons red wine vinegar	1	small sliced green pepper
1	tablespoon brown mustard	1	teaspoon salt
		½	teaspoon pepper

Blend ingredients at least ½ hour before serving. Before serving, blend again. Serve artichokes cold with dressing.

VEGETABLE ASPIC

Make ahead

2	tablespoons gelatin	1	teaspoon Tabasco
½	cup cold water	1½	teaspoons celery salt
½	cup boiling consommé	⅛	teaspoon paprika
2	cups cold consommé	1	cup chopped celery
6	ounces tomato juice	1	8½-ounce can artichoke
4	teaspoons Worchstershire		hearts, quartered
	sauce	1	10½-ounce can asparagus
3	tablespoons lemon juice		tips

Soften gelatin in water. Add boiling consommé to dissolve. Cool. Add remaining cold consommé, tomato juice, Worcestershire sauce, lemon juice, Tabasco, celery salt, and paprika. Chill until nearly set, stirring occasionally. Fold in celery, artichoke hearts, and asparagus. Pour into a 5-cup wet and chilled mold and refrigerate. Serve with mayonnaise.

TOMATO ASPIC WITH CREAM CHEESE

Make ahead   Serves 10 to 12

1	quart tomato juice	⅛	teaspoon red pepper
2	cloves garlic, pressed	3	tablespoons gelatin
½	teaspoon dry mustard	¾	cups bouillon
2½	teaspoons salt	6	ounces cream cheese,
2½	teaspoons sugar		softened
5	tablespoons lemon juice	3	tablespoons grated onion
1	teaspoon paprika	½	teaspoon Tabasco
1	bay leaf		

In a saucepan, bring tomato juice, garlic, mustard, salt, sugar, lemon juice, paprika, bay leaf, and pepper to a boil. Continue cooking 3 minutes. Remove from fire. Soften gelatin in bouillon. Add gelatin mixture to tomato juice and stir to dissolve. Remove bay leaf. Pour into 1½-quart mold and refrigerate. Combine cream cheese with onion and Tabasco and roll into small balls. Chill. When aspic becomes slightly firm, arrange cheese balls in mold. When all is firm, unmold and serve with mayonnaise.

FETA CHEESE DRESSING

Makes 4 cups

Make ahead

2 cups crumbled Feta cheese
2 cups mayonnaise
2 small cloves garlic, minced
½ cup red wine vinegar
1 teaspoon salad herbs
1 teaspoon oregano

1 tablespoon Worcestershire sauce
2 tablespoons olive oil
Freshly ground pepper to taste
2 tablespoons minced green onion tops

Blend ingredients until smooth. Stores well in refrigerator.

ITALIAN CHEESE DRESSING

Can be made ahead

Makes 1½ cups

½ cup oil
¼ cup tarragon vinegar
½ cup mayonnaise
½ cup grated Romano cheese, *or* mixture of Parmesan and Romano cheese

¼ teaspoon salt
Freshly ground pepper to taste

With a wire whisk beat together all ingredients. Refrigerate. Mix before serving.

MINT DRESSING

Makes 1 cup

5 tablespoons lemon juice
4 tablespoons dry sherry
8 sprigs fresh mint, chopped

2 tablespoons honey
1 teaspoon celery seed

Combine all ingredients and serve over fruit salad.

GREEN GODDESS DRESSING   Makes 2 cups

1   clove garlic, pressed
1   cup sour cream
1   cup anchovies, *or* 2
    tablespoons anchovy
    paste
3   tablespoons finely
    chopped green onion tops

1   tablespoon lemon juice
3   tablespoons cider vinegar
1   cup mayonnaise
⅓   cup finely chopped fresh
    parsley
    Salt to taste
    Pepper to taste

In blender, mix above ingredients. Refrigerate. Stores well in refrigerator.

CELERY SEED DRESSING   Makes 2 cups

1   cup sugar
1   teaspoon salt
1   teaspoon paprika
1   teaspoon grated onion

⅓   cup catsup
1   cup oil
⅓   cup cider vinegar
½   teaspoon celery seed

In blender, combine sugar, salt, paprika, onion, and catsup. Blend at medium speed, slowly adding oil and vinegar alternately. Add celery seed. Good on grapefruit sections or congealed fruit salad. Stores well in refrigerator.

REMOULADE SAUCE   Makes 2 cups

Make ahead

2   large cloves garlic,
    pressed
1   hard-boiled egg
3   anchovies
¾   cup olive oil
¼   cup vinegar
1   tablespoon lemon juice
½   cup catsup

2   tablespoons
    Worcestershire sauce
8   teaspoons Creole mustard
2   teaspoons dry mustard
2   teaspoons Dijon mustard
1   tablespoon paprika
    Salt to taste
    Pepper to taste

In a food processor, using metal blade, blend garlic, egg, and anchovies to a smooth paste. Transfer to a bowl. Stir in oil, vinegar, lemon juice, catsup, Worcestershire sauce, mustards, paprika, salt, and pepper. Stores well in refrigerator.

LEMON BUTTER SAUCE

Makes 1 cup

3 tablespoons lemon juice
1 tablespoon Dijon mustard
1 egg yolk

¼ teaspoon salt
⅛ teaspoon white pepper
¾ cup oil, warmed

In a bowl, combine juice, mustard, yolk, salt, and pepper. Slowly add oil in a stream. Whisk until sauce is thick. Good over vegetables, meat, fish, and chicken.

HOLLANDAISE SAUCE

Makes ¾ cup

3 egg yolks
2 tablespoons lemon juice
1 stick butter, cut into pieces

⅛ teaspoon cayenne pepper
⅛ teaspoon salt

In a double boiler over low heat, place all ingredients. Stir constantly with wooden spoon until sauce is creamy, about 5 to 8 minutes. NEVER let water in double boiler come to boil. When sauce is thickened, remove from heat. Cover and set entire double boiler on back of stove until ready to serve. Sauce will thicken while sitting. Recipe doubles well.

BEARNAISE SAUCE

Makes ¾ cup

¾ cup Hollandaise Sauce
5 tablespoons coarsely chopped green onion
1 tablespoon pepper
1 cup dry vermouth, *or* dry white wine

¾ cup cider vinegar
1½ tablespoons tarragon
1 tablespoon fresh parsley
2 tablespoons chervil, optional

Prepare Hollandaise Sauce.

In blender or food processor, place remaining ingredients. Blend at high speed 30 seconds. Pour into a heavy saucepan and boil until liquid is gone, about 30 minutes. Cool. Beat 1 teaspoon of this essence into Hollandaise Sauce. Remaining essence may be frozen or refrigerated several weeks.

MARCHAND DE VIN SAUCE

Makes 4 cups

4	tablespoons butter	1	tablespoon chopped garlic
4	tablespoons flour	2	bay leaves
3	cups beef stock	¾	teaspoon thyme
½	cup chopped onion	¼	pound mushrooms,
¼	cup chopped celery		coarsely chopped
¼	cup chopped ham	2	tablespoons butter
2	tablespoons chopped	½	cup Madeira, *or* red wine
	fresh parsley	¼	teaspoon lemon juice

In a large skillet, heat butter and gradually add flour, stirring constantly until roux becomes dark brown. Place 1 cup beef stock in blender or food processor with onion, celery, ham, parsley, and garlic. Blend 30 seconds and add to roux. Stir in remaining 2 cups stock; add bay leaves and thyme. Simmer 30 minutes. In a small skillet, sauté mushrooms in butter. Add to stock base and simmer 10 minutes, stirring occasionally. Add Madeira and simmer 5 minutes. Add lemon juice and remove bay leaves. Blend well.

The longer the roux and stock simmer, the better sauce will be. If sauce is not thick enough, blend 1 tablespoon softened butter with 1 tablespoon flour. Add to sauce and simmer several minutes.

ROCKEFELLER SAUCE

For 5 dozen oysters

Freezes well

3	10-ounce bags fresh	4	cups water
	spinach	1	cup grated Parmesan
1	bunch green onions		cheese
	Leaves from ½ bunch of	1	cup bread crumbs
	celery	1	pound butter, melted
1	whole bulb garlic, peeled	1	jigger Pernod (anise
	and separated		liqueur)
1	bunch fresh parsley		

In a large pot, boil spinach, onions, celery leaves, garlic, and parsley in water 20 minutes. Drain and chop in a food processor. Return to pot and add cheese, bread crumbs, and melted butter. Mix. Add Pernod and stir. Serve over oysters.

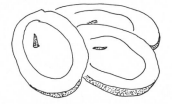

SECRET MAYONNAISE

Makes 1 quart

1 quart mayonnaise
1 tablespoon vinegar
2 tablespoons lemon juice
1 teaspoon salt
1 teaspoon black pepper
¼ teaspoon red pepper
1 tablespoon horseradish
1 tablespoon prepared
  yellow mustard

1 tablespoon
  Worcestershire sauce
¼ teaspoon basil
¼ teaspoon thyme
1 clove garlic, pressed
1 tablespoon grated onion

In a bowl, combine all ingredients and mix well. Cover and refrigerate.

CREOLE MAYONNAISE

Makes 2 cups

1½ cups oil
1 egg
3 tablespoons chopped
  onion
1 tablespoons Creole
  mustard
3 tablespoons vinegar, *or*
  lemon juice

¼ teaspoon paprika
  Tabasco to taste
1 teaspoon prepared yellow
  mustard
1 teaspoon salt

In blender or food processor, place ¼ cup oil. Add remaining ingredients and blend on high speed until smooth. Immediately add remaining oil, a little at a time, until all is used.

SWEET HOT MUSTARD

Makes 1 pint

Begin a day ahead

4 ounces dry mustard
1 cup cider vinegar, *or*
  tarragon vinegar

3 eggs
1 cup sugar

In a bowl, mix mustard and vinegar. Cover and refrigerate overnight. The next day, beat eggs. In top of double boiler, combine eggs and sugar. Stir in mustard mixture and cook, stirring occasionally until mixture thickens, approximately 10 minutes. Cool. Stores well in refrigerator.

FRENCH BUTTER PECAN SAUCE   Makes 1 cup

½   cup butter, melted
2   tablespoons chives
½   teaspoon salt
¼   teaspoon pepper

¼   teaspoon marjoram
3   tablespoons lemon juice
½   cup chopped pecans

Combine all ingredients; heat. Serve over cooked vegetables or fish.

SOUR CREAM CHEESE SAUCE   Makes 1¾ cups

½   cup mayonnaise
½   cup sour cream
½   teaspoon Worcestershire
     sauce
¼   teaspoon salt

White pepper to taste
½   cup grated cheddar, or
     Parmesan cheese
½   cup finely chopped green
     onions

In a small bowl, combine mayonnaise, sour cream, Worcestershire sauce, salt, and pepper. In a separate bowl, combine cheese and green onions. Add cream mixture to cheese and onions; mix well. Pour over warm vegetables and bake 2 minutes at 350°.

WHITE WINE SAUCE   Makes 1 cup

¼   cup white wine vinegar
¼   cup dry white wine
¼   cup minced green onions
1   tablespoon heavy cream
1½ sticks butter, cut into 6
     pieces

⅓   teaspoon salt
¼   teaspoon pepper
½   teaspoon lemon juice
⅛   teaspoon celery salt

In a small, heavy saucepan, combine vinegar, wine, and onions. Simmer until it is almost a glaze. Remove from heat. Add cream. Return to low heat and whisk in butter, 1 piece at a time. Add each additional piece of butter before previous one has completely melted, stirring constantly. Do not let sauce get too hot or it will liquify. Add salt, pepper, lemon juice, and celery salt. Pour over warm seafood and serve immediately.

BARBECUE SAUCE

Makes 3½ cups

Freezes well

2	sticks butter	½	cup Worcestershire sauce
¾	cup chopped onion	14	ounces catsup
½	cup light brown sugar	2	tablespoons chili sauce
¼	teaspoon cayenne pepper	2	cloves garlic, minced
1	cup oil	¼	cup lemon juice
1	teaspoon dry mustard	3	drops Tabasco

In a large saucepan, melt butter. Add onion and sauté until clear, about 3 minutes. Add remaining ingredients, stirring constantly. Simmer 15 minutes, stirring frequently. Stores well in refrigerator.

TARTAR SAUCE

Makes 1¼ cups

1	cup mayonnaise	½	clove garlic, minced
½	teaspoon dry mustard	1	teaspoon capers, optional
4	teaspoons finely chopped green onions	1	teaspoon tarragon vinegar or lemon juice
1	tablespoon chopped sweet pickle, drained		Salt to taste
			Cayenne pepper to taste

Mix all ingredients. Stores well in refrigerator.

TOMATO RELISH

Makes 5 pints

6	pounds ripe tomatoes (about 12 large ones)	1	cup cider vinegar
3	cups finely chopped onions	2	cups sugar
		1	teaspoon cinnamon
1	cup finely chopped green pepper	2	teaspoons salt
		½	teaspoon ground cloves
			Cayenne pepper to taste

Peel, chop, and drain tomatoes. Add remaining ingredients. Bring to boil. Lower heat and simmer 2 hours, stirring occasionally. Seal in sterile jars.

ORANGE JEZEBEL SAUCE

Makes 2½ pints

1   18-ounce jar apple jelly
1   18-ounce jar pineapple, *or*
    apricot preserves
3   tablespoons dry mustard
4   tablespoons horseradish

¾   teaspoon finely grated
    orange rind
½   teaspoon pepper
¼   teaspoon poppy seeds, *or*
    mustard seeds

Combine all ingredients. Stir well, cover, and refrigerate. Stores well in refrigerator.

Good with cheese and crackers, as a condiment with meats, or as a dip for egg rolls and won ton.

BREAD AND BUTTER PICKLES

Makes 6 pints

12 medium cucumbers,
    peeled and sliced
6   medium yellow onions,
    thinly sliced
1   cup salt
2½ cups cider vinegar

2   cups sugar
2   teaspoons mustard seed
2   teaspoons turmeric
2   teaspoons celery seed
¼   teaspoon ground cloves

In a large bowl layer cucumbers, onions, and salt. Cover with cold water and let stand 2 hours. Drain well. In a large pot, combine vinegar, sugar, and seasonings; bring to boil. Add cucumbers and onions and boil 10 minutes. Seal in sterile jars.

YELLOW SQUASH PICKLES

Makes 8 pints

25 yellow squash, sliced
8   cups chopped onions
2   cups chopped green
    peppers
½   cup salt

5   cups sugar
5   cups cider vinegar
2   tablespoons mustard seeds
½   tablespoon ground cloves
1   teaspoon turmeric

In a large stainless steel bowl, combine squash, onions, green peppers, and salt; let stand 3 hours. Drain. In a large stainless steel or enamel pot, combine sugar, vinegar, mustard seeds, cloves, and turmeric. Bring to a boil. Add vegetables and return to a boil. Remove from heat. Seal in sterile jars. Place in hot water bath for 5 minutes.

PICKLED OKRA

Makes 16 pints

Best made ahead

7	pounds okra (small pods are best)	1	gallon cider vinegar
6	tablespoons alum (available at drug store)	1	pound light brown sugar
		1	cup salt
4	quarts water	1	teaspoon peppercorns
16	hot green peppers	1	teaspoon mustard seeds
48	cloves garlic	1	teaspoon pickling spice

Do not wash okra before using. Trim okra stems, not exposing seeds, and soak in a mixture of alum and water 2 hours. Rinse well in cold water. Arrange okra in sterile pint jars. Place 1 hot green pepper and 3 cloves garlic in each jar. In a large saucepan, combine remaining ingredients and boil 10 minutes. Pour over okra and seal. Turn jars regularly. Okra is best if allowed to sit several days before eating.

CAPTAIN'S RELISH

Makes 12 pints

3	heads cabbage, cored	3	cups sugar
3	large Bermuda onions	1	cup minus 1 tablespoon flour
3	large green peppers, seeded	1	teaspoon turmeric
2	large cauliflower	9	tablespoons dry mustard
¾	cup salt	2	tablespoons salt
1	gallon water	3	quarts cider vinegar

Shred cabbage, onions, and peppers. Separate cauliflower into florets or slice thinly. Put vegetables in a 5-quart pot and cover with salt. Pour boiling water over vegetables; soak 1 hour. Drain; cover vegetables with ice water; let stand 30 minutes. Drain. Combine remaining ingredients in another large pot and boil 5 minutes. Add vegetables and simmer 30 minutes. Seal in sterile jars.

APPLE BUTTER

Makes 2 pints

2½	pounds tart cooking apples, peeled, cored, and quartered
3	cups water
1	cup apple juice
1	cup honey
1	cup sugar

2½	tablespoons lemon juice
¾	teaspoon ground cloves
1	teaspoon ground allspice
1	teaspoon cinnamon
½	teaspoon nutmeg
½	teaspoon grated lemon rind

In an enamel or stainless steel kettle, combine apples and water and bring to a boil. Cook ½ hour, until apples are tender. Purée apple mixture and return to kettle. Add remaining ingredients, mix well, and bring to a boil. Reduce heat and simmer at least 1½ hours, stirring occasionally, until thickened. Seal in sterile jars and store in a cool, dark place.

CRANBERRY RELISH

Makes 5 pints

2	pounds fresh cranberries
6½	cups sugar
1	pound raisins
2	large oranges, rind and juice, finely chopped
1	tablespoon lemon juice, *or* chopped lemon rind

1	cup cider vinegar
½	teaspoon ground cloves
2	teaspoons ground cinnamon

In a large pot, mix ingredients and cook over low heat until cranberries pop, about 30 minutes. Seal in sterile jars.

PEAR CHUTNEY

Makes 2½ pints

1	lemon, seeded and chopped
1	clove garlic, minced
5	cups peeled, chopped cooking pears
1	pound dark brown sugar
1	cup raisins
2	ounces crystalized ginger

1½	teaspoons salt
2	cups cider vinegar
⅓	cup chopped onion
1	tablespoon mustard seeds
¼	teaspoon cinnamon
⅛	teaspoon allspice
¼	teaspoon cayenne pepper

In a large saucepan, combine ingredients and cook until fruit is tender and syrup is thick, about 45 minutes. Seal in sterile jars.

HOT PEPPER JELLY

Makes 7 pints

1 ⅓   **cups finely chopped hot green peppers, seeded**
2 ½   **cups finely chopped green peppers, seeded**

3   **cups cider vinegar**
13   **cups sugar**
12   **ounces liquid pectin**
     Green or red food coloring

Caution: Wear rubber gloves when cleaning and preparing peppers.

In a large pot, place peppers, vinegar, and sugar. Bring to a boil and boil 1 minute. Lower heat and cook 5 minutes. Remove from heat and add pectin. Stir well. Add a few drops of food coloring. Seal in sterile jars.

PARSLEY JELLY

Makes 3 pints

Begin a day ahead

1 ½   **cups packed flat-leaf parsley, leaves only**
3 ½   **cups water**
2   **tablespoons lemon juice**

1   **1¾-ounce box Sure-Gel**
4   **cups sugar**
     Green food coloring

Chop parsley and place in a large bowl. Boil water and pour over parsley. Cool, cover, and refrigerate overnight.

The next day, strain parsley mixture through cheese cloth. In a large pot, combine lemon juice, Sure-Gel, and 3 cups parsley essence. Bring to a full boil, stirring occasionally, and immediately add sugar. Stir and add food coloring. Cook, stirring, until mixture returns to a rolling boil that cannot be stirred down. Boil 1 minute. Remove from heat. Skim off foam with a metal spoon and pour immediately into hot sterile jars and seal. Serve with lamb, pork, or game.

Mint Jelly: Substitute 1½ cups packed mint leaves for parsley.

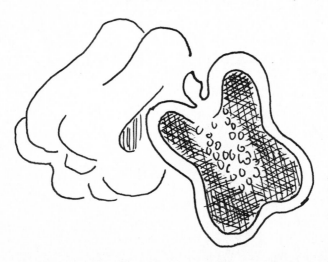

Eggs & Cheese

SCRAMBLE JAMBALAYA

Serves 4

Preheat broiler

4	tablespoons butter	½	teaspoon salt
¾	cup chopped onion	¼	teaspoon pepper
1½	cups chopped ham	¾	cup grated cheddar cheese
2½	cups cooked rice		
2	eggs	1	tablespoon minced fresh parsley
¼	cup finely chopped green pepper		
⅓	cup grated Parmesan cheese		

In an ovenproof skillet, melt butter and sauté onion until transparent. Remove from heat; add ham and rice, gently tossing with a fork until well blended. In a small bowl, beat eggs with green pepper, Parmesan cheese, salt, and pepper. Return skillet to heat and stir in eggs, cooking until done. Sprinkle with cheese and parsley. Broil to melt cheese.

EGG BRUNCH

Serves 10 to 12

Preheat oven to 275°

Sauce

4	slices bacon, diced
½	pound chipped beef, coarsely shredded
4	tablespoons butter
1	8-ounce can sliced mushrooms
½	cup flour
¼	teaspoon pepper
1	quart milk

In a large skillet, sauté bacon. Remove from heat; add chipped beef, butter, and most of mushrooms. Stir to melt butter. Sprinkle flour and pepper over mixture. Return to heat; gradually stir in milk; cook until thick and smooth, stirring constantly.

Egg Mixture

16	eggs
¼	teaspoon salt
1	cup evaporated milk
¼	cup butter

In a large bowl, beat eggs with salt and milk. Melt butter in a large skillet and gently scramble eggs. In an 11 × 13 baking dish, place half the egg mixture and top with half the sauce. Repeat this step and garnish with remaining mushrooms. Cover with foil and bake 1 hour.

BAKED ARTICHOKE HEART AND SHRIMP OMELETTE

Preheat oven to 400°

Serves 4

6	eggs
½	teaspoon salt
⅛	teaspoon cayenne pepper
2	tablespoons olive oil
¾	cup chopped green onions
1	14-ounce can artichoke hearts, drained and quartered
1	cup cooked, peeled shrimp
1	tablespoon butter
¾	cup grated Jarlsburg cheese
¼	cup grated Parmesan cheese

In a bowl, beat eggs with salt and cayenne pepper. Heat oil in a skillet and sauté onions until wilted. Add artichokes and cook 2 to 3 minutes. Remove from heat and stir in shrimp. Pour artichoke mixture into eggs and blend well. Pour all into a buttered 1½-quart baking dish. Sprinkle cheeses evenly over top. Bake in upper portion of oven 15 to 20 minutes until omelette is firm and a knife inserted in center comes out clean.

CRAWFISH OMELETTE

Serves 1

1   basic 3-egg omelette

Filling

¾   cup crawfish tails, boiled
     and seasoned (about 2
     pounds whole)
3   tablespoons butter
3   tablespoons minced green
     onions

1   tablespoon chopped fresh
     parsley
1   teaspoon Worcestershire
     sauce
⅛   teaspoon cayenne pepper
⅛   teaspoon salt

When peeling crawfish, reserve as much fat as possible. Coarsely chop crawfish. In a small skillet, lightly sauté onions in butter. Add crawfish, fat, and parsley and stir until blended. Season with Worcestershire sauce, cayenne, and salt. Keep filling warm while preparing omelette. When omelette is set, spread filling over half and fold. Serve immediately.

MAPLE SYRUP SOUFFLÉED OMELETTE

Preheat oven to 350°

Serves 2

3   eggs, separated
6   tablespoons maple syrup
½   teaspoon vanilla
     Pinch of salt

3   tablespoons butter
¼   cup blanched almonds
4   slices bacon, cooked and
     crumbled

Beat yolks until frothy; add 3 tablespoons syrup, vanilla, and salt. In another bowl, beat egg whites until stiff peaks form. Fold into first mixture. In a 12-inch ovenproof skillet, melt butter. Add almonds; pour in egg mixture and cook over low heat 8 minutes. Place pan in oven and cook 8 to 10 minutes. To serve, fold omelette and transfer to a hot serving dish. Pour remaining 3 tablespoons syrup over omelette; garnish with bacon; serve immediately.

CRABMEAT QUICHE

Serves 6 to 8

Preheat oven to 425°

1	10-inch pastry shell		1	tablespoon tomato paste
4	tablespoons butter		½	teaspoon salt
⅓	cup chopped green onions		⅛	teaspoon red pepper
½	cup chopped fresh mushrooms		1	cup fresh crabmeat
			2	tablespoons dry vermouth
3	large eggs		½	cup grated cheddar cheese
1	cup heavy cream			

Prick pastry shell and bake 12 minutes. Remove shell and reduce temperature to 375°. In skillet, melt butter; sauté onions and mushrooms 5 minutes. In a bowl, beat eggs and cream; add tomato paste, salt, and pepper; mix well. Stir crabmeat and vermouth into mushroom mixture and cook over low heat serveral minutes. Pour crabmeat mixture into eggs and cream and stir until combined. Pour all ingredients into pastry shell and bake. After 35 minutes, sprinkle with cheese and return to oven until knife inserted in center comes out clean, approximately 10 minutes.

SPINACH QUICHE

Serves 4 to 6

Preheat oven to 400°

1	10-inch pastry shell		¼	teaspoon nutmeg
2	tablespoons butter, melted		⅛	teaspoon cayenne pepper
¾	cup chopped white onion		1	tablespoon Worcestershire sauce
⅓	cup chopped green onions			
¼	cup chopped fresh parsley		2	eggs, beaten
1	10-ounce package frozen chopped spinach, cooked and well drained		1	cup grated Swiss, Jarlsburg, *or* Gruyère cheese
2	tablespoons flour		⅓	cup grated Parmesan cheese
1	teaspoon salt			
¼	teaspoon black pepper		1¼	cups milk

Prick pastry shell and bake 8 minutes. Remove shell and reduce temperature to 350°. In butter, sauté onions and parsley. Add spinach and cook 2 minutes. Add flour, salt, pepper, nutmeg, cayenne, and Worcestershire sauce; mix well. In a bowl, combine eggs, cheeses, and milk; mix well; add to spinach mixture. Pour into pastry shell and bake 45 minutes to 1 hour, until knife inserted in center comes out clean.

APPLE SAUSAGE QUICHE

Serves 6 to 8

Preheat oven to 350°

½	pound ground pork sausage	1	tablespoon brown sugar
⅓	cup chopped onion	3	eggs
¼	teaspoon thyme	1¼	cups light cream
1¼	cups peeled and diced apple	½	cup grated cheddar cheese
1	tablespoon lemon juice	1	10-inch pastry shell

In a skillet, cook sausage and drain on absorbent paper. Cook onion and thyme in sausage drippings. In a bowl, toss apple with lemon juice and sugar. In a separate bowl, beat eggs; add cream, cheese, apple mixture, sausage, and onion. Pour all ingredients into pastry shell and bake 50 minutes, until a knife inserted in center comes out clean.

ARTICHOKE QUICHE

Serves 6

Preheat oven to 400°

1	9-inch pastry shell	1	cup grated hot pepper cheese
2	tablespoons butter, melted	1	cup grated cheddar cheese
⅓	cup chopped green onions		
2	eggs		
1	tablespoon flour		
⅔	cup light cream		
1	14-ounce can artichoke hearts, drained and coarsely chopped		

Prick pastry shell and bake 12 minutes. Remove shell and reduce temperature to 350°. In butter, sauté onion. In a large bowl, beat eggs, flour, and cream. Stir in artichokes, pepper cheese, onion-butter mixture, and cheddar cheese, reserving 3 tablespoons. Stir until well blended. Pour into pastry shell and bake 35 minutes. Sprinkle top with remaining 3 tablespoons cheddar cheese, and bake until knife inserted in center comes out clean, approximately 10 minutes.

MUSHROOM QUICHE

Serves 6

Preheat oven to 425°

1   9-inch pastry shell

Filling

4   slices bacon, cooked and
     crumbled
½   cup sliced white onion
1   cup water
1½   teaspoons salt
¾   cup grated Swiss cheese
2   cups sliced fresh
     mushrooms
2   tablespoons butter

Custard

1   tablespoon butter
1   tablespoon flour
1   cup milk, warmed
2   eggs well beaten
½   teaspoon salt
⅛   teaspoon cayenne pepper
⅛   teaspoon nutmeg

Prick pastry shell and bake 12 minutes. Remove shell and reduce temperature to 350°. Sprinkle bacon on bottom of pastry shell. Cook onion in salted water until limp. Drain onion and place on top of bacon. Sprinkle cheese over bacon and onion. Sauté mushrooms in butter. Drain and spread over cheese.

Custard: In a saucepan, over low heat, melt butter. Remove from heat; add flour, stirring constantly until smooth. Return pan to heat and cook 3 minutes. Add milk, stirring with wire whisk. Cook slowly until slightly thickened. Cool 5 minutes; stir in eggs. Season with salt, cayenne, and nutmeg. Pour into pastry shell and bake at 350° 40 minutes, or until knife inserted in center comes out clean.

SAUSAGE QUICHE

Serves 6

Preheat oven to 425°

1   10-inch pastry shell
1½   cups grated Swiss cheese
1½   cups grated cheddar
     cheese
½   cup grated Parmesan
     cheese

1   pound ground hot sausage,
     browned and drained
½   cup grated onion
3   eggs
½   cup light cream
1   cup sour cream

Prick pastry shell and bake 12 minutes. Remove shell and reduce temperature to 375°. In a large bowl, mix cheeses, sausage, and onion. In a smaller bowl, beat eggs with creams. Combine ingredients and pour into pastry shell. Bake at 375° 50 to 60 minutes, or until knife inserted in center comes out clean.

BRIE QUICHE

Serves 6 to 8

Preheat oven to 400°

1	9-inch pastry shell, unbaked	4	tablespoons butter, softened
8	ounces softened Brie cheese, rind removed	6	tablespoons heavy cream
8	ounces cream cheese, softened	4	eggs, beaten
		4	dashes Tabasco
		1	tablespoon minced chives

Prick pastry shell and bake 12 minutes. Remove and reduce temperature to 375°. Blend Brie, cream cheese, butter, and cream. Add eggs and blend well. Season with Tabasco; stir in chives. Pour into pastry shell and set in upper third of oven. Bake 25 to 30 minutes or until quiche has puffed and top is brown.

BAKED ZUCCHINI PIE

Serves 8

Preheat oven to 350°

1¼	pounds zucchini	1	tablespoon olive oil
2	teaspoons salt	¼	teaspoon minced garlic
4	egg yolks, lightly beaten	¼	teaspoon pepper
½	cup grated onion	¼	teaspoon nutmeg
¾	cup grated Parmesan cheese	4	egg whites, stiffly beaten
1	large potato, boiled, peeled, and mashed, to equal 1 cup		

In a bowl, grate zucchini; sprinkle with 1½ teaspoons salt. Let stand 15 minutes. Drain very well. In a bowl, combine zucchini, egg yolks, onion, ½ cup cheese, potato, oil, garlic, ½ teaspoon salt, pepper, and nutmeg. Fold whites into zucchini mixture, blending gently but thoroughly. Pour mixture into a lightly-greased 10-inch pie plate. Sprinkle with remaining ¼ cup cheese and bake 30 minutes, until knife inserted in center comes out clean.

BLACK OLIVE AND TOMATO PIE

Serves 6

Preheat oven to 425°

1   9-inch pastry shell
2   medium tomatoes, sliced in 7-½ inch thick slices
¾   teaspoon salt
¼   cup flour
¼   teaspoon pepper
2   tablespoons olive oil
½   cup sliced black olives

1   cup minced green onions
3   ounces Provolone cheese, thinly sliced
2   eggs, slightly beaten
1   cup grated cheddar cheese
1   cup heavy cream

Prick pastry shell and bake 12 minutes. Remove shell and reduce temperature to 375°. Place tomato slices on absorbent paper and sprinkle with ¼ teaspoon salt. Drain 15 minutes, turning once. Dip in flour seasoned with ½ teaspoon salt and pepper; sauté quickly in heated oil. Arrange olives and all but 2 tablespoons onion in bottom of pastry shell. Cover with Provolone slices and top with tomatoes. In a bowl, mix eggs, cheddar cheese, and cream. Pour over tomatoes. Bake 45 minutes, or until knife inserted in center comes out clean. Sprinkle with remaining 2 tablespoons onions and cool 5 minutes before cutting.

CHEESEY EGG FLOAT WITH SHRIMP

Preheat oven to 350°

Serves 4

3   tablespoons butter
3   tablespoons flour
1½   cups milk
½   teaspoon salt
½   teaspoon curry powder
1   tablespoon minced onion
¼   teaspoon celery seeds

1   cup cooked shrimp
5   eggs
1   cup grated cheddar cheese
5   slices buttered toast, *or* English muffins
    Fresh parsley

In a saucepan, melt butter. Blend in flour and add milk, salt, curry powder, onion, and celery seeds. Stir constantly over low heat, until sauce boils and thickens. Stir in shrimp. Pour mixture in a shallow, buttered baking dish. Break eggs and drop on surface. Sprinkle with cheese and bake 15 to 20 minutes, until eggs are done to desired firmness and cheese is toasted. Serve on muffins and garnish with parsley. Diced ham or crawfish may be substituted for shrimp.

EGGS CAVIAR

Makes 20 stuffed eggs

10	hard-boiled eggs
6	ounces blue cheese, softened
⅓	cup black caviar
1	tablespoon chopped chives
1½	teaspoons minced fresh parsley
⅛	teaspoon cayenne pepper
½	cup mayonnaise
1	tablespoon lemon juice
5	black olives, sliced

Slice eggs in half lengthwise; remove yolks and mash. In a separate bowl, mash cheese and mix with caviar, chives, parsley, cayenne, mayonnaise, and lemon juice. Blend with yolks and spoon into egg whites. Garnish with an olive slice.

CREOLE SCRAMBLE

Serves 4

1	tablespoon olive oil
½	pound smoked sausage, thinly sliced
½	teaspoon finely chopped garlic
⅛	teaspoon cayenne pepper
½	cup sliced green onions
¾	cup fresh tomatoes, peeled and quartered
½	cup thinly sliced green pepper
⅓	cup cold water
⅛	teaspoon black pepper
6	eggs, slightly beaten

In a skillet, heat oil. Add sausage, garlic, cayenne, and onions. Cook until sausage is lightly browned, stirring frequently. Add tomatoes, green pepper, water, and black pepper; cook quickly until most of liquid has evaporated. Green pepper should remain crisp. Pour eggs into sausage mixture and stir over very low heat, until soft and creamy. Serve immediately.

FANCY EGG SCRAMBLE

Serves 8

Make ahead

Preheat oven to 350°

Cheese Sauce

2 tablespoons butter	2 cups milk
2 tablespoons flour	1 cup grated cheddar cheese
½ teaspoon salt	
⅛ teaspoon pepper	

In a saucepan, melt butter and gradually stir in flour. Add salt and pepper. Gradually add milk; stir until sauce thickens. Add cheese and stir until melted. Remove from heat.

Filling

1 cup diced Canadian bacon, *or* ham, *or* bacon	2 cups cheese sauce
¼ cup chopped green onions	2 tablespoons butter, melted
3 tablespoons butter	2¼ cups bread crumbs
12 eggs, beaten	⅛ teaspoon paprika
1 8-ounce can sliced mushrooms, drained	

In a skillet, cook Canadian bacon and onions in butter until tender. Add eggs and scramble, over **very low heat,** until set. Remove from heat and stir in mushrooms and cheese sauce. Pour mixture into greased 12 × 7 × 2 baking dish. Combine butter, bread crumbs, and paprika and sprinkle over top. Bake, uncovered, 30 minutes.

SPANISH EGGS

Serves 6

6 slices bacon, cooked and crumbled	¼ teaspoon salt
3 tablespoons bacon grease	¼ teaspoon cayenne pepper
1 cup corn chips, small size	8 large eggs, beaten
1 cup chopped onion	1 15-ounce can chili, heated
½ cup thinly sliced green pepper	1 cup grated sharp cheddar cheese

In skillet, over medium heat, stir corn chips in bacon grease 2 minutes. Add onion and green pepper, stirring until onion becomes transparent. Mix bacon, salt, and cayenne with eggs; combine with corn chip mixture; cook over medium-low heat stirring constantly. Place mixture in 1-quart casserole. Pour heated chili over eggs; sprinkle with cheese and serve immediately.

WEST INDIAN EGGS

Serves 8

1½ cups tomato sauce
¼ cup minced green onions
¼ cup minced green pepper
2 tablespoons flour
1 cup grated cheddar cheese
2 dashes Tabasco
1 teaspoon lemon juice

⅛ teaspoon tarragon
2 cups peeled and cubed avocados
12 eggs
⅔ cup light cream
½ teaspoon salt
4 tablespoons butter

In a saucepan, blend tomato sauce, green onions, green pepper, and flour. Bring to a boil and cook, stirring 2 to 3 minutes. Stir in ⅔ cup cheese, Tabasco, lemon juice, and tarragon. Remove from heat and add avocado cubes. DO NOT COOK, but keep warm.

In large bowl, beat eggs with cream and salt. Melt butter in large skillet, and scramble eggs until set. Season tomato sauce with Tabasco, lemon juice and tarragon. Transfer to a warmed serving platter and spoon tomato sauce over eggs. Sprinkle with remaining ⅓ cup cheese. Serve immediately.

BACON CHEESE SOUFFLÉ

Serves 6

6 slices bacon, cooked and crumbled
2 tablespoons bacon grease
⅓ cup chopped white onion
5 eggs, separated
3 tablespoons flour
2 dashes Tabasco
1¼ cups milk

¼ teaspoon paprika
1½ cups grated Swiss cheese
¼ teaspoon salt
1 cup grated cheddar cheese
1 tablespoon chopped fresh parsley

In bacon grease, sauté onion. In a large bowl, combine egg yolks, flour, Tabasco, milk, and paprika; beat until smooth. Stir in Swiss cheese. In a small bowl, beat egg whites with salt until stiff, but not dry. Fold whites into cheese mixture. Place skillet over *very low heat* and pour cheese mixture over onions. Cover and cook 12 to 15 minutes, or until almost set. Sprinkle with cheddar cheese and bacon; cover and cook 5 minutes longer, until firmly set. Sprinkle with parsley and serve immediately.

SAUSAGE AND EGG PUFF

Serves 6

Make a day ahead

1	pound ground hot sausage	½	teaspoon salt
2	slices white bread, diced	1	drop Tabasco
1	cup grated sharp cheddar cheese	1	teaspoon dry mustard
6	eggs	1	teaspoon Worcestershire sauce
1⅔	cups milk		

In a skillet, brown sausage, making sure that there are no large lumps. Drain. In a 2-quart casserole, layer sausage, bread, and cheese. In a bowl, beat eggs with milk, salt, Tabasco, mustard, and Worcestershire sauce. Pour mixture over sausage, bread, and cheese. Cover and refrigerate 12 hours, or overnight. Remove from refrigerator 1 hour before cooking. Preheat oven to 350°; bake, uncovered, 45 minutes, or until firm and golden on top.

SOUFFLÉED CHEESE TOAST

Serves 6

Preheat oven to 375°

6	slices white bread, crusts removed	¼	teaspoon Worcestershire sauce
2½	tablespoons butter, softened	⅛	teaspoon cayenne pepper
6	slices ham	1	cup grated sharp cheddar cheese
18	asparagus spears, cooked	¼	teaspoon salt
4	eggs, separated		Pimiento strips, thinly sliced
1	teaspoon dry mustard		

Toast bread and lightly butter one side. Place on greased baking sheet, topping each slice with 1 slice ham and 3 asparagus spears. In a bowl, beat egg yolks with dry mustard, Worcestershire sauce, and cayenne. Stir in cheese. In another bowl, beat egg whites with salt until stiff. Fold small amount of egg whites into cheese mixture. Fold in remaining whites. Spoon soufflé mixture over asparagus. Bake 10 minutes, or until puffed and lightly browned. Garnish with pimiento strips.

CHEESE SOUFFLÉ

Serves 6 to 8

Preheat oven to 325°

6	tablespoons butter	¼	teaspoon dry mustard
6	tablespoons flour	¼	teaspoon nutmeg
2	cups milk	2	cups grated sharp cheddar cheese
¾	teaspoon salt		
¼	teaspoon white pepper	8	egg yolks, well beaten
10	drops Tabasco	8	egg whites, stiffly beaten

In top of double boiler, melt butter; stir in flour. Gradually add milk, stirring until thickened. Add salt, pepper, Tabasco, mustard, nutmeg, and cheese. Stir until cheese melts. Stir 2 tablespoons of hot cheese mixture into beaten egg yolks. Pour yolk mixture back into cheese mixture; return to double boiler and whisk 30 seconds. Remove from heat and when slightly cool, fold egg whites into cheese mixture. Pour into a 3-quart, ungreased soufflé dish. Place in pan of warm water. Make a half inch cut around surface of soufflé, 1 inch from edge. Bake approximately 55 minutes, until set in middle and golden on top. Serve immediately.

DEVILED EGGS WITH BÉCHAMEL SAUCE

Can be made ahead

Serves 12 to 14

18	hard-boiled eggs	2	teaspoons lemon juice
¾	cup mayonnaise	16	ripe olives, chopped
¼	cup hot mustard	16	pimiento stuffed olives, chopped
4	dashes Tabasco		
½	teaspoon white pepper	½	teaspoon paprika
4	tablespoons butter	1	cup grated cheddar cheese
6	tablespoons flour		
½	teaspoon salt	1½	tablespoons minced fresh parsley
2	cups chicken stock		
1¼	cups half and half cream		

Slice eggs in half lengthwise; remove yolks and mash. Add mayonnaise, mustard, Tabasco, and pepper; mix well. Spoon into egg whites. Place in shallow baking dish and set aside. May be made ahead up to this point.

Preheat oven to 350°. In top of double boiler, melt butter; blend in flour and salt. Slowly add stock and cream; stir constantly until thick. Add lemon juice, olives, paprika, and cheese and stir until cheese is melted. Spoon sauce over eggs and sprinkle with parsley. Bake 15 minutes. Sauce can be frozen.

SWISS TOAST

Serves 10 to 12

Preheat oven to 375°

1½ cups butter, softened
½ cup chopped white onion
1½ pounds fresh mushrooms, sliced
½ cup white wine
2 cups half and half cream
¾ cup flour
1 teaspoon lemon juice
½ teaspoon salt

⅛ teaspoon white pepper
12 slices toasted bread
24 slices ham
24 slices Swiss cheese
Paprika
Chopped fresh parsley
Pimiento strips, thinly sliced

In a saucepan, sauté onion in ½ cup butter. Add mushrooms and wine; cover and continue cooking 10 to 15 minutes. Remove mushrooms with a slotted spoon and add cream. Remove from heat. In a small bowl, mix flour and another ½ cup butter. Add to cream and cook over very low heat about 5 minutes, stirring frequently until smooth and thick. Stir in mushrooms, lemon juice, salt, and pepper. Butter toast with remaining ½ cup butter and place slices on 2 jelly-roll pans. Cover each slice with 1 slice ham. Spoon mushroom mixture on top and cover with another slice ham and 2 slices cheese. Sprinkle with paprika. Bake until cheese is melted, about 7 minutes. Garnish with parsley and pimiento.

BROILED CHEESE MUFFINS

Serves 4

Preheat broiler

2 cups grated cheddar cheese
4 hard-boiled eggs, chopped
½ cup mayonnaise
1 2-ounce jar diced pimiento, drained
1 tablespoon chopped celery

1 tablespoon chopped green onions
1 teaspoon horseradish
¼ teaspoon salt
3 dashes Tabasco
4 English muffins, split
1 tablespoon chopped fresh parsley

In a large bowl, combine cheese, eggs, mayonnaise, pimiento, celery, onions, horseradish, salt, and Tabasco. Blend well. Spread muffins with cheese mixture and sprinkle with parsley. Place muffins on baking sheet and broil until golden brown, about 7 minutes.

EGGS IN TOMATOES FLORENTINE Serves 6

Spinach

2	10-ounce packages frozen chopped spinach, thawed	2	teaspoons chives
1	cup sour cream	¼	teaspoon black pepper
½	teaspoon garlic salt	⅛	teaspoon cayenne pepper
½	teaspoon celery salt	¼	teaspoon nutmeg
2	teaspoons Worcestershire sauce	½	cup grated Parmesan cheese

Squeeze moisture out of spinach. In a saucepan, combine spinach with remaining ingredients, and warm over low heat.

Tomatoes

6	ripe, firm tomatoes (approximately 3 inches in diameter)	¼	cup seasoned bread crumbs
1	teaspoon salt	¼	cup grated Parmesan cheese
6	teaspoons butter	6	teaspoons melted butter
6	teaspoons finely chopped green onions	6	slices bacon, cooked and crumbled
6	large eggs		

Preheat oven to 400°. Slice top off each tomato. Scoop out and discard pulp. Salt inside and invert on a rack to drain 20 minutes. Place tomatoes right side up in a lightly buttered 10 × 12 casserole. Put 1 teaspoon butter in each tomato and top with 1 teaspoon onion. Break an egg into each tomato and bake 10 minutes. Remove and transfer to a buttered 10 × 12 shallow baking dish lined with spinach mixture. Loosely cover with foil and bake 15 minutes, or until whites are set. Top each egg with 2 teaspoons each bread crumbs, Parmesan cheese, and 1 teaspoon melted butter. Broil until crumbs are lightly browned. Remove from oven and sprinkle with bacon.

Seafood

SHRIMP AND SAUSAGE JAMBALAYA

Preheat oven to 350°   **Serves 10**

1	pound smoked sausage, thinly sliced	2	bay leaves
3	tablespoons olive oil	2	teaspoons oregano
⅔	cup chopped green pepper	1	tablespoon Creole seasoning*
2	cloves garlic, minced	½	teaspoon salt
¾	cup chopped fresh parsley	¼	teaspoon cayenne pepper
1	cup chopped celery	¼	teaspoon black pepper
2	16-ounce cans tomatoes	2	cups long grain converted rice, washed
2	cups chicken broth		
1	cup chopped green onions	3	pounds raw shrimp, peeled
1½	teaspoons thyme		

In 4-quart heavy pot, sauté sausage; remove with slotted spoon. Add oil to drippings and sauté green pepper, garlic, parsley, and celery 5 minutes. Chop tomatoes and reserve liquid. Add tomatoes with liquid, broth, and onions. Stir in spices. Add rice which has been washed and rinsed three times. Add sausage and cook 30 minutes, covered, over low heat, stirring occasionally. After most liquid has been absorbed by rice, add shrimp and cook until pink. Transfer mixture to an oblong baking dish; bake approximately 25 minutes.

*A mixture of salt, red pepper, black pepper, chili powder, and garlic powder.

SHRIMP FETTUCINE

Serves 4 to 6

5 green onions, chopped	8 ounces noodles
2 cups sliced mushrooms	¾ cup grated Romano cheese
2 cloves garlic, minced	
1 stick butter	¾ cup grated Parmesan cheese
2 tablespoons oil	
1 pound peeled, raw shrimp	1 cup heavy cream
2 teaspoons salt	¼ cup chopped fresh parsley

In a large skillet, sauté onions, mushrooms, and garlic in ½ stick butter and oil. Add shrimp and sauté until pink. Pour off excess liquid. Season with salt; cover and keep warm.

Cook noodles in salted, boiling water. Drain. In saucepan, melt remaining ½ stick butter. Add noodles, cheeses, and cream. Mix well and combine with shrimp mixture. Sprinkle with parsley, toss, and serve immediately.

SHRIMP CLEMENCEAU

Serves 4

4 pounds raw, unpeeled shrimp	2 cups peeled and cubed potatoes, sautéed until tender
1 pound butter	
2 cups small fresh mushroom caps	2 cups small green peas
1½ teaspoons minced garlic	2 teaspoons minced fresh parsley
2 teaspoons lemon juice	
2 tablespoons Worcestershire sauce	

Peel and devein shrimp.

In a large skillet, melt butter and sauté mushrooms and garlic 3 to 5 minutes. Add shrimp, lemon juice, Worcestershire sauce, and potatoes. Sauté 6 to 8 minutes or until shrimp turn pink. Add peas and parsley and heat thoroughly.

SHRIMP AND RICE CASSEROLE   Serves 12

Preheat oven to 375°

1	stick plus 3 tablespoons butter	½	teaspoon pepper
3	pounds peeled, raw shrimp	2	teaspoons Worcestershire sauce
½	cup chopped green pepper	¼	teaspoon Tabasco
1	cup chopped yellow onion	1	tablespoon chopped chives
¼	pound fresh mushrooms, sliced	1	tablespoon chopped pimiento
6	cups cooked rice	½	cup dry bread crumbs
1	teaspoon thyme	½	cup heavy cream
1	teaspoon salt		

In a large skillet, melt 1 stick butter. Add shrimp, green pepper, onion, and mushrooms. Sauté, stirring constantly, 3 to 5 minutes. Stir in rice, thyme, salt, pepper, Worcestershire sauce, and Tabasco. Gently mix over low heat. Fold in chives and pimiento. Put mixture into 3-quart casserole. Melt remaining 3 tablespoons butter and combine with bread crumbs. Top casserole with crumbs. Pour cream around edge of casserole. Bake 25 to 30 minutes.

SHRIMP ORIENTAL CASSEROLE   Serves 6

Preheat oven to 350°

1	stick butter	2	teaspoons salt
½	cup flour	2	teaspoons soy sauce
½	cup chopped green pepper	½	teaspoon white pepper
½	cup chopped celery	2	tablespoons lemon juice
2	cups light cream	3	pounds shrimp, cooked, peeled, and deveined
1	cup dry white wine		
1	cup grated cheddar cheese	3	cups steamed rice, *or*
½	pound fresh mushrooms, sliced	6	patty shells

In a large skillet, melt butter. Add flour; blend well. Add green pepper and celery. Cook until soft, but not brown, about 5 to 7 minutes. After vegetables are soft, gradually add cream and wine. Stir in cheese, mushrooms, salt, soy sauce, pepper, and lemon juice. Simmer 2 minutes; add shrimp. Pour into a 2-quart casserole. Bake 20 to 25 minutes. Serve over steamed rice or in patty shells.

SHRIMP AND CHICKEN CURRY

Serves 6

1 pound raw shrimp	1 tablespoon tomato paste
4 large chicken breasts, skinned and boned	½ cup cubed banana
4 tablespoons butter	1 cup peeled and cubed apple
½ cup finely chopped yellow onion	1 cup chicken broth
1 small garlic clove, crushed	1 teaspoon salt
½ cup finely diced celery	½ teaspoon pepper
2 tablespoons curry powder	3 cups steamed rice

Peel shrimp, rinse, and drain. Cut chicken into 1-inch cubes.

In a large skillet, melt 2 tablespoons butter; add onion and garlic. Cook briefly and add celery. Cook, stirring, 1 minute. Sprinkle with curry powder and continue stirring, adding tomato paste, banana, and apple. Gradually pour in broth, blending well. Add salt and simmer 10 minutes.

In saucepan, melt remaining butter. Add chicken and sprinkle with salt and pepper. Cook, stirring occasionally, 2 to 3 minutes. Add shrimp and simmer, stirring constantly, 2 minutes. Transfer chicken and shrimp with a slotted spoon into a 1½-quart casserole. Pour curry sauce over chicken and shrimp. Bake 20 to 25 minutes. Serve over rice.

SHRIMP DEWEY

Serves 6

4 tablespoons butter	⅓ cup white wine
1½ cups chopped green onions	1 cup sour cream
¾ cup canned Italian tomatoes, and ½ cup liquid	1½ teaspoons salt
	¼ teaspoon basil
1½ pounds raw shrimp, peeled and deveined	½ teaspoon oregano
1 cup sliced mushrooms	¼ teaspoon pepper
¼ cup chopped fresh parsley	Tabasco to taste
3 tablespoons cornstarch dissolved in ¼ cup water	6 patty shells, heated

In a large skillet, melt butter and sauté onions. Add tomatoes and liquid; cook 5 minutes, mashing well. Add shrimp and simmer 5 minutes. Add mushrooms and parsley; cook a few minutes longer. Slowly stir in cornstarch. When thickened, add wine, sour cream, salt, basil, oregano, pepper, and Tabasco. Heat, but do not boil. Spoon in patty shells.

COLD SHRIMP CURRY

Serves 8

4 tablespoons butter
1 cup peeled and chopped apple
2 cups chopped green onions
1 teaspoon crushed coriander seed
1 teaspoon ginger
1 tablespoon curry powder
1 teaspoon flour
1 large orange, peeled and chopped

½ cup coconut liquid, *or* milk mixed with 1½ teaspoons sugar
2 cups mayonnaise
Salt to taste
Pepper to taste
Dash cayenne pepper
2 tablespoons lemon juice
3 pounds peeled, cooked shrimp

In a skillet, melt butter and sauté apple and onions until soft, approximately 8 to 10 minutes. Add coriander seed, ginger, curry powder, and flour. Mix well. Add orange. Add coconut liquid, one teaspoon at a time, using just enough to form a smooth paste. Cool and mix paste with mayonnaise. Add salt, pepper, cayenne, and lemon juice. Combine sauce and shrimp. Chill.

Variation: Can be served in scooped-out pineapple halves. Garnish with cubed pineapple and toasted, grated coconut.

CRAB AND SHRIMP ÉTOUFFÉ

Serves 6

3 pounds raw, unpeeled shrimp
1½ sticks butter
1 cup finely chopped onion
¼ cup finely chopped green pepper
¼ cup finely chopped celery
4 cloves garlic, minced
4 teaspoons cornstarch
1-1½ cups chicken stock
½ cup white wine
4 teaspoons tomato paste

¼ cup finely chopped green onions
¼ cup finely chopped fresh parsley
1 tablespoon Worcestershire sauce
Salt to taste
Pepper to taste
Tabasco to taste
1 pound crabmeat
3 cups steamed rice

Peel and devein shrimp.

In Dutch oven, melt butter. Add onion, green pepper, and celery; cook until tender. Add garlic. Dissolve cornstarch in 1 cup stock. Add to sautéed vegetables. Add wine, stirring constantly. Add tomato paste, onions, parsley, and Worcestershire sauce. Blend well. Add shrimp and cover. Simmer 10 minutes, stirring occasionally. If necessary, add more stock. Add salt, pepper, and Tabasco. Add crabmeat, stirring gently, and continue cooking until thoroughly heated. Serve on bed of steamed rice.

SHRIMP AND SPAGHETTI

Serves 6-8

4 pounds raw, unpeeled shrimp
2 sticks butter
1 cup chopped onion
5 cloves garlic, minced
⅔ cup coarsely chopped celery
1 green pepper, cut in strips
¼ cup dry white wine
¼ cup water

2 bay leaves
1 teaspoon thyme
Salt to taste
Pepper to taste
Tabasco to taste
1 pound thin spaghetti
½ cup chopped fresh parsley
Freshly grated Romano cheese

Peel and devein shrimp.

In a Dutch oven, melt 1½ sticks butter; sauté onion and garlic until tender. Add celery and green pepper and cook 2 minutes. Add shrimp and cook until pink, about 5 minutes. With a slotted spoon, remove shrimp and vegetable mixture to heated bowl and keep warm. Add wine and water to Dutch oven and boil 5 minutes. Reduce heat; add bay leaves, thyme, salt, pepper, and Tabasco; simmer 20 minutes. Add remaining ½ stick butter and shrimp and vegetable mixture. Remove bay leaves. Cover and keep warm.

Cook spaghetti in salted, boiling water, al dente. Drain thoroughly and put in a large, heated shallow dish. Add parsley to warmed shrimp and pour over spaghetti. Toss well with 2 large forks. Sprinkle with cheese and serve immediately.

SHRIMP VERMOUTH

Serves 4

5 pounds raw, unpeeled shrimp
2 sticks butter
2 cloves garlic, split
6 tablespoons chopped fresh parsley
1 teaspoon tarragon

1 cup dry vermouth
2 teaspoons salt
¼ teaspoon cayenne pepper
½ teaspoon black pepper
1 teaspoon paprika
Garlic bread or toast points

Peel and devein shrimp.

In a large skillet, heat butter; add garlic and cook 2 minutes, mashing with back of a wooden spoon. Remove garlic. Add shrimp and sauté 5 minutes, or until pink. Remove shrimp to a hot platter. Add parsley, tarragon, and vermouth. Increase heat and simmer 30 seconds. Add shrimp. Season with salt, cayenne, black pepper, and paprika. Serve on rounds of garlic bread or toast points.

SHRIMP ARTICHOKE CASSEROLE   Serves 4

Preheat oven to 375°

1	14-ounce can artichoke hearts, drained and quartered	½	cup milk
1½	pounds boiled shrimp, peeled and deveined	1	teaspoon salt
		½	teaspoon pepper
1	stick butter	¼	cup dry sherry
½	pound fresh mushrooms, sliced	1	tablespoon Worcestershire sauce
¼	cup flour	¼	cup freshly grated Parmesan cheese
1	cup heavy cream	¼	teaspoon paprika

In bottom of well-greased 1½-quart casserole, place artichoke hearts and cover with shrimp. In half stick butter sauté mushrooms 6 to 8 minutes. Pour over shrimp. Melt remaining half stick butter. Add flour and cook over low heat 3 to 5 minutes, stirring constantly. Gradually add cream and milk, cooking until thick. Add salt, pepper, sherry, and Worcestershire sauce. Stir until smooth. Pour over casserole; top with cheese and paprika. Bake 25 minutes, until light brown and bubbly.

SHRIMP CREOLE   Serves 4

2½	pounds raw, unpeeled shrimp	1	clove garlic, minced
1½	tablespoons bacon grease	3	dashes Tabasco
1½	tablespoons flour	2	tablespoons Worcestershire sauce
½	cup finely chopped onion	1	teaspoon sugar
⅓	cup finely chopped green pepper	2	teaspoons salt
¼	cup finely chopped celery	¼	teaspoon pepper
1	8-ounce can tomato sauce	2	tablespoons chopped fresh parsley
1	16-ounce can Italian plum tomatoes with basil, reserving liquid	¾	cup chopped green onions
		2	cups steamed rice

Peel and devein shrimp.

In a large pot, heat bacon grease and add flour, stirring constantly until roux is golden brown. Add onion, green pepper, and celery; cook until tender. Pour in tomato sauce, tomatoes, and liquid. Blend well. Add garlic, Tabasco, Worcestershire sauce, sugar, salt, and pepper. Simmer 30 minutes, stirring occasionally. Add shrimp, parsley, and green onions; cook 30 minutes. Serve over rice.

SHRIMP MOUSSE WITH HORSERADISH SAUCE

Preheat oven to 350°   **Serves 4 to 6**

1¼	pounds peeled, raw shrimp	¼	teaspoon nutmeg
2	eggs whites	¼	teaspoon Tabasco
1½	teaspoons salt	2	cups heavy cream
½	teaspoon pepper	2	tablespoons butter

In food processor or blender, purée shrimp, reserving 6 for garnish. With motor running, add egg whites, one at a time. Add salt, pepper, nutmeg, and Tabasco. If using food processor, gradually add cream, 1 tablespoon at a time, until all is incorporated. If using blender, remove purée to a bowl and work in cream with wooden spoon. Pour mixture into a buttered 1-quart mold, and cover with buttered wax paper. Set in a pan of hot water, reaching half way up sides of mold. Bake 30 minutes.

In butter, sauté remaining 6 shrimp until pink. Pour off excess butter. Keep warm.

At end of cooking time, remove mousse from oven and run knife around inside of mold. Invert on warm serving platter, and spoon on horseradish sauce. Garnish with shrimp. Serve immediately.

Horseradish Sauce

1	tablespoon butter	2	egg yolks, lightly beaten
1	tablespoon flour	¼	cup heavy cream, lightly whipped
½	cup milk		
1	whole clove	1½	teaspoons horseradish
1	small bay leaf		

In saucepan, melt butter and blend in flour. Slowly add milk, blending until smooth; add clove and bay leaf. Cook over low heat, stirring constantly, until sauce thickens. Stir a few spoonfuls of hot sauce into egg yolks. Add egg mixture back to sauce, blending thoroughly. Add cream and horseradish. Heat thoroughly, but do not boil. Remove clove and bay leaf.

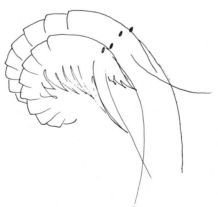

BARBECUED SHRIMP

Serves 8

Preheat oven to 450°

1	pound butter	3	cloves garlic, minced
2	cups olive oil	1	teaspoon paprika
¾	cup Worcestershire sauce	4	teaspoons salt
6	tablespoons pepper	8	pounds raw, unpeeled,
4	lemons, sliced		jumbo shrimp
½	teaspoon Tabasco		
1	tablespoon Italian seasoning		

In a 2-quart saucepan, heat butter and oil. Add Worcestershire sauce, pepper, lemons, Tabasco, Italian seasoning, garlic, paprika, and salt. Mix thoroughly. Simmer 5 to 7 minutes. Divide shrimp between 2 Dutch ovens and pour sauce over each. Cook 6 to 8 minutes, or until shrimp begin to turn pink. Bake 10 minutes, turning shrimp once. Serve with French bread.

SEAFOOD STUFFED EGGPLANT

Serves 8

Preheat oven to 350°

4	medium eggplants	¼	teaspoon Tabasco
	Salted water	1½	teaspoons Worcestershire
1	cup chopped onion		sauce
2	teaspoons minced green onions	¼	teaspoon pepper
		2	cups steamed rice
2	cloves garlic, minced	¼	cup lemon juice
½	cup minced celery	¼	cup chopped fresh parsley
½	teaspoon oregano	1	pound crabmeat
6	tablespoons bacon grease	1	cup bread crumbs
1½	pounds shrimp, peeled and chopped	6	tablespoons melted butter
		½	cup grated Parmesan
½	teaspoon salt		cheese

Wash eggplants, cut in half lengthwise, and boil in water 10 minutes, or until tender. When cool, scoop out pulp, leaving a shell ¼ inch thick. Finely chop pulp. In a Dutch oven, sauté onions, garlic, celery, and oregano in bacon grease 20 minutes. Lower heat, add eggplant; cover and simmer about 15 minutes. Add shrimp and cook until pink. Remove from heat and stir in salt, Tabasco, Worcestershire sauce, pepper, rice, and lemon juice. Gently fold in parsley and crabmeat. Arrange shells in lightly-greased baking dishes. Spoon mixture into shells. Combine bread crumbs, butter, and cheese. Sprinkle evenly over eggplant. Bake until hot and browned on top, about 30 minutes.

OYSTER AND ARTICHOKE CASSEROLE

Can be made ahead   **Serves 6 to 8**

Preheat oven to 350°

6-8 boiled artichokes (1 per person)
1 stick butter
2½ cups finely chopped green onions
½ cup finely chopped celery
1 10-ounce can cream of mushroom soup
1 tablespoon Worcestershire sauce
1 teaspoon salt
¼ teaspoon Tabasco
1 tablespoon grated lemon rind
¼ teaspoon pepper
4 pints oysters, drained on paper towels
½ cup bread crumbs
Lemon slices
Parsley

Scrape artichoke leaves; mash scrapings with fork. Keep artichoke hearts whole. In a heavy skillet, melt butter; sauté onions and celery. Reduce heat; add soup, Worcestershire sauce, salt, Tabasco, lemon rind, and pepper; simmer 10 minutes. Add artichoke scrapings and oysters to mixture and simmer 10 minutes. Arrange artichoke hearts on bottom of 2-quart casserole. Pour oyster mixture over hearts and top with bread crumbs. Bake 30 minutes. If necessary, spoon off excess liquid. Broil 3 to 5 minutes, or until bread crumbs turn brown. Garnish with lemon slices and parsley.

BAKED OYSTERS ITALIAN   **Serves 6**

Preheat oven to 425°

1¼ sticks butter
½ cup olive oil
½ cup chopped green onions
¼ cup chopped fresh parsley
2 tablespoons minced garlic
1⅓ cups seasoned bread crumbs
½ cup grated Parmesan cheese
1 teaspoon salt
½ teaspoon black pepper
¼ teaspoon cayenne pepper
1 teaspoon basil
1 teaspoon oregano
4 pints oysters, drained on paper towels

In a large skillet, heat butter and oil. Sauté onion, parsley, and garlic. In a bowl, combine bread crumbs, cheese, salt, black pepper, cayenne, basil, and oregano. Add to skillet and mix well. Remove from heat and add oysters. Stir gently; put into a 2-quart baking pan. Bake 15 minutes, or until brown and crusty.

OYSTERS AND SPAGHETTI

Serves 8

1	package Vermicelli	2	small cans anchovies
1	cup olive oil	1	teaspoon salt
4	cups sliced mushrooms	1	teaspoon pepper
4	cups chopped green onions	2	sticks butter
1	pod garlic, minced	¼	pound fresh Parmesan
1	cup chopped fresh parsley		cheese, grated
2	quarts oysters, drained		

In boiling, salted water, cook Vermicelli, al dente. Drain and keep warm in colander over hot water.

In a Dutch oven, heat oil; sauté mushrooms, green onions, and garlic until tender. Add parsley, oysters, and anchovies. Cook until oysters begin to curl. Remove from heat. Season with salt and pepper and keep warm.

In a large pot, melt butter; add Vermicelli and cheese. Mix well. Add oyster mixture and toss thoroughly with 2 large forks. Serve immediately.

OYSTERS DUFOSSAT

Serves 6

Preheat broiler

3	pints oysters, drained	½	cup melted butter, flavored
1½	cups bread crumbs		with ¼ teaspoon pressed
½	teaspoon dry mustard		garlic
	Dash cayenne pepper	8	slices bacon, cooked and
½	teaspoon paprika		crumbled
1	teaspoon salt		Lemon wedges
3	tablespoons grated		
	Parmesan cheese		

Place oysters on paper towels to dry. In a shallow dish, combine bread crumbs, mustard, cayenne, paprika, salt, and cheese. Roll oysters in mixture. Place on greased baking pan in single layer. Baste oysters with half the butter and broil until golden brown. Turn and baste with remaining half butter, and continue broiling until that side is brown. Serve topped with bacon and garnished with lemon wedges.

OYSTERS IN RAMEKINS

Serves 6

Preheat oven to 350°

2	sticks butter	½	cup oyster liquid
½	cup flour	4	pints oysters, drained on
¼	cup finely chopped celery		paper towels
¼	cup finely chopped green		Salt to taste
	pepper		Pepper to taste
¼	cup minced fresh parsley	¼	cup Worcestershire sauce
2	cups finely chopped	2	cups coarsely crushed
	onions		cracker crumbs

In large heavy pot, heat butter and gradually add flour, stirring constantly until roux is golden brown. Add celery, green pepper, parsley, and onions and sauté until onion becomes transparent. Stir in oyster liquid a little at a time until sauce has consistency of smooth, thick gravy. Add oysters, salt, and pepper. Cook, stirring occasionally, until edges of oysters begin to curl. Remove from heat and add Worcestershire sauce. Divide oysters into individual ramekins. May be prepared ahead up to this point and refrigerated for several hours or overnight. Just before serving, top with cracker crumbs and bake 10 to 15 minutes until brown and bubbly.

OYSTERS ROCKEFELLER CASSEROLE

Preheat oven to 375°　　　　　　　　　　　　　　　**Serves 10**

3	sticks butter	¾	cup chopped fresh parsley
1	teaspoon thyme	½	cup grated Parmesan
1⅔	cups chopped green onions		cheese
1	cup chopped celery	2	tablespoons Pernod (anise
1	large clove garlic, pressed		liqueur)
1	tablespoon	3	10-ounce packages frozen
	Worcestershire sauce		chopped spinach, cooked
1	teaspoon anchovy paste		and drained
1½	cups seasoned bread	½	teaspoon salt
	crumbs	¼	teaspoon black pepper
4	pints oysters, drained,	¼	teaspoon cayenne pepper
	reserving ½ cup liquid		

In a large skillet, melt butter; add thyme, onions, celery, and garlic. Sauté 5 minutes; add Worcestershire sauce, anchovy paste, and bread crumbs. Stir 5 minutes until bread crumbs are toasted. Fold in oysters, liquid, parsley, cheese, and Pernod. Cook until oysters curl, about 3 minutes. Add spinach. Season with salt, black pepper, and cayenne. Place in a 3-quart casserole and bake 20 to 25 minutes. May be served in individual ramekins as an appetizer.

SPINACH CRABMEAT CASSEROLE   Serves 6

Preheat oven to 350°

1	stick butter	1	teaspoon salt
1	cup chopped yellow onion	¼	teaspoon white pepper
¼	cup chopped green onions	1	teaspoon Worcestershire
2	10-ounce packages		sauce
	frozen chopped spinach,	¼	teaspoon Tabasco
	cooked and drained	1	pound lump crabmeat
1	pint sour cream	1	cup boiled and peeled
½	cup grated Parmesan		shrimp
	cheese		
1	7-ounce can artichoke		
	hearts, drained		

In skillet, melt butter; sauté onions 5 to 8 minutes. Add spinach, sour cream, and cheese. Reduce heat and simmer 2 to 3 minutes. Add artichoke hearts, salt, pepper, Worcestershire sauce, and Tabasco; simmer 3 minutes. Gently fold in crabmeat and shrimp. Blend well. Pour mixture into a 2-quart casserole and bake 20 to 30 minutes.

SOFT SHELL CRAB AMANDINE   Serves 6

6	medium soft shell crabs,	2	tablespoons oil
	cleaned	¾	cup sliced almonds
⅔	cup flour	2	tablespoons lemon juice
½	teaspoon salt	3	tablespoons dry white
½	teaspoon black pepper		wine
⅛	teaspoon garlic powder		Worcestershire sauce to
½	teaspoon cayenne pepper		taste
1½	sticks butter		

Dredge crabs lightly in flour seasoned with salt, pepper, garlic powder, and cayenne. In a large skillet, melt butter and oil. When mixture is very hot, add crabs, one at a time, being sure not to overcrowd. Cook 6 minutes. Turn and cook 4 to 5 minutes more. Transfer to a heated platter and keep hot. To pan juices, add almonds; sauté until lighlty browned. Add lemon juice, wine, and Worcestershire sauce. Mix; heat. Pour over crabs.

CRABMEAT CAROLINE

Serves 4

Preheat oven to 350°

2	tablespoons butter	1	teaspoon salt
2	tablespoons flour	¼	teaspoon Tabasco
¼	cup minced green onions	⅓	cup grated Gruyère
¼	cup minced green pepper		cheese
1	clove garlic, minced	⅛	teaspoon dry mustard
⅛	teaspoon rosemary	1	pound lump crabmeat
1	tomato, peeled and	3	tablespoons grated
	chopped		Mozzarella cheese
¼	cup dry white wine	3	tablespoons grated
1	cup heavy cream		Parmesan cheese

In a large skillet melt butter and gradually blend in flour. Cook 2 minutes, stirring constantly. Add onions, green pepper, garlic, rosemary, and tomato; sauté 2 to 3 minutes. Add wine and continue cooking until vegetables are tender. Lower heat, and gradually add cream, salt, and Tabasco. Blend well. Remove from heat and stir in Gruyère cheese and mustard. Gently fold crabmeat into sauce and spoon into individual buttered ramekins. Combine cheeses and sprinkle on top. Bake 10 to 15 minutes, until browned and bubbly.

STUFFED CRABS

Serves 8

Preheat oven to 350°

6	tablespoons butter		Cayenne pepper to taste
¼	cup minced celery leaves	¼	teaspoon Tabasco
½	cup minced onion	2	cups French bread cubes
2	cloves garlic, minced	1	cup chicken broth
1	pound crab meat	2	eggs, beaten
¼	cup minced fresh parsley	8	crab shells
1	teaspoon black pepper	4	teaspoons bread crumbs
1	teaspoon salt	4	teaspoons butter
3	bay leaves		
2	teaspoons Worcestershire		
	sauce		

In a Dutch oven, melt butter and sauté celery leaves, onion, and garlic until tender. Add crabmeat, parsley, pepper, salt, bay leaves, Worcestershire sauce, cayenne, and Tabasco. Simmer 8 minutes. Remove bay leaves. Soak bread in broth; mix in eggs. Stir into crab mixture and heat thoroughly, about 5 minutes. Spoon into shells, sprinkling each with ½ teaspoon bread crumbs, and dotting each with ½ teaspoon of butter. Bake 15 to 20 minutes.

CRABMEAT CASSEROLE

Serves 6

Preheat oven to 350°

1	stick butter	1	teaspoon seasoned salt
½	cup chopped green onions	¼	teaspoon Tabasco
½	cup chopped yellow onion	1	teaspoon salt
5	tablespoons flour	¼	teaspoon pepper
1½	cups milk	¼	cup chopped fresh parsley
½	cup dry sherry	1	pound lump crabmeat
1	6-ounce can mushrooms, drained	1	14-ounce can artichoke hearts, drained
1	cup grated sharp cheddar cheese	¼	cup seasoned bread crumbs
2	bay leaves	½	cup freshly grated Parmesan cheese
3	lemons, seeded		
1	teaspoon Worcestershire sauce		

In a large skillet, melt butter; add onions; sauté until soft, about 3 minutes. Add flour and cook, stirring constantly, until thick and bubbly. Add milk alternately with sherry and mushrooms. Simmer, stirring constantly. Add cheddar cheese, stirring until melted. Add bay leaves, lemon slices, Worcestershire sauce, seasoned salt, Tabasco, salt, pepper, and parsley; simmer 5 minutes. Remove from heat.

Arrange artichoke hearts in bottom of a 2-quart casserole and cover with crabmeat. Remove lemon and bay leaves and pour sauce over crabmeat. Gently blend; do not stir. Top with bread crumbs and Parmesan cheese. Bake 30 minutes until bubbly.

CRAWFISH IN RAMEKINS

Serves 4

Preheat oven to 350°

1¾ sticks butter
1 cup chopped onion
2 cloves garlic, minced
1 tablespoon catsup
1 bay leaf
1 tablespoon Italian
  seasoning
1 pound crawfish tails
1 stick butter
2 teaspoons lemon juice

¾ teaspoon salt
½ teaspoon pepper
¼ teaspoon Tabasco
2 tablespoons minced fresh
  parsley
2 tablespoons bread crumbs
  Parsley
  Lemon wedges
  French bread, toasted

In a large, heavy skillet, melt ¾ stick butter; sauté onion and garlic until tender. Add catsup, bay leaf, and Italian seasoning. Stir. Add crawfish, remaining 1 stick butter, lemon juice, salt, pepper, Tabasco, and parsley. Heat thoroughly. Remove bay leaf. Spoon into individual ramekins and top with bread crumbs. Broil until golden brown. Garnish with parsley and lemon wedges; serve with French bread.

CRAWFISH ÉTOUFFÉ

Serves 6

2 pounds crawfish tails
2 teaspoons salt
1 teaspoon pepper
¼ teaspoon paprika
1 stick butter
1½ cups chopped yellow
  onions
1 clove garlic, minced
1½ teaspoons flour
1¾ cups water

¼ cup brandy
¾ cup chopped green onions
2 tablespoons chopped
  fresh parsley
2 teaspoons grated lemon
  rind
2 teaspoons lemon juice
  Tabasco to taste
3 cups steamed rice

Season crawfish tails with salt, pepper, and paprika. In a large skillet, heat butter; add crawfish tails and sauté 3 minutes. Add yellow onions and garlic; cook 10 minutes, stirring frequently. Sprinkle with flour and blend. Add water, brandy, green onions, parsley, lemon rind, lemon juice, and Tabasco. Simmer 10 minutes. Serve over rice.

CRAWFISH CARDINALE

Preheat oven to 350°   **Serves 6**

5   tablespoons butter
¼   cup minced onion
1   clove garlic, minced
5   tablespoons flour
1   tablespoon tomato paste
1¼   cups chicken broth, *or* 1
       cup clam juice and ¼ cup
       water
1   teaspoon salt

      Pinch of thyme
¼   teaspoon nutmeg
½   teaspoon Tabasco
1   bay leaf
1   cup light cream
2   tablespoons lemon juice
2   tablespoons brandy
1   pound crawfish tails

In a large skillet, melt butter; sauté onion and garlic until tender, but not brown. Blend in flour. Add tomato paste and cook 2 minutes. Gradually stir in liquid. Add salt, thyme, nutmeg, Tabasco, and bay leaf. Mix well. Stir in cream, lemon juice, and brandy. Add crawfish. Remove bay leaf. Spoon into individual ramekins and bake until bubbly, approximately 10 minutes.

SPICY FRIED CRAWFISH TAILS   **Serves 6**

Begin ahead

Preheat oven to 250°

6   tablespoons flour
2   teaspoons salt
1   teaspoon black pepper
2   tablespoons liquid crab
       boil
2   eggs, beaten

2   tablespoons milk
2   pounds crawfish tails
½   teaspoon salt
¼   teaspoon cayenne pepper
1   quart oil

In bowl, mix flour, salt, pepper, crab boil, and eggs. Add milk, a teaspoon at a time, until batter is thick. Season crawfish with salt and cayenne. Add to batter and let stand at least an hour.

In Dutch oven, heat oil until a wooden kitchen match floating on top ignites. Drop crawfish into hot oil, a handful at a time, making sure to separate them as they cook. Fry until golden brown, about 1 minute. Drain on a platter lined with paper towels, and keep warm in oven. When all crawfish have been fried, serve immediately.

POACHED FISH PROVENÇALE

Serves 6

3	pounds white fish filets, cut in 2-inch pieces	⅛	teaspoon basil
		1	bay leaf
	Salt		Salt to taste
	Pepper		Pepper to taste
¼	cup olive oil	1½	cups water
2	cups chopped onions	1½	cup dry white wine
¾	cup chopped green onions	12	black olives, sliced
¼	cup chopped fresh parsley	2	tablespoons capers
4	ounces tomato paste	3	cups steamed rice
3	cloves garlic, minced		Lemon wedges
⅛	teaspoon thyme		

Season fish with salt and pepper. In a Dutch oven, heat oil and sauté onions and parsley until tender. Add tomato paste and cook, stirring frequently, until it loses its bright red color. Add garlic, thyme, basil, bay leaf, salt, pepper, and water. Cover and simmer 30 minutes. Add wine, olives, and fish. Cover and poach 10 to 15 minutes, until it flakes easily. Remove bay leaf. Sprinkle capers into sauce and spoon mixture over rice. Serve with lemon wedges.

BAKED FISH BEATRICE

Serves 4

Preheat oven to 350°

2	pounds white fish filets	1	cup mayonnaise
	Salt to taste	¼	cup prepared yellow mustard
	Pepper to taste		
½	cup thinly sliced onion	2	tablespoons dry vermouth
2	tablespoons butter		

In a shallow baking dish, salt and pepper fish liberally; cover with sliced onion; dot with butter. Bake 20 minutes or until fish flakes easily. In a small bowl, mix mayonnaise, mustard, and vermouth. Pour over fish and broil 2 to 3 minutes, until brown and bubbly.

TROUT NANTUA

Serves 6

Preheat oven to 400°

5	tablespoons butter		Pepper
3	pounds trout filets	1	cup sliced onion
	Salt	¾	cup dry white wine

Grease baking dish with 2 tablespoons butter. Salt and pepper filets well on both sides, and arrange in single layer in dish. Arrange onion on top and dot with remaining butter. Add wine and bake 15 minutes, until fish flakes easily. Remove and reduce temperature to 375°.

Sauce Nantua

6	tablespoons butter	1	pound crawfish tails*
3	tablespoons flour	½	cup heavy cream
1	cup finely chopped green onions	½	teaspoon Tabasco
¼	cup finely chopped fresh parsley	½	teaspoon salt
⅓	cup chopped celery	¼	cup freshly grated Parmesan cheese

In a large skillet, heat 4 tablespoons butter and gradually add flour, stirring constantly until roux is light brown. Add green onions, parsley, and celery and sauté until tender. Add crawfish and cook until pink. Remove from fire.

Drain fish juices from baking dish into crawfish mixture. Return skillet to heat and cook until sauce is thick and bubbly. Remove from heat and gradually add cream, stirring constantly. Add Tabasco and salt, blending well. Pour sauce over fish, dot with remaining 2 tablespoons butter, and sprinkle with cheese. Bake 15 minutes, then brown under broiler.

*Variation: 1 pound lump crabmeat, or 1 pound raw, peeled shrimp may be substituted for crawfish.

TROUT FLORENTINE

Serves 6

Preheat oven to 150°

2	cups hollandaise sauce (page 46)	1	cup sour cream
3	tablespoons butter	⅛	teaspoon minced garlic
½	cup chopped green onions	¼	teaspoon nutmeg
2	cups cooked spinach, well drained		Salt to taste
			Pepper to taste
			Tabasco to taste

Prepare hollandaise sauce.

In a skillet, sauté onions in butter. Add spinach, sour cream, garlic, nutmeg, salt, pepper, and Tabasco. Mix well. Purée. Spread spinach in bottom of buttered baking dish. Place in oven.

4	green onions, chopped		Water
2	teaspoons salt	3	pounds trout filets
6	peppercorns	½	cup grated Swiss cheese
½	cup dry white wine	¼	cup grated Parmesan cheese
¼	cup lemon juice		

In a skillet, place onions, salt, peppercorns, wine, lemon juice, and water to cover filets. Bring to a boil. Add filets, lower heat, and simmer 5 minutes or until fish flakes easily. With a slotted spoon, remove and transfer to spinach-filled baking dish. Preheat broiler. Spoon hollandaise sauce on top. Sprinkle with cheeses. Broil until golden brown.

TROUT ORLEANS

Serves 6

Preheat broiler

3	pounds trout filets	¼	cup finely chopped celery
	Garlic salt	¼	cup chopped green onions
	Salt to taste	½	cup sliced water chestnuts
	Pepper to taste	1	pound crabmeat
	Lemon juice	¼	teaspoon tarragon
1¼	sticks butter		

Season filets generously with garlic salt, pepper, and lemon juice.

In a heavy skillet, heat 4 tablespoons butter until bubbly. Quickly sauté celery, onion, and water chestnuts. Vegetables should remain crunchy. Add crabmeat and tarragon; blend until thoroughly heated.

In a single layer, place filets in baking dish. Dot with remaining butter. Broil 5 minutes, basting with butter in dish. Remove from broiler, and top with crabmeat. Baste and return to broiler for 4 minutes or until fish flakes easily. Serve immediately.

TROUT AUDUBON

Serves 4

2	pounds trout filets	2	sticks butter
1	cup milk	1	cup sliced mushrooms
¾	cup flour	1	cup quartered artichoke
3	tablespoons salt		hearts, drained
2	tablespoons black pepper	2	tablespoons minced fresh
	Dash cayenne pepper		parsley
¾	cup fine bread crumbs	¼	cup dry white wine

Dip filets in milk; roll in flour seasoned with salt, black pepper, and cayenne; dip in milk again, and coat with bread crumbs. In a large skillet, over high heat, melt butter and brown filets on both sides. Remove to a heated serving platter. Lower heat. Add mushrooms, artichokes, and parsley; cook 3 minutes. Stir in wine. Spoon sauce over fish and serve immediately.

RED SNAPPER MAISON

Serves 6

Preheat broiler

Sauce Maison

4	tablespoons butter	4	tablespoons lemon juice
4	tablespoons flour	⅛	teaspoon Tabasco
1	tablespoon chopped fresh parsley	⅛	teaspoon Worcestershire sauce
1	green onion, chopped	½	cup dry white wine
2	cups chicken stock	3	egg yolks, beaten
½	cup sliced mushrooms		

In a saucepan, melt butter. When butter starts to brown, add flour, blending thoroughly. Add parsley and onion. Cook 1 minute. Slowly add stock, stirring constantly until thick and creamy. Add mushrooms, lemon juice, Tabasco, and Worcestershire sauce; blend well. Add wine. Slowly stir in yolks until sauce begins to thicken. Keep warm.

3	pounds red snapper filets	1	rib celery, finely chopped
1	stick butter		Salt to taste
3	green onions, finely chopped		Pepper to taste
2	tablespoons chopped fresh parsley		

Lightly grease a baking pan large enough to hold filets in single layer. In a saucepan, melt butter, and add onions, parsley, and celery. Warm thoroughly, but do not brown. Lightly salt and pepper fish; place in baking pan, and brush with half of the butter sauce. Broil 4 minutes. Do not place so close to flame that fish browns. Turn fish, brush with remaining half of butter sauce and broil 2 minutes. Transfer to a warm platter, spoon Sauce Maison over fish, and serve immediately.

COLD REDFISH WITH SAUCE VERTE   Serves 8

Courtbouillon

2	cups white wine	1	teaspoon peppercorns
2	tablespoons chopped fresh parsley	2	bay leaves
			Pinch of thyme
2	cups chopped green onions	⅛	teaspoon Tabasco
		4	tablespoons lemon juice
1	tablespoon salt		Water to cover redfish

In a fish poacher or roasting pan, combine all ingredients and simmer, covered, 30 minutes.

1	6 to 7 pound redfish	Salt and pepper

Wash and dry fish; sprinkle inside and out with salt and pepper. Wrap in cheesecloth and secure with string. Place in courtbouillon, cover, and simmer, 6 to 8 minutes per pound, until fish flakes easily. Lift fish out of liquid, remove cheesecloth, and place on serving platter. Allow to cool enough to handle. Remove skin and row of bones along top and bottom, and any dark meat. Refrigerate.

Sauce Verte

1	cup water	6	tablespoons white wine vinegar
¼	cup chopped spinach leaves	2	teaspoons salt
¼	cup chopped green onions	½	teaspoon pepper
¼	cup chopped fresh parsley	3	cups oil
¼	cup chopped watercress	1½	tablespoons gelatin
1	tablespoon tarragon	½	cup white wine
2	tablespoons chervil	1	tablespoon water
4	eggs		

In a saucepan, boil water; add spinach and onions; boil 1 minute. Add parsley, watercress, tarragon, and chervil; boil 1 minute more. Drain in fine strainer and turn out on paper towels to dry. Blend eggs and vinegar in blender or food processor. Add greens, salt and pepper, and blend more. Transfer to electric mixer. On high speed, gradually add oil until mixture thickens. Refrigerate.

Soften gelatin in wine. Place in a small saucepan, over low heat. Add water and stir until gelatin is dissolved. Cool; blend into the chilled Sauce Verte. Spread mixture over fish. Refrigerate or serve immediately. Serve extra sauce on the side.

May be decorated with flowers cut from lemon peel, using parsley for stems and leaves. Use black olive slice for eye. Garnish platter with lettuce, cucumbers, cherry tomatoes, and lemon wedges.

Poultry & Game

DUCK JAMBALAYA

Serves 4 to 6

Ducks

2	large ducks	1	onion, quartered
	Water to cover	2	ribs celery
1	tablespoon salt	1	bay leaf
1	teaspoon pepper		

In large pot, cook ducks in water seasoned with salt, pepper, onion, celery, and bay leaf for about 1½ hours, until tender. Remove ducks and cool. Remove meat from bone, and cut into bite-size pieces. This should equal about 4 cups.

Jambalaya

3	tablespoons bacon grease	1	cup chopped green pepper
3	tablespoons flour	2	cloves garlic, minced
2	medium onions, chopped	2	cups chicken stock
1	cup chopped green onions	1	cup rice
2	tablespoons chopped	2	teaspoons salt
	fresh parsley	½	teaspoon cayenne pepper
1	cup chopped celery	4	cups duck meat

In a large heavy pot, heat bacon grease and gradually add flour, stirring constantly until roux is dark brown. Add onions, parsley, and garlic. Cook until soft. Add water, rice, salt, pepper, and duck meat. Bring to a boil, then lower heat as much as possible. Cook 1 hour, covered tightly. Stir occasionally. When rice is done, remove lid and cook a few more minutes so rice will steam dry.

CHICKEN AND SAUSAGE JAMBALAYA

Serves 8 to 10

1	small fryer	1	cup chopped yellow onion
1	rib celery with leaves	¾	cup chopped green pepper
1	onion, halved	¼	cup chopped fresh parsley
1	clove garlic	2	cloves garlic, minced
2	cups converted long grain rice	1	6-ounce can tomato paste
		1	large bay leaf
1	pound smoked sausage, sliced into 1/2 inch pieces	¼	teaspoon thyme
		2	teaspoons salt
1	pound ham, cubed	½	teaspoon pepper
½	stick butter	¼	teaspoon Tabasco

In a large pot, cover chicken with water; add celery, onion, garlic; boil until tender, about 1 hour. Reserve stock. Remove meat from bones. In 5 cups stock, cook rice until all liquid is absorbed, about 25 minutes.

In a Dutch oven, fry sausage and ham until lightly browned, about 3 to 5 minutes. Remove meat. Add butter to pan and sauté onion, pepper, and parsley until tender, about 3 minutes. Add chicken, sausage, and ham; stir in garlic, tomato paste, bay leaf, thyme, salt, pepper, and Tabasco. Add rice and mix thoroughly. Cook over low heat 15 minutes, stirring frequently. Remove bay leaf and serve.

CHICKEN TRIÈSTE

Serves 6

6	chicken breasts	½	pound fresh mushrooms, sliced
½	teaspoon salt		
½	teaspoon pepper	1	cup dry white wine
⅛	teaspoon thyme	½	teaspoon tarragon
4	tablespoons butter	1	cup sour cream
½	cup sliced green onions		

Dry chicken well; season with ¼ teaspoon salt, ¼ teaspoon pepper, and thyme. In a large skillet, melt butter; brown chicken. Remove chicken and sauté onions and mushrooms. Add wine, tarragon, ¼ teaspoon salt and ¼ teaspoon pepper. Return chicken to pan and simmer 45 minutes. Transfer to warm platter.

Boil pan juices 3 minutes. Remove from heat and cool a few minutes. Add sour cream and mix well. Cook until hot, stirring frequently. Do not allow sauce to boil. Pour sauce over chicken and serve immediately.

CREOLE CHICKEN PIE

Serves 6

Preheat oven to 425°

1	3-pound fryer	½	teaspoon salt
1	quart water	¼	teaspoon pepper
½	teaspoon poultry seasoning	1	onion, quartered
		2	ribs celery, sliced

Simmer chicken in water seasoned with remaining ingredients 45 to 60 minutes, until tender. Remove chicken from bone and dice. Skim fat from stock; strain, reserving 1½ cups.

Pastry

2	cups flour	5	tablespoons ice water
1	teaspoon salt	1	egg yolk, beaten
⅔	cup solid vegetable shortening		

In a bowl, combine flour, salt, and shortening. Cut shortening into flour with pastry blender or 2 knives until mixture resembles corn meal. Sprinkle 5 tablespoons water over dough and toss lightly with a fork. Add more ice water if necessary to bind dough. Chill.

Sauce

⅓	cup oil	1½	teaspoons salt
½	cup flour	¼	teaspoon pepper
¾	cup chopped celery	¼	teaspoon thyme
¼	cup chopped green pepper	1	teaspoon Worcestershire sauce
¾	cup chopped onion		
½	cup chopped green onions	1	pound mushrooms, sliced
1	clove garlic, minced	2	tablespoons butter
1½	cups chicken stock, heated	¼	cup finely chopped fresh parsley
1	bay leaf	2	teaspoons chopped pimiento
¼	teaspoon Tabasco		

In a heavy skillet, heat oil and gradually add flour, stirring constantly until roux is dark brown. Add celery, green pepper, onion, green onions, and garlic; cook 5 minutes, stirring frequently. Slowly add stock to roux, stirring constantly until smooth. Add bay leaf, Tabasco, salt, pepper, thyme, and Worcestershire sauce. Simmer 20 minutes, stirring occasionally. In a small skillet, sauté mushrooms in butter. Add mushrooms, parsley, pimiento, and diced chicken to sauce. Simmer 20 minutes. Remove bay leaf.

Divide dough in half and roll each half between 2 sheets of waxed paper until dough is ½ inch larger than a 9 inch pie pan. Line pie pan with 1 piece of dough and trim excess. Fill with chicken and sauce and top with second piece of dough. Trim excess dough and pinch edges to seal. Brush top with yolk. Place pie on baking sheet. Bake 30 minutes. If necessary, brown under broiler.

CHICKEN WITH OYSTER DRESSING

Preheat oven to 375°   **Serves 4**

1	clove garlic, minced
¼	cup finely chopped onion
2	tablespoons finely chopped green onions
1	tablespoon finely chopped green pepper
¼	cup finely chopped celery
3	tablespoons minced fresh parsley
4	tablespoons plus 2 teaspoons butter
1	cup oysters, drained and chopped, reserving 1/2 cup liquid

1	cup plus 2 tablespoons unseasoned bread crumbs
1¼	teaspoons salt
½	teaspoon black pepper
⅛	teaspoon cayenne pepper
⅛	teaspoon thyme
1	tablespoon lemon juice
1	teaspoon Worcestershire sauce
2	1½ pound fryers, halved, *or* Cornish hens, halved
½	cup water

In a large skillet, sauté garlic, onion, green onions, green pepper, celery, and parsley in 2 tablespoons butter 5 minutes. Add oysters; sauté 3 minutes. Remove from heat; add oyster juice, 1 cup bread crumbs, ¾ teaspoons salt, ¼ teaspoon black pepper, cayenne, thyme, lemon juice, and Worcestershire sauce. Mix well.

In a large baking dish, arrange chicken in one layer with skin side up. Place 1 teaspoon butter on each. Add water and bake 20 minutes. Broil until skin is lightly browned. Remove, sprinkle with ½ teaspoon salt and ¼ teaspoon pepper, and place skin side down in baking dish. Fill each cavity with oyster dressing. Sprinkle with remaining 2 tablespoons bread crumbs and dot each half with 1 teaspoon butter. Bake 25 minutes. Broil until brown.

CHICKEN À L'ORANGE

Serves 4

Preheat oven to 350°

1	3-pound fryer, cut in pieces	1	cup sliced mushrooms, sautéed in 1 teaspoon
1½	teaspoons salt		butter and ½ teaspoon
¼	teaspoon pepper		Worcestershire sauce
¼	teaspoon paprika	2	cups orange juice
¼	cup flour	¼	cup dry sherry
2	tablespoons butter	2	tablespoons brown sugar
1	tablespoon oil	2	teaspoons freshly grated
1	medium onion, thinly sliced into rings		orange rind
		¼	cup water
4	thin slices green pepper, cut into rings	2	tablespoons cornstarch

Combine ½ teaspoon salt, pepper, paprika, and flour. Roll chicken in flour and lightly brown in butter and oil. Arrange in single layer in a shallow baking dish. Place onions, green pepper, and mushrooms over chicken.

In a saucepan, mix juice, sherry, sugar, 1 teaspoon salt, and orange rind. Bring to a boil and remove from heat. Blend water and cornstarch; add to juice mixture, stirring well. Simmer 5 minutes, stirring frequently, until mixture thickens. Pour over chicken and bake 1 hour, basting every 20 minutes.

CHICKEN DIABLO

Serves 6

8	chicken breasts, skinned and boned	3	tablespoons Dijon mustard
½	teaspoon salt	1	teaspoon Worcestershire sauce
¼	teaspoon pepper	1½	cups bread crumbs
3	tablespoons dry white wine	4	tablespoons butter
		1	cup oil

Place chicken between sheets of waxed paper and pound lightly. Sprinkle with salt and pepper. In a small bowl, combine wine, mustard, and Worcestershire sauce. Brush chicken on all sides with mustard mixture, then roll in bread crumbs. In a large skillet, over medium heat, heat butter and oil. Brown chicken on both sides until fully cooked.

CHICKEN CARONDELET

Serves 6

¾	cup finely chopped onion	⅛	teaspoon Tabasco
1	clove garlic, minced	½	pound mushrooms, sliced
5	tablespoons butter	3	cups cooked, diced
¼	cup flour		chicken
1½	cups chicken stock, heated	6	slices bacon, cooked and crumbled
¼	cup dry white wine	½	cup sour cream
1	teaspoon salt	6	patty shells, warmed
¼	teaspoon pepper		

Sauté onion and garlic in 4 tablespoons butter until soft. Add flour and cook 3 minutes, stirring constantly. Slowly add stock and whisk until smooth. Add wine, salt, pepper, and Tabasco; simmer 5 minutes, stirring occasionally. In a small skillet, sauté mushrooms in remaining 1 tablespoon butter.

Add chicken, bacon, mushrooms, and sour cream. Simmer 20 minutes, stirring occasionally. Do not allow sauce to boil. Serve in patty shells.

CHICKEN CURRY

Serves 4

4	chicken breasts	2	tablespoons flour
3	cups water	1½	teaspoons curry powder
½	cup chopped celery	2	tablespoons mango chutney
1	cup chopped onion		
½	teaspoon poultry seasoning	2	tablespoons black currant jelly
¾	teaspoon salt	1	cup chopped apple
½	teaspoon pepper	¼	cup raisins
4	tablespoons butter	2	cups steamed rice

Simmer chicken in water with celery, ½ cup onion, poultry seasoning, ½ teaspoon salt, and ¼ teaspoon pepper 30 minutes. When tender, skin and debone; reserve stock. Melt butter in skillet; sauté remaining ½ cup onion until soft, stirring frequently. Blend in flour and curry powder and cook 3 minutes, stirring constantly. Heat stock and add slowly, stirring until well blended. Bring sauce to boiling point and simmer 5 minutes until thickened. Add chutney and jelly; blend. Season with ¼ teaspoon salt and ¼ teaspoon pepper.

Add chicken to sauce. Cover and simmer 10 minutes. Stir in apple and raisins; cover and continue to simmer 10 minutes. Serve over rice.

CHICKEN AND GARLIC STEW

Serves 4

Preheat oven to 375°

6	chicken thighs	½	cup chopped celery and
¾	teaspoon salt		leaves
¾	teaspoon white pepper	½	cup chopped fresh parsley
20	cloves garlic	⅛	teaspoon thyme
3	cups water	1	cup dry white wine
2	tablespoons olive oil		French bread

Season chicken with ¼ teaspoon salt and ¼ teaspoon pepper. Separate cloves of garlic and drop unpeeled into boiling water 1 minute. Drain and rinse under cold water, then peel. In a shallow 2-quart casserole, add oil, coating bottom of dish. Add garlic, celery, parsley, ½ teaspoon salt, ½ teaspoon pepper, and thyme. Add wine and stir. Add chicken, skin side down, and baste. Cover tightly and cook 35 minutes. Turn chicken, baste, and cook 40 minutes. Serve with hot French bread.

CHICKEN BONNE FEMME

Serves 4

1	fryer, cut in pieces	1	large white onion, thinly
1½	teaspoons salt		sliced
½	teaspoon pepper	½	pound mushrooms, sliced
½	cup oil	1	tablespoon grated
2	large baking potatoes,		Parmesan cheese
	thinly sliced	1	teaspoon chopped fresh
2	tablespoons butter		parsley

Dry chicken thoroughly and season with ½ teaspoon salt and ¼ teaspoon pepper. Heat oil in large skillet and fry chicken until cooked. Remove from skillet, drain on paper towels, and keep warm. Fry potatoes in hot oil until brown. Drain and keep warm. Pour oil out of skillet. Add butter and sauté onions and mushrooms until onions are soft. Remove and drain.

Assemble chicken on a heated platter. Arrange potatoes around chicken. Spread mushrooms and onions over chicken; season with 1 teaspoon salt and ¼ teaspoon pepper. Sprinkle with cheese and parsley.

CHICKEN FILETS IN WINE SAUCE   Serves 4

6	chicken breasts, skinned and boned	½	cup flour
½	teaspoon salt	5	tablespoons butter
¼	teaspoon pepper	1	tablespoon oil
		⅔	cup dry white wine

To prepare filet of chicken, first divide skinned and boned whole breast in half along midline. Remove loose piece with tendon and cut off tendon. Place remaining large piece on cutting board with side next to bone facing down. Press down on chicken with palm of hand and slice with knife blade parallel to cutting board. Large piece should be divided into 2 equal portions. Each chicken breast half will yield 3 filets.

Sprinkle each filet with salt and pepper. Dredge in flour. In a large skillet, heat 3 tablespoons butter and oil. Sauté filets until light brown, without crowding skillet. Remove pieces and keep warm.

Pour wine into skillet and cook over high heat about 2 minutes, until sauce thickens slightly. Stir to loosen pan drippings. Remove from heat and add 1 tablespoon butter. When melted, add remaining table-spoon butter. When melted, pour sauce over chicken and serve immediately.

TARRAGON CHICKEN   Serves 6

Preheat oven to 350°

6	chicken breasts, skinned and boned	¾	cup dry white wine
4	tablespoons butter	¾	teaspoon crushed dried tarragon, *or* 1 tablespoon chopped fresh tarragon
¼	cup brandy		
¼	cup minced onion	½	teaspoon salt
2	tablespoons flour	¼	teaspoon pepper
1	tablespoon tomato paste		Dash Tabasco
½	cup chicken broth		

In a large skillet, brown chicken in 3 tablespoons butter. Warm brandy, ignite, and pour over chicken. When flames die, place chicken in shallow 2-quart casserole. Reduce brandy until it barely coats skillet. Add remaining tablespoon butter and sauté onion 3 minutes. Add flour and cook 3 minutes, stirring constantly. Slowly stir in tomato paste, broth, and wine. Simmer briefly, stirring constantly, until sauce is smooth. Add tarragon, salt, pepper, and Tabasco. Cover and bake 30 minutes or until tender.

CHICKEN PROVENÇALE

Serves 4

Preheat oven to 350°

1	fryer, cut in pieces	4	cloves garlic, minced
½	cup flour	3	tablespoons chopped
2½	teaspoons salt		fresh parsley
½	teaspoon pepper	½	cup dry white wine
½	cup olive oil	1	bay leaf
1	cup boiling water	6	medium tomatoes, peeled,
2	chicken bouillon cubes		seeded, and cut in strips
½	cup chopped green pepper	½	cup ripe olives, halved
12	small white onions, peeled	¼	teaspoon thyme
¼	cup chopped green onions	¼	teaspoon Tabasco

Dry chicken thoroughly. Mix flour, ½ teaspoon salt, ¼ teaspoon pepper. Roll chicken in flour. In a large skillet, heat oil; slowly brown chicken. Transfer chicken to a shallow, 2-quart casserole. Dissolve bouillon in water. Pour out all but 1 tablespoon oil. Add green pepper, onions, green onions, and garlic; sauté 5 minutes. Add 2 tablespoons parsley, wine, bouillon, bay leaf, tomatoes, olives, thyme, 2 teaspoons salt, ¼ teaspoon pepper, and Tabasco. Simmer 5 minutes. Pour over chicken. Cover and bake 45 minutes. Remove bay leaf and garnish with remaining tablespoon parsley.

CHICKEN CLEVELAND

Serves 8

Preheat oven to 350°

10	chicken breasts, skinned and boned	1	clove garlic, pressed
1	stick butter	¼	cup flour
6	tablespoons dry sherry	2	cups chicken stock, heated
½	teaspoon salt	½	cup dry white wine
⅛	teaspoon pepper	1	cup slivered almonds,
½	pound fresh mushrooms, sliced and sautéed		toasted (4 ounces)

In a large skillet, brown chicken breasts, a few at a time, in 6 table-spoons butter. Remove to a heated platter. When all are brown, return to skillet. In a small pan, warm sherry, ignite, and pour over chicken. When flames die, transfer chicken to a plate; sprinkle with salt and pepper.

Add remaining 2 tablespoons butter to pan and sauté mushrooms and garlic 3 minutes. When lightly browned, stir in flour. Cook 3 minutes, stirring constantly. Remove from heat and pour in stock. Return to heat and stir constantly until sauce is smooth. Slowly add wine, stirring until sauce begins to bubble.

Turn chicken and simmer, covered, 20 to 25 minutes, or until tender. Sprinkle almonds over chicken when ready to serve.

COQ AU VIN   Serves 4

¼	pound thick-sliced bacon, cut into 1 inch pieces
6	cups water
1	stick butter
1	3-pound fryer, cut in pieces
1½	teaspoons salt
½	teaspoon pepper
⅛	teaspoon thyme
24	small white onions, peeled
2	cloves garlic, pressed
½	pound fresh mushrooms, halved
⅓	cup brandy
2	cups red wine, preferably Burgundy
1	cup chicken broth
1	bay leaf
4	tablespoons flour
2	teaspoons finely chopped fresh parsley

In a saucepan, simmer bacon in water 10 minutes. Drain, rinse in cold water, and dry on paper towels. In a Dutch oven, sauté bacon in 4 tablespoons butter 10 minutes. Dry chicken well and season with ½ teaspoon salt, ¼ teaspoon pepper, and thyme. Remove bacon and brown chicken. Remove chicken and sauté onions and garlic 5 minutes. Remove onions and garlic and sauté mushrooms 3 minutes. Remove mushrooms and discard remaining butter.

In a small saucepan, warm brandy. Remove from heat, ignite, and pour into Dutch oven. After flames die, add wine, broth, bay leaf, 1 teaspoon salt, and ¼ teaspoon pepper. Return bacon, onions, garlic, mushrooms, and chicken to pot. Cook until sauce begins to bubble. Cover, reduce heat, and simmer 45 minutes.

Remove chicken and onions from pot. In a separate pot, melt remaining 4 tablespoons butter and gradually add flour, stirring constantly until roux is dark brown. Remove bay leaf. Add to sauce, mix well. Return chicken and onions to pot and simmer 15 minutes. Transfer to a deep dish and sprinkle with parsley.

ROLLED CHICKEN BREASTS

Serves 6

Preheat oven to 350°

½	pound mushrooms, sliced	½	teaspoon pepper
1	stick butter	1	tablespoon oil
6	chicken breasts, skinned	1	cup chicken broth, heated
	and boned	¼	cup dry white wine
6	thin slices ham		Tabasco to taste
6	slices Swiss cheese	¼	cup slivered almonds,
6	tablespoons flour		toasted
½	teaspoon salt		

In a small pan, sauté mushrooms in 2 tablespoons butter. Pound chicken breasts until ¼ inch thick. Place a slice of ham and a slice of cheese on each piece of chicken. Starting at narrow end, roll lengthwise toward wider end. Secure with toothpicks. Mix flour, ¼ teaspoon salt and ¼ teaspoon pepper. Coat chicken with flour. Reserve flour. In a large skillet, heat 4 tablespoons butter and oil and brown chicken. Arrange in 1 layer in a greased, shallow 2-quart casserole.

Discard butter and oil from skillet and add remaining 2 tablespoons butter. Gradually add 2 tablespoons seasoned flour, stirring constantly until roux is light brown. Slowly add broth, stirring constantly until smooth. Add wine, ¼ teaspoon salt, ¼ teaspoon pepper, Tabasco, and mushrooms. Simmer 5 minutes. Pour over chicken, cover, and bake 30 minutes. Sprinkle with almonds.

CHICKEN CRÊPES

Serves 12

2	whole chickens	½	cup chopped green onions
2	onions, quartered	¼	pound mushrooms,
½	cup coarsely chopped		chopped
	celery tops	¼	cup dry sherry
2	carrots, chopped	¼	cup finely chopped fresh
2½	teaspoons salt		parsley
1	stick plus 3 tablespoons	¼	teaspoon white pepper
	butter	¼	teaspoon Tabasco
1	cup flour	24	crêpes (page 237)
3½	cups chicken stock,	1½	cups hollandaise sauce
	heated		(page 46)

In a large pot, cover chicken with water. Add onions, celery tops, carrots, and 1½ teaspoons salt. Simmer 45 minutes, until tender. Skin, debone, and dice. Skim fat from stock, strain and reserve.

Preheat oven to 350°.

In a large skillet, melt 9 tablespoons butter. Add flour and blend. Cook 3 minutes without browning flour, stirring constantly. Remove from heat and slowly add stock, blending well. Return to low heat and simmer 5 minutes until smooth, stirring frequently.

In a small skillet, sauté green onions and mushrooms in 2 tablespoons butter. Add to sauce, along with chicken, sherry, parsley, 1 teaspoon salt, pepper, and Tabasco. Mix gently.

Fill each crêpe with ⅓ cup chicken filling. Roll and place seam-side down in shallow 3-quart baking dish. Cover and heat 30 minutes. Serve with hollandaise sauce.

COLD CHICKEN AND SPAGHETTI   Serves 4

Make ahead

4	chicken breasts	2	tablespoons white wine vinegar
2	teaspoons salt		
¼	teaspoon poultry seasoning	½	teaspoon Dijon mustard
		½	cup chopped green onion tops
1	onion, quartered		
1	rib celery, chopped	½	cup chopped celery
½	pound mushrooms, sliced	½	cup mayonnaise
1	tablespoon lemon juice	⅛	teaspoon cayenne pepper
6	ounces thin spaghetti	¼	teaspoon black pepper
¼	cup olive oil	¼	teaspoon paprika

In a large pot, simmer chicken breasts in water to cover with 1 teaspoon salt, poultry seasoning, onion, and celery 45 minutes, or until tender. Skin, debone, and dice. Refrigerate 1 hour. Sprinkle mushrooms with lemon juice.

Cook spaghetti al dente. Place in colander; rinse under cold water; transfer to a 3-quart bowl. In a small bowl, combine oil and vinegar; beat well. Pour over spaghetti and toss lightly until well coated. Return to colander and drain.

Combine chicken, mushrooms, mustard, onion tops, celery, and mayonnasie. Add spaghetti, 1 teaspoon salt, cayenne pepper, and black pepper; toss well. Sprinkle with paprika. Refrigerate 4 to 6 hours.

MISTLETOE CHICKEN

Serves 6

4	chicken breasts	½	teaspoon salt
4	cups water	¼	teaspoon pepper
1	onion, quartered	¼	teaspoon poultry
1	rib celery, chopped		seasoning

Simmer chicken in water with onion, celery, salt, pepper, and poultry seasoning 45 minutes, or until tender. Skin, debone, and dice. Skim fat from stock and strain; reserve.

Sauce

1	cup chopped green onions	½	teaspoon salt
1	clove garlic, minced	¼	teaspoon pepper
2	tablespoons minced fresh parsley	⅛	teaspoon Tabasco
1	stick plus 1 tablespoon butter	½	teaspoon Worcestershire sauce
7	tablespoons flour	½	pound mushrooms, sliced
3¼	cups chicken stock, heated	1	pound shrimp, boiled, peeled, and deveined
¼	cup dry sherry	6	patty shells, warmed

In a Dutch oven, sauté onions, garlic, and parsley in 7 tablespoons butter until soft. Gradually add flour and cook about 3 minutes, stirring constantly. Add stock and whisk until smooth. Add sherry, salt, pepper, Tabasco, and Worcestershire sauce. Simmer 5 minutes, stirring occasionally. In a separate pan, sauté mushrooms in remaining 2 tablespoons butter. Add to sauce along with chicken and shrimp. Simmer 10 minutes. Serve in patty shells.

LEMON CHICKEN

Serves 4

4	chicken breasts, skinned and boned	¼	teaspoon salt
2	tablespoons butter	⅛	teaspoon pepper
1	tablespoon oil	1	cup half and half cream
2	tablespoons dry sherry	4	lemon slices, seeded
2	tablespoons lemon juice	1	tablespoon minced fresh parsley

In a skillet, sauté chicken in butter and oil. When brown, remove chicken and discard butter and oil. Add sherry, lemon juice, salt, and pepper. Simmer 2 minutes, stirring constantly. Remove from heat and slowly add half and half. Heat until sauce begins to bubble. Add chicken and simmer 20 minutes, until tender. Transfer to a serving dish and pour sauce over top. Garnish with lemon slices and parsley.

CHICKEN AND ARTICHOKE CASSEROLE

Preheat oven to 350°　　　　　　　　　　　　　　**Serves 4**

1	3-pound fryer	1	cup half and half cream, heated
1	quart water		
2	teaspoons salt	1	cup milk, heated
2	cups chopped celery and celery tops	¼	teaspoon white pepper
1	large onion, quartered	1	teaspoon Worcestershire sauce
3	large artichokes		
½	pound mushrooms, sliced	¼	teaspoon Tabasco
7	tablespoons butter	2	tablespoons grated fresh Parmesan cheese
½	cup chopped green onions		
1	clove garlic, pressed	¼	cup grated Swiss cheese
¼	cup flour	2	tablespoons bread crumbs

Simmer chicken 1 hour in water seasoned with 1 teaspoon salt, celery and celery tops, and onion. Skin, debone, and cube. Boil artichokes 1 hour in salted water. When done, scrape leaves and dice hearts. In a small skillet, sauté mushrooms in 2 tablespoons butter.

In a large skillet, melt remaining 5 tablespoons butter and sauté onions, garlic, and artichoke scrapings 3 minutes. Add flour and cook 3 minutes, stirring constantly. Remove from heat and slowly add half and half and milk, stirring constantly until smooth. Heat sauce until it begins to bubble. Remove from heat and add 1 teaspoon salt, pepper, Worcestershire sauce, Tabasco, and cheeses. Stir until melted. Sauce may be heated, but do not allow sauce to boil.

Gently stir in chicken, artichoke hearts, and mushrooms. Transfer to a greased 2-quart casserole, and sprinkle with breadcrumbs. Bake 30 minutes.

CHICKEN AND WILD RICE

Serves 12

Preheat oven to 350°

2	3-pound chickens	2	6-ounce boxes long grain white and wild rice
1	cup water	1	stick butter
1	cup dry sherry	1	pound mushrooms, sliced
2	ribs celery	1	cup sour cream
1½	teaspoons salt	1	can cream of mushroom soup
1	yellow onion, quartered		
½	teaspoon curry powder		
¼	teaspoon pepper		
¼	teaspoon poultry seasoning		

Simmer chickens in water, sherry, celery, salt, onion, curry powder, pepper, and poultry seasoning. Cover. Turn every 15 minutes. Skin, debone, and cube. Reserve stock and use to cook rice, according to package directions. Add water to make required amount of liquid.

In a small skillet, melt butter and sauté mushrooms. In a 4-quart casserole dish, combine rice, chicken, and mushrooms with sour cream and soup. Cover and bake 20 to 25 minutes.

CHICKEN AND RICE CASSEROLE

Serves 10

Preheat oven to 375°

1	stick butter	½	teaspoon Tabasco
½	cup finely chopped yellow onion	1	teaspoon salt
½	cup minced green pepper	¼	teaspoon pepper
½	pound mushrooms, sliced	1	cup sour cream
¼	cup chopped fresh parsley	1½	cups chicken stock
½	cup chopped celery	3	cups cooked, diced chicken
1	clove garlic, pressed	3	cups steamed rice
1	teaspoon beau monde	½	cup slivered almonds, toasted
1	teaspoon thyme		
1	teaspoon Worcestershire sauce		

In a large skillet, melt butter. Sauté onion, green pepper, and mushrooms 10 minutes. Add parsley, celery, and garlic. Simmer 5 minutes. Add beau monde, thyme, Worcestershire sauce. Tabasco, salt, and pepper and mix well. Stir in sour cream; slowly pour in stock. Fold in chicken and rice. Place mixture in 2½-quart casserole and sprinkle with almonds. Bake 30 minutes.

PERSIAN CHICKEN WITH PEACHES   Serves 4

Preheat oven to 350°

⅓	cup flour	2	tablespoons butter
1¼	teaspoons salt	¼	cup oil
1	teaspoon pepper	¾	cup finely chopped onion
1¼	teaspoons marjoram	¼	cup lemon juice
2	tablespoons finely	1	tablespoon honey, optional
	chopped fresh parsley	1	cup peach syrup
4	chicken breasts	8	canned peach halves
½	cup milk		

Mix flour, salt, pepper, marjoram, and parsley. Dip chicken in milk; roll in seasoned flour. In a large skillet, heat butter and oil; brown chicken until crisp. Transfer chicken to a 2-quart baking dish, arranging in 1 layer. Add onion to skillet and sauté until soft. Sprinkle over chicken.

Add remaining seasoned flour to skillet and brown. Add lemon juice, honey, and peach syrup; cook 5 minutes until slightly thickened, stirring frequently. Arrange peach halves on top of onions and chicken. Cover with sauce and bake 45 minutes.

TURKEY NOODLE CASSEROLE   Serves 6

Preheat oven to 350°

½	pound fine noodles,	2	cups cooked, diced turkey
	cooked and drained	¾	teaspoon salt
¼	cup butter, melted	¼	teaspoon pepper
1	4-ounce can mushrooms, drained		

Mix noodles with butter; transfer to a shallow, 2-quart casserole. In a bowl, combine mushrooms, turkey, salt, and pepper. Place on top of noodles.

Sauce

¼	cup butter	2	cups chicken stock
¼	cup flour	½	cup grated fresh Parmesan
½	teaspoon salt		cheese
¼	teaspoon pepper	1	cup grated Swiss cheese

In a saucepan, melt butter; blend in flour, salt, and pepper. Add stock and cook, stirring frequently, until thick and smooth, about 5 minutes. Add Parmesan cheese and mix well. Pour sauce over chicken. Top with Swiss cheese. Bake 30 minutes.

QUAIL SUPREME

Serves 4

Preheat oven to 350°

8	quail, cleaned and washed	8	green onions, chopped
	Salt	½	cup dry sherry
	Pepper	2	cups chicken stock
6	tablespoons butter	1	cup heavy cream

Salt and pepper quail inside and out. In a Dutch oven, melt butter; brown quail and onions. Pour sherry over quail and ignite. Stir over low heat until flame dies. Pour stock over quail and bake 10 minutes. Add cream and bake 20 minutes more until tender.

QUAIL WITH MUSHROOMS

Serves 6

Preheat oven to 325°

12	quail, cleaned and washed	1	bay leaf
5	tablespoons oil	½	teaspoon thyme
½	teaspoon salt	1	teaspoon salt
½	teaspoon pepper	1	teaspoon freshly ground
1½	sticks butter		pepper
½	cup flour	1	cup peeled, chopped
½	cup finely chopped onion		carrots
½	cup finely chopped green onions	2	cups water
		1	pound mushrooms, sliced
2	cloves garlic, minced	2	cups chicken stock
½	cup finely chopped fresh parsley	1	cup dry white wine

One hour before cooking, wash and dry quail and rub with 2 table-spoons oil. Season with salt and pepper inside and out. In a heavy Dutch oven (not iron), brown quail in 3 tablespoons oil. Remove and place breast-side down in a deep baking pan. Cover and keep warm.

In Dutch oven, melt butter and gradually add flour, stirring constantly until roux is golden brown. Add onion, green onions, garlic, parsley, bay leaf, thyme, salt, and pepper. Cook until tender, about 15 minutes.

Cook carrots in water 10 minutes. Add carrots, mushrooms, stock, and wine to Dutch oven. Stir and cook 5 minutes. Remove bay leaf. Pour sauce over quail. Cover and bake 45 minutes.

QUAIL IN WINE SAUCE

Serves 8

Preheat oven to 325°

8	quail, cleaned and washed	8	squares of aluminum foil

Sauce

1	stick butter, melted	¼	teaspoon pepper
¾	cup dry red wine	¼	cup soy sauce
¼	teaspoon salt		

Put each quail in the middle of a piece of foil and fold foil around, leaving opening at top. In a saucepan, mix sauce ingredients. Pour equal amounts of sauce over each and close tightly. Bake 1 hour.

DOVES ON TOAST

Serves 6

½	cup butter		Cayenne pepper
2	cloves garlic	½	teaspoon salt
12	doves, cleaned and washed	½	teaspoon pepper
			Toast points

In a large, heavy skillet, melt butter and add garlic. Sprinkle doves with cayenne. Brown doves in butter. Season with salt and pepper. Cover tightly and cook over low heat 1 hour. Serve on toast points.

DOVES WITH WINE

Serves 8

2	tablespoons butter	2	teaspoons pepper
1	cup chopped onion	16	doves, cleaned and washed
1½	cups flour		
4	teaspoons salt	1	cup port or dry sherry

In a large skillet, melt butter and sauté onion until slightly brown. Season flour with salt and pepper. Dust doves with flour, add to skillet and brown on all sides over high flame. Reduce heat and pour in wine. Cover and simmer 20 minutes, until doves are done, turning once. Add more wine if necessary. Transfer doves to a warmed serving platter. Scrape all brown bits from bottom and sides of skillet, and stir. Pour sauce over doves and serve.

MARINATED DOVES SUPREME

Serves 4

Begin ahead

8	doves, cleaned and washed	1	cup water

Marinade

1	stick butter, melted	1	tablespoon chopped fresh parsley
½	cup oil		
⅓	cup lemon juice	½	teaspoon salt
¼	cup soy sauce	¼	teaspoon pepper
1	teaspoon oregano	1	clove garlic, minced

Place doves in shallow baking dish. Combine marinade ingredients; pour over doves; cover and refrigerate overnight.

Preheat oven to 375°. Drain marinade and reserve. Place doves in shallow baking dish; add water and bake ½ hour, until browned. Baste generously with marinade. Cover and cook another 15 minutes, or until tender.

Recipe can be used for quail, duck breasts, and back strap of venison.

DOVES WITH CURRY

Serves 4

Begin ahead

1	tablespoon soy sauce	¼	cup chopped white onion
¼	teaspoon salt	2	cloves garlic, minced
½	teaspoon pepper	⅓	cup chopped celery
1	cup olive oil	⅓	cup chopped green pepper
1	tablespoon wine vinegar	⅓	cup chopped green onions
8	doves, cleaned and washed	1	small piece fresh ginger, chopped
2	cups water	1½	tablespoons Madras curry powder
1	tablespoon butter		

Place doves in shallow baking dish. Combine soy sauce, salt, pepper, ½ cup oil, and vinegar; pour over doves. Cover and refrigerate 3 hours or overnight.

In a skillet, brown doves in remaining ½ cup oil. Place doves in a Dutch oven. Pour water in skillet and stir well. Pour over doves. Stir with wooden spoon. Melt butter in skillet; sauté onion, garlic, celery, green pepper, green onions, and ginger until brown. Add curry powder; blend well. Add to doves. Cover and simmer 1½ hours, until tender.

LOUISIANA HONEY-GLAZED CANARD   Serves 4

4	small ducks, preferably teal or gray, cleaned and washed	2	bay leaves
		1	teaspoon thyme
		4	slices bacon
	Salt	¾	cup honey
	Pepper	1	tablespoon cider vinegar
	Chicken stock to cover (about 1½ quarts)	1	teaspoon dry mustard
1	large onion, coarsely chopped		

Generously salt and pepper ducks inside and out. In a large Dutch oven, place stock, onion, bay leaves, and thyme. Bring to a boil and add ducks, making sure they are covered with liquid. Cover and simmer until ducks are tender. Place breast-side up in a roasting pan.

Preheat oven to 375°. Combine honey, vinegar, and mustard. Baste ducks with mixture; place bacon on top. Bake 30 minutes, until bacon is crisp. Baste several times during last 15 minutes. Transfer to a warmed platter and cover with remaining sauce.

DUCK WITH ORANGE SAUCE   Serves 2

1	cup orange marmalade		Salt to taste
½	cup orange juice		Pepper to taste
2	tablespoons freshly grated orange rind	1	orange, sliced
		1	small onion, sliced
2	tablespoons orange flavored liqueur	2	cloves garlic
1	4-pound duck or 2 teal, cleaned and washed	2	cups water

In saucepan, combine marmalade, juice, rind and liqueur and cook over low heat until smooth. Keep warm.

Prick skin of duck in several places. Generously sprinkle cavity with salt and pepper. Place orange, onion, and garlic in a Dutch oven. Place duck on top. Add water. Cover and simmer 2½ to 3 hours, until tender. (The duck may be cooked in advance up to this point and refrigerated.)

Preheat oven to 425°. Transfer duck to a heat-proof platter. Wipe and prick skin again. Pour off all fat and liquid. Brush duck with orange sauce. Roast 20 to 30 minutes, until skin is brown and crisp, basting occasionally.

WILD DUCK WITH MUSHROOM STUFFING

Preheat oven to 400°   Serves 6

6	teal or 3 large ducks, cleaned and washed	2	tablespoons chopped fresh parsley
¼	cup chopped yellow onion	4	slices bacon, cooked and crumbled
¼	cup chopped green onions		
¼	cup chopped celery	½	teaspoon salt
¼	cup chopped green pepper	1	teaspoon pepper
2	cloves garlic, minced	2	tablespoons dry sherry
3	tablespoons butter		Salt to taste
1	cup chopped mushrooms		Pepper to taste
1	onion, chopped	1¾	cups water
½	pound chicken livers, chopped		

In a bowl, mix celery, green pepper, and garlic.

In a skillet, melt butter and sauté mushrooms and onions. Add livers and simmer 5 to 10 minutes. Add parsley, bacon, salt, pepper, and sherry. Mix well and simmer until all liquids have evaporated.

Lightly salt and pepper each duck. Fill each cavity with stuffing. Place ducks, breast side down, in a Dutch oven. Pour water around ducks, but do not cover. Sprinkle with chopped vegetables. Cover and bake 45 minutes. Uncover; baste. Cook uncovered another 45 minutes, basting every 15 minutes. Split large ducks.

COLD DUCK SALAD   Serves 4

5	ducks, cleaned and washed	2	bay leaves
	Water to cover	½	cup chopped green onions
		1	cup chopped celery
2	tablespoons salt	2	cups mayonnaise
1	teaspoon pepper	½	cup finely chopped chutney
3	onions, quartered		
3	ribs celery		

Place ducks in a large pot and cover with water. Season with salt, pepper, onions, celery, and bay leaves. Bring to a boil and simmer 1 hour, until tender. Skin, debone, and cube. Refrigerate. When cold, mix with green onions, celery, mayonnaise, and chutney. May be served with crackers as an hors d'oeuvre.

Meat

'Way Down Yonder In New Orleans

Moderate Bounce

Verse

By HENRY C...
and J. TURNE...

SAUSAGE AND HAM JAMBALAYA   Serves 6

2	cups sliced smoked sausage	1	teaspoon salt	
1	cup finely chopped yellow onion	½	teaspoon thyme	
¾	cup diced green pepper	¼	teaspoon basil	
1	large clove garlic	¼	teaspoon marjoram	
2	cups diced ham	¼	teaspoon paprika	
½	cup dry white wine	¼	teaspoon Tabasco	
1	16-ounce can tomatoes, undrained	2	tablespoons chopped fresh parsley	
		1	cup long grain converted rice	

In a Dutch oven, sauté sausage 10 minutes. Remove with slotted spoon and drain on paper towels. Add onion, green pepper, and garlic to drippings. Sauté until tender, about 5 minutes. Stir in sausage, ham, wine, tomatoes with their liquid, salt, thyme, basil, marjoram, paprika, and Tabasco. Bring to a boil. Reduce heat; add parsley and rice; mix well. Cover and simmer 25 minutes.

BEEF WELLINGTON

Serves 10

Begin a day ahead

Preheat oven to 350°

1	5-pound filet of beef, well-trimmed	½	teaspoon pepper
1	teaspoon salt	1	clove garlic, sliced lengthwise

Rub filet with salt, pepper, and garlic. Place on a rack in a large, shallow roasting pan. Insert meat thermometer. Cook 50 minutes, or until thermometer registers 130°. Cool, cover, and refrigerate overnight.

Prepare forcemeat and pastry

Forcemeat

4	tablespoons unsalted butter	1	egg, slightly beaten
½	cup finely chopped yellow onion	¼	cup heavy cream
1	cup finely chopped mushrooms, liquid extracted by squeezing tightly through a dishtowel	¼	cup finely chopped fresh parsley
		½	teaspoon powdered thyme
		½	teaspoon powdered rosemary
¼	cup brandy	½	teaspoon dried basil
½	pound ground pork	1½	teaspoons salt
½	pound ground veal	½	teaspoon pepper

In a large, heavy skillet, melt butter, and sauté onion 3 minutes. Reduce heat; stir in mushrooms and brandy; simmer 3 minutes. Transfer to a bowl; add pork, veal, egg, cream, parsley, thyme, rosemary, basil, salt, and pepper; mix well. Cool, cover, and refrigerate overnight.

Pastry

2	sticks unsalted butter, softened	1	teaspoon salt
⅔	cup solid shortening	⅔	cup ice water
4	cups flour, sifted	3	tablespoons flour, unsifted
		2	egg whites, slightly beaten

In a large bowl, combine butter and shortening; cut mixture into flour and salt until mixture resembles large bread crumbs. Sprinkle water over mixture, and work quickly into flour mixture until it forms a ball. Sprinkle with 2 tablespoons flour, wrap in waxed paper, and refrigerate overnight.

On day of serving, remove pastry from refrigerator 3 hours before rolling. Preheat oven to 425°. Set 2 sheets of waxed paper side by side, and sprinkle with remaining tablespoon flour. Rub rolling pin with flour. Roll out most of pastry (large enough to enclose beef), cutting off uneven edges to make a perfect rectangle, allowing 1 inch for overlapping under filet. Lay filet along one edge of pastry. Tuck in tail of meat. Spread forcemeat evenly over filet. Lift pastry up over filet, overlapping it under meat, and pinch edges to seal. Cut designs from remaining dough, moisten, and decorate pastry. Brush with egg whites. Place on ungreased baking sheet (avoid non-stick sheets). In upper third of oven, cook 40 minutes. Transfer to a heated serving platter, cover loosely with foil, and let rest 20 minutes. Carve in ¾ inch slices and serve.

INDIVIDUAL BEEF WELLINGTON   Serves 8

Can be made ahead

Preheat oven to 450°

8	5 to 6 ounce filets	4	ounces pâté de foie gras
2	tablespoons oil	1	egg white, room
1	teaspoon salt		temperature
½	teaspoon pepper	1	teaspoon water
3	tablespoons flour		
2	10-ounce packages of 6 puff patty shells, thoroughly defrosted		

Place filets in freezer 20 minutes. Remove and brush with oil. In a hot skillet, sear filets 3 minutes on each side. Remove, sprinkle with salt and pepper, and refrigerate 20 minutes. Lightly flour each patty shell and rolling pin. On waxed paper, roll out to ⅛ inch thickness. Shape pâté into small, flat circles and place in center of dough. Place filets on top of pâté, and fold dough around meat. Pinch to seal. Place in a shallow roasting pan, sealed-side down. Make a small hole in center of crust. Cut designs from remaining dough, moisten, and decorate top of crusts. *(At this point, Wellingtons may be covered with foil and refrigerated overnight.)* Place Wellingtons 1 inch apart on baking sheet (avoid non-stick sheets). Beat egg white with water and, just before cooking, brush crusts. In upper third of oven, cook 10 minutes for rare, 12 minutes for medium rare, or 15 minutes for medium. If crusts are not brown, place on a *low* rack under broiler 2 or 3 minutes until golden. Transfer to a heated platter and serve.

STUFFED TENDERLOIN OF BEEF

Serves 10

Preheat oven to 500°

1	5-pound tenderloin of beef, well trimmed	18	pitted black olives, finely chopped
1	teaspoon salt	½	cup cooked chopped ham
1	teaspoon pepper	¼	pound mushrooms, finely chopped
1	tablespoon oil		
2	coarsely chopped carrots	¼	cup finely chopped fresh parsley
1	coarsely chopped yellow onion		
		2	egg yolks, slightly beaten
1½	cups finely chopped yellow onions	⅛	cup brandy
		½	cup whole pine nuts, shelled, optional
1	clove garlic, finely chopped	3	tablespoons Tawny Port

Cut tenderloin *almost* all the way through in ¾ inch slices. Dry meat with paper towels. Sprinkle with salt and pepper.

In a large, shallow roasting pan, over high heat, heat oil, and sauté carrots and coarsely chopped onion, stirring constantly 2 minutes. Remove from heat. Place tenderloin on top. In a bowl, combine finely chopped onions, garlic, olives, ham, mushrooms, parsley, egg yolks, brandy, and pine nuts; mix well. Spread equal amounts of stuffing between each slice of tenderloin. Roast 5 minutes. Reduce heat to 350° and cook 35 minutes. Transfer to a heated serving platter, cover loosely with foil, and let rest 20 minutes. Place pan on stove top; add port. Boil 3 minutes. Strain and serve with tenderloin.

FILET OF BEEF WITH OYSTER STUFFING

Preheat oven to 500°　　　　　　　　　　**Serves 8 to 10**

1　5 to 6 pound filet of beef,
　　well trimmed

Slit filet lengthwise, stuff and tie tightly with thick string at 1 to 2 inch intervals.

Or

Alternate method: slice a 1-inch wide, 2-inch deep wedge along top length of filet; remove wedge. Fill cavity with stuffing and replace wedge.

Stuffing

4　tablespoons butter	¾　cup dry bread crumbs
1　cup finely chopped green 　　onions	1½　teaspoons finely chopped 　　fresh parsley
½　pound mushrooms, finely 　　chopped	1　egg, slightly beaten
1　pint oysters, drained and 　　quartered	1　teaspoon salt
	½　teaspoon pepper

In a Dutch oven, heat butter; sauté onions, stirring constantly 3 minutes. Add mushrooms and oysters, and cook, stirring 3 minutes. Remove from heat. Add bread crumbs, parsley, egg, salt, and pepper; mix well.

Basting sauce

1　stick butter	¼　cup dry mustard
½　cup brandy	

In a small saucepan, melt butter; add brandy and mustard; cook, stirring constantly 3 minutes.

Roast filet 5 minutes. Reduce heat to 350° and cook, basting frequently with sauce, for 35 minutes. Remove from oven, cover loosely with foil, and let rest 20 minutes. Carve in ¾-inch slices; arrange on a heated platter; serve.

122

FILET DE BOEUF EN GELÉE

Serves 10

Begin a day ahead

Horseradish Sauce

1	cup sour cream	1	teaspoon lemon juice
1	cup mayonnaise	1	teaspoon Worcestershire
⅓	cup horseradish		sauce
¼	cup finely chopped fresh	1	teaspoon coarse salt
	parsley	½	teaspoon pepper
1	teaspoon prepared yellow		
	mustard		

In a bowl, combine all ingredients and refrigerate 24 hours.

1	3-pound filet of beef, well	3	tablespoons
	trimmed		Worcestershire sauce
1	tablespoon prepared	1	teaspoon coarse salt
	yellow mustard		

Place filet in a shallow roasting pan. Coat filet on underside *only* with mustard. Sprinkle Worcestershire sauce over meat. Cover tightly with foil and refrigerate 24 hours.

Preheat oven to 400°. Remove filet from refrigerator at least 1 hour prior to cooking. Roast 50 minutes; remove from oven; sprinkle with salt. Transfer to a platter to cool. When cool carve in ¼ inch slices. Refrigerate.

Gelée

1	tablespoon gelatin	2	cups beef consommé
¼	cup dry Madeira		

In a bowl, sprinkle gelatin over surface of Madeira. DO NOT STIR. Soak 5 minutes until gelatin has absorbed all wine. In a saucepan, heat consommé, just to boiling point. Stir consommé into gelatin, until dissolved. Cool to room temperature. When gelée has begun to thicken, use a *chilled* spoon to spoon a small amount over beef, and chill until firm. Repeat, spooning and chilling, until all gelée is used. Refrigerate until ready to serve. Serve with horseradish sauce.

FILET OF BEEF
WITH GREEN PEPPERCORN SAUCE

Serves 8

Preheat oven to 500°

1	tablespoon oil	1	4-pound filet of beef, well
2	coarsely chopped carrots		trimmed
1	coarsely chopped medium yellow onion		

In a large, shallow roasting pan, on stove top, over high heat, heat oil; sauté carrots and onion, stirring constantly 2 minutes. Remove from heat. Place filet on top of vegetables. Roast 5 minutes. Reduce heat to 350° and cook 40 minutes. Transfer to a carving board, cover loosely with foil, and let rest 20 minutes.

Green Peppercorn Sauce

7	tablespoons butter	¼	cup green peppercorns,
4	tablespoons flour		drained
1½	cups beef stock	1	teaspoon lemon juice
⅓	cup Madeira	1	teaspoon salt
3	tablespoons brandy	½	teaspoon Tabasco
1	cup heavy cream		

In a Dutch oven, heat 4 tablespoons butter and gradually add flour, stirring constantly until roux is light brown. Remove from heat, and gradually stir in ¾ cup stock. Over low heat, stir in remaining ¾ cup stock and Madeira; simmer 15 minutes. Keep warm. *(Sauce may be prepared ahead of time up to this point.)*

Add pan drippings, brandy, and cream to sauce and bring to a boil. Cook, stirring 2 minutes. Reduce heat; add peppercorns, lemon juice, salt, Tabasco, and remaining 3 tablespoons butter; cook, stirring constantly 5 minutes. Carve filet in ¾ inch slices; arrange on a heated platter and spoon some green peppercorn sauce over slices. Serve remaining sauce in a heated sauceboat.

FILET FLAMBÉ

Serves 4

6	tablespoons butter	1	tablespoon Madeira
½	pound mushrooms, thinly sliced	4	tablespoons unsalted butter, softened
½	teaspoon salt	1	tablespoon Dijon mustard
½	teaspoon pepper	4	5 to 6 ounce filets, 1 inch thick
1	tablespoon brandy		
1	tablespoon sherry		

In a skillet, heat 3 tablespoons butter; sauté mushrooms 5 minutes. Add salt and pepper; remove from heat. In a small saucepan, over low heat, warm brandy, sherry, and Madeira. Ignite and pour flaming liquid into skillet. Shake skillet until flames die. In a small bowl, cream unsalted butter with mustard. Stir into skillet. Over low heat, cook sauce, stirring constantly 5 minutes until slightly thickened. Keep sauce warm. Dry filets thoroughly with paper towels. In a large, heavy skillet, over high heat, heat remaining 3 tablespoons butter and, just as butter browns, cook steaks 3 minutes on each side for rare, 4 minutes on each side for medium rare, or 5 minutes on each side for medium. Remove filets to a heated platter, pour sauce over meat, and serve immediately.

BARBEQUED BEEF

Serves 8

2	pounds boneless beef chuck roast	3	cloves garlic, finely chopped
3	tablespoons oil	¾	cup tomato paste
2½	cups water	3	tablespoons Worcestershire sauce
2	cups finely chopped yellow onions	3	tablespoons cider vinegar
1½	cups finely chopped celery	2	teaspoons Tabasco
¾	cup finely chopped green pepper	2	teaspoons salt

Dry roast on paper towels. In a Dutch oven, heat oil and brown beef on all sides. Add remaining ingredients. Cover and simmer 3 to 4 hours, stirring occasionally until beef is easily shredded and liquid has been absorbed. Serve on hot buttered buns.

STEAK WITH SAUCE BERCY

Serves 4

4	8-ounce steaks (top loin strip or tenderloin), 1 inch thick, well trimmed	1	tablespoon oil
		½	teaspoon salt
2	tablespoons butter	½	teaspoon pepper

Cut small incisions around steaks where there is a layer of gristle. Dry steaks with paper towels. In a large, heavy skillet, heat butter and oil. When very hot, cook steaks 3 minutes on each side for rare, 4 minutes on each side for medium rare, or 6 minutes on each side for medium. Transfer to a heated serving platter, sprinkle with salt and pepper, and keep warm.

Sauce Bercy

6	tablespoons unsalted butter, softened	1	tablespoon lemon juice
2	tablespoons finely chopped green onions	2	tablespoons finely chopped fresh parsley
½	cup dry vermouth	¼	teaspoon salt
		¼	teaspoon white pepper

Pour off fat from skillet. Over low heat, melt 1 tablespoon butter; stir in onions; cook, stirring 1 minute. Remove from heat. Add vermouth, and over high heat, deglaze pan, scraping brown bits from bottom and sides, until liquid is reduced to almost a syrup, 4 to 5 minutes. Remove from heat; cool 1 minute. Whisk in remaining 5 tablespoons butter, 1 tablespoon at a time until sauce has thickened. Beat in lemon juice, parsley, salt, and pepper. Spread over steaks; serve immediately.

STEAK AU POIVRE FLAMBÉ Serves 4

4	8-ounce steaks (club, tenderloin, or top sirloin), 1 inch thick, well trimmed	½	teaspoon coarse salt
		¼	cup finely chopped green onions
2	tablespoons crushed pepper	2	tablespoons brandy
½	cup beef broth	½	cup dry red wine
1	tablespoon cornstarch	1	teaspoon Worcestershire sauce
1	tablespoon Dijon mustard		
5	tablespoons unsalted butter	2	teaspoons lemon juice
		2	teaspoons finely chopped fresh parsley

Dry steaks with paper towels. Press steaks into pepper, and with back of a spoon, work pepper into steaks. Allow steaks to sit at room temperature 1 hour. In a bowl, blend stock, cornstarch, and mustard. In a large, heavy skillet, over high heat, melt 3 tablespoons butter. When butter begins to brown, sear steaks 1 minute on each side. Reduce and continue cooking 2 minutes more on each side for rare, 3 minutes on each side for medium rare, or 4 minutes on each side for medium. Transfer steaks to a heated platter, sprinkle with salt, and keep warm.

Pour off fat from skillet. In same skillet, over low heat, melt one tablespoon butter; sauté onions, stirring constantly 1 minute. Remove pan from heat. In a small saucepan, over low heat, warm brandy, ignite, and pour into pan. Stir until flames die. Add wine, and over high heat, bring to a boil, stirring constantly and scraping brown bits on bottom and sides of pan, reducing liquid by half, about 3 minutes. Stir in broth mixture; bring to a boil. Reduce heat and continue cooking, stirring constantly, until sauce thickens, about 3 minutes. Reduce to low heat; add remaining tablespoon butter, Worcestershire sauce, and lemon juice; cook, stirring 1 minute. Pour sauce over steaks and sprinkle with parsley.

STUFFED FLANK STEAK

Serves 6

Begin a day ahead

1   3-pound flank steak,
    butterflied

Lightly pound steak with a meat tenderizer. Place steak in a large shallow roasting pan.

Marinade

¼   cup olive oil
¼   cup soy sauce
¼   cup lemon juice
2   cloves garlic, pressed
1   tablespoon powdered
    rosemary

1   teaspoon powdered thyme
1   tablespoon salt
2   teaspoons pepper

In a small bowl, combine all ingredients, mix well, and pour over steak. Cover with foil and refrigerate 24 hours, turning several times. Remove from refrigerator at least 1 hour prior to cooking.

Stuffing

8   slices bacon, cooked and
    crumbled (reserve 4
    tablespoons grease)
1   cup finely chopped yellow
    onion
¾   cup unpeeled, grated
    zucchini squash
¾   cup unpeeled, grated
    yellow squash

¼   teaspoon oregano
½   cup fresh bread crumbs
2   tablespoons finely
    chopped fresh parsley
1   tablespoon lemon juice
1   egg, slightly beaten
¼   teaspoon salt
¼   teaspoon pepper

In a Dutch oven, heat grease; sauté onion, stirring 5 minutes. Add squash and oregano; sauté, stirring 5 minutes. Remove from heat and add bacon, bread crumbs, parsley, lemon juice, egg, salt, and pepper. Moisten with 3 tablespoons reserved marinade; mix well.

Preheat oven to 450°. Place steak flat and spread stuffing to within 1 inch from each edge. Roll, jellyroll fashion, and with thick string, tie tightly at 1-inch to 2-inch intervals. Return steak to roasting pan, and baste with marinade. Roast 20 minutes for rare, 30 minutes for medium rare, or 40 minutes for medium. Every 10 minutes, turn and baste. Carve in ½ inch slides; arrange on a heated platter and serve.

MARINATED FLANK STEAK

Serves 4

Begin a day ahead

2	**pounds beef flank steak**	**2**	**tablespoons seasoned**
2	**tablespoons garlic salt**		**pepper**

Marinade

½	**cup Worcestershire sauce**	**¼**	**cup olive oil**
¼	**cup soy sauce**	**¼**	**cup lemon juice**

Sprinkle flank steak with garlic salt and pepper. Place steak in a large, shallow roasting pan. In a small bowl, combine marinade ingredients, mix well, and pour over steak. Cover pan and marinate in refrigerator 24 hours, turning several times. Remove from refrigerator 1 hour prior to cooking. Reserve marinade. Dry meat with paper towels.

To barbecue: Charcoal broil 4 minutes on each side for rare, or 5 minutes on each side for medium rare. Baste with marinade while cooking.

To broil in oven: Broil 1 inch from heat, 3 minutes on each side for rare, or 4 minutes on each side for medium rare. Baste with marinade while cooking.

To carve, beginning at small end of steak, thinly slice diagonally with grain of meat.

BAKED BRISKET

Serves 8

Preheat oven to 275°

4	pounds beef brisket, untrimmed	6	carrots, peeled and quartered
2	teaspoons garlic salt	1½	teaspoons salt
3	tablespoons flour	1	teaspoon pepper
3	tablespoons oil	2	tablespoons finely chopped fresh parsley
4½	cups water		
24	small red potatoes, unpeeled		

Dry brisket with paper towels. Sprinkle all sides of brisket with garlic salt; lightly coat with flour. In a Dutch oven, over high heat, heat oil. Brown meat. Remove pot from heat, cover, and cook in oven 4 hours. After 2 hours, in separate saucepans, with 2 cups boiling water in each, cook potatoes 15 minutes; carrots 5 minutes. Drain broth. After 2½ hours of cooking, turn meat; add potatoes, carrots, ½ cup water, salt, and pepper. When cooking is completed, remove brisket and trim excess fat. Carve across grain into very thin slices. Arrange slices on a large heated platter surrounded by potatoes and carrots. Sprinkle parsley over vegetables and serve with Mustard Cream Sauce.

Mustard Cream Sauce

2	tablespoons dry mustard	1	teaspoon white vinegar
2	tablespoons cold water	¼	teaspoon salt
½	cup sour cream		

In a small bowl, place mustard; *very* gradually add water, stirring constantly until mixture is creamy. Let stand 15 minutes. Stir in sour cream, vinegar, and salt.

POT ROAST

Serves 8

1	4-pound rump roast	⅓	cup sherry
½	cup flour	¼	cup tomato sauce
2	tablespoons oil	¼	teaspoon powdered
1	teaspoon salt		rosemary
½	teaspoon pepper	¼	teaspoon dry mustard
2	yellow onions, thickly	¼	teaspoon marjoram
	sliced	¼	teaspoon powdered thyme
2	teaspoons finely chopped	1	bay leaf
	garlic	½	pound mushrooms, thinly
½	cup water		sliced

Dry roast with paper towels. Dredge roast in flour. In a Dutch oven, heat oil; brown meat on all sides. Remove roast and sprinkle with salt and pepper. Reserve 2 tablespoons of pan drippings, and pour off excess. In reserved drippings, sauté onions, stirring 3 minutes. Add garlic and sauté, stirring 2 minutes. Add water, sherry, tomato sauce, rosemary, mustard, marjoram, thyme, and bay leaf; stir. Return roast to pot, reduce heat, cover, and simmer 3½ hours. Transfer roast to a carving board, cover loosely with foil, and let rest 15 minutes. To the pot, add mushrooms, and over moderate heat, cook 10 minutes. Over very low heat, keep gravy warm. Carve roast in thin slices; arrange on a large, heated platter. Pour some gravy over slices and serve remaining gravy in a heated sauceboat.

SPAGHETTI SAUCE

Serves 12

1½	cups sliced hot sausage	2	teaspoons salt
1½	cups sliced Italian sausage	½	teaspoon pepper
2	tablespoons butter	1	teaspoon garlic powder
1½	cups chopped onions	1	teaspoon oregano
1	cup chopped green pepper	1	teaspoon basil
½	cup chopped fresh parsley	2-3	bay leaves
2	pounds ground beef	1	quart water
18	ounces tomato paste		

Render sausage in boiling water 20 minutes. In a Dutch oven, melt butter and sauté onions, green pepper, and parsley 5 minutes. Add beef and cook until browned. Add sausage, tomato paste, and seasonings. Stir in water and simmer 1 hour.

BEEF AND NOODLE CASSEROLE   Serves 6

Preheat oven to 350°

1	5-ounce package noodles
2	tablespoons butter
1	large clove garlic, pressed
1	pound ground beef
¼	pound fresh mushrooms, sliced
2	cups tomato sauce
1	teaspoon salt
1	teaspoon sugar
3	ounces cream cheese, softened
1	cup sour cream
1	cup chopped green onions
½	cup grated cheddar cheese

Cook noodles, rinse, and drain.

In a skillet, melt butter and sauté garlic 1 minute. Add meat and brown. Drain fat. Add mushrooms, tomato sauce, salt, and sugar. Cook over low heat 20 minutes. In a bowl, blend cream cheese, sour cream, and onions. Combine meat and cream cheese mixture. In a 1½-quart casserole, layer half noodles and half meat mixture. Repeat layer and top with cheese. Bake until hot and bubbly, about 30 minutes.

SPICY FRIED LIVER   Serves 4

2	pounds calves liver, ½-inch thick
2	cloves garlic, pressed
1	tablespoon white vinegar
1	teaspoon turmeric
1	teaspoon ground ginger
¼	teaspoon cayenne pepper
¼	teaspoon pepper
4	tablespoons butter
1	teaspoon lemon juice
1	teaspoon salt
3	yellow onions, thinly sliced

Rinse liver and pat dry with paper towels. In a small bowl, combine garlic, vinegar, turmeric, ginger, cayenne, and pepper; mix well. Rub liver on both sides with mixture. In a large, heavy skillet, heat 2 tablespoons butter and when very hot, fry liver 1 minute on one side; turn and fry 3 minutes on other side. Transfer liver to a heated platter, sprinkle with lemon juice and salt, and keep warm. In same skillet, melt remaining 2 tablespoons butter and sauté onions, stirring until soft and golden, about 8 minutes. Place onions over liver and serve immediately.

BLANQUETTE DE VEAU

Serves 8 to 10

4   pounds boneless veal shoulder or breast, cut in 1½ inch cubes, well trimmed
2   teaspoons paprika
½   teaspoon powdered rosemary
6   tablespoons butter
1   tablespoon oil
2   pounds mushrooms, thinly sliced
2   teaspoons salt
1   teaspoon white pepper
1   cup finely chopped yellow onion

4   cloves garlic, pressed
2   cups veal or chicken stock
2   tablespoons flour
1   cup dry white wine
12   small white onions, peeled
3   egg yolks
2   cups sour cream, room temperature
2   tablespoons lemon juice
¼   teaspoon nutmeg
2   tablespoons finely chopped fresh parsley

Dry meat with paper towels. Sprinkle with paprika and rosemary. In a Dutch oven, heat 2 tablespoons butter and oil; brown veal in small batches. With a slotted spoon, remove veal as it browns. In a skillet, heat 2 tablespoons butter and sauté mushrooms, 3 minutes. After all meat is browned and removed, sprinkle with salt and pepper. In Dutch oven, sauté onions, stirring 3 minutes; add garlic and sauté, stirring 2 minutes. Return meat, stir in stock, and add mushrooms. In a cup, stir flour into wine until well blended; stir into pot. Cover and simmer 1½ hours, or until meat is tender. Remove from heat. In a saucepan, heat remaining 2 tablespoons butter; add onions. Cover and cook 8 minutes; add to pot. In a bowl, whisk egg yolks, sour cream, and lemon juice; gradually stir into pot. Add nutmeg. Over very low heat, continue cooking, stirring occasionally, 10 minutes more to thicken sauce slightly, **but do not allow to simmer.** Serve in a heated deep dish or platter surrounded with rice or noodles. Sprinkle with parsley.

VEAL BIRDS

Preheat oven to 350°

1½	pounds veal cutlets, ⅜-inch thick slices, cut in 3 × 5 inch pieces	1	teaspoon pepper
1	cup milk	¼	teaspoon nutmeg
5	strips bacon, cooked and crumbled	¼	cup flour
1	cup dry bread crumbs	1	tablespoon olive oil
1	egg yolk, slightly beaten	1	cup dry white wine
¼	teaspoon Worcestershire sauce	1	cup chicken broth
¼	teaspoon thyme	½	pound mushrooms, thinly sliced
7	tablespoons butter	¼	cup finely chopped green pepper
1	cup finely chopped yellow onion	¼	cup finely chopped green onions
½	cup finely chopped celery	2	tablespoons brandy
¼	pound pork sausage	1	cup heavy cream
1	teaspoon salt	1	teaspoon finely chopped fresh parsley

In a large, deep dish, soak cutlets in milk 1 hour. Dry with paper towels. Place cutlets between 2 sheets of waxed papper and pound lightly with a smooth meat mallet to ¼-inch thickness.

In a bowl, combine bacon, bread crumbs, egg yolk, Worcestershire sauce, and thyme; mix well. In a large, heavy skillet, melt 2 tablespoons butter; sauté onion, celery, and sausage, stirring 10 minutes. Combine with bread crumb mixture.

Place equal amounts of stuffing in center of each cutlet. Roll up cutlets and tie with string. Combine salt, ½ teaspoon pepper, nutmeg, and flour; roll birds in mixture. Shake off excess. In skillet, heat 3 table-spoons butter and oil and brown birds quickly on all sides. As birds brown, transfer to a deep ovenproof dish.

Remove skillet from heat. Add wine, and over high heat, deglaze pan, scraping brown bits on botton and sides of pan, until liquid is reduced by half, about 3 minutes. Reduce heat, stir in broth and cook 3 minutes. In a skillet, melt remaining 2 tablespoons butter; sauté mushrooms, green pepper, and green onions, stirring 3 minutes. Place over birds. Sprinkle with remaining ½ teaspoon pepper. Pour sauce over top and cover with foil. In oven, cook 45 minutes. Transfer birds to a large, heated platter, and remove string. Keep warm. Return sauce to skillet. In a small saucepan, warm brandy, ignite, and pour flaming liquid into skillet. Shake skillet until flames die. Over high heat, stir in cream and cook to desired consistency, 4 to 5 minutes. Pour sauce over birds, sprinkle with parsley, and serve immediately.

VEAL WITH ARTICHOKES AND MUSHROOMS

Serves 4

1	pound veal cutlets, 8 slices, ⅜-inch thick	2	cups sliced artichoke bottoms
1	teaspoon salt	½	pound mushrooms, thinly sliced
1	teaspoon white pepper		
3	tablespoons flour	2	tablespoons finely chopped green onions
1	egg		
2	tablespoons water	1	tablespoon lemon juice
5	tablespoons butter	1	tablespoon finely chopped fresh parsley
1	tablespoons olive oil		

Between 2 sheets of waxed paper, pound cutlets lightly with a smooth meat mallet to ¼-inch thickness. Pat cutlets dry with paper towels. Combine salt, pepper, and flour; dredge cutlets on both sides. Shake off excess. Lightly beat egg with water; brush both sides of cutlets. In a large, heavy skillet, heat 2 tablespoons butter with olive oil, and when very hot, sauté cutlets 2 minutes on each side. As cutlets are sautéed, transfer to a heated platter, and keep warm. In a Dutch oven, heat remaining 3 tablespoons butter; sauté artichoke, mushrooms, and green onions, stirring 5 minutes. Add lemon juice and parsley, and cook, stirring 2 minutes more. Spoon over cutlets and serve immediately.

VEAL VERMOUTH

Serves 4

1	pound veal cutlets, 8 slices, ⅜-inch thick, *or* 1 pound boneless veal rounds, ⅜-inch thick, cut in 8 pieces, well trimmed	3	tablespoons flour
2	cloves garlic, sliced lengthwise	2	tablespoons butter
1	teaspoon salt	1	tablespoon olive oil
1	teaspoon white pepper	½	pound mushrooms, thinly sliced
		½	cup dry vermouth
		2	teaspoons lemon juice
		2	tablespoons finely chopped fresh parsley

Between 2 sheets of waxed paper, lightly pound veal with a smooth meat mallet to ¼-inch thickness. Pat veal dry with paper towels. Rub veal with cut side of garlic. Combine salt, pepper, and flour; dredge veal on both sides. Shake off excess. In a Dutch oven, heat butter and oil, and when very hot, sauté veal 2 minutes on each side. As veal browns, remove meat from pan. After all veal has browned, return meat to pan. Place mushrooms over veal and add vermouth. Reduce heat, cover, and simmer 25 minutes. Remove to a heated platter, sprinkle with lemon juice and parsley, and serve immediately.

VEAL TAORMINA

Serves 8 to 10

Preheat oven to 350°

2	eggs, beaten	2	teaspoons sugar
1½	cups seasoned bread crumbs	1	teaspoon oregano
1	large eggplant, pared and sliced into ¼-inch slices	½	teaspoon basil
¾	cup olive oil	½	teaspoon salt
1½	pounds veal, ground once	½	cup grated Parmesan cheese
3	8-ounce cans tomato sauce	8	ounces Mozzarella cheese, sliced

Dip eggplant slices in eggs and then into bread crumbs. Fry in oil and drain on paper towels. Shape veal into a large patty and brown 5 minutes on each side. Break patty into chunks and stir in tomato sauce, sugar, oregano, basil, and salt. Simmer 10 minutes. Place ⅓ eggplant into a greased 13 x 9 x 2 baking dish, cover with ⅓ of meat sauce, add ⅓ of Parmesan cheese, and then ⅓ of Mozzarella cheese. Repeat until all ingredients are used. Cook 40 minutes, or until cheese is bubbly.

VEAL WITH MUSHROOMS, PROSCUITTO AND CHEESE

Preheat broiler   **Serves 6**

1½ pounds veal cutlets, 12
    slices, ⅜-inch thick
1   teaspoon salt
1   teaspoon freshly ground
    white pepper
3   tablespoons flour
7   tablespoons butter
1   tablespoon olive oil
4   tablespoons finely
    chopped green onions
½   cup dry white wine

2   cups heavy cream
3   cups finely chopped
    mushrooms
¼   cup finely grated Swiss
    cheese
⅓   cup finely grated
    Parmesan cheese
12 slices proscuitto, *or*
    cooked ham, *very* thinly
    sliced

Between 2 sheets of waxed paper, lightly pound cutlets with a smooth meat mallet to ¼-inch thickness. Pat cutlets dry with paper towels. Combine salt, pepper, and flour; dredge veal. Shake off excess. In a large, heavy skillet, heat 3 tablespoons butter with oil and, when very hot, sauté cutlets 2 minutes on each side. As veal is browned, transfer to a heated baking sheet and keep warm. After all cutlets have browned, reduce heat; add 2 tablespoons onions and cook, stirring constantly 1 minute. Remove skillet from heat. Add wine and, over high heat, deglaze skillet, scraping brown bits from bottom and sides of pan, until liquid is reduced by half, about 2 minutes. Reduce heat and gradually stir in 1½ cups cream. Over high heat, stirring constantly, reduce sauce by half. Keep warm.

In a separate skillet, heat remaining 4 tablespoons butter and remaining 2 tablespoons onions; cook, stirring constantly 1 minute. Add mushrooms and sauté, stirring until all moisture has evaporated, 3 to 4 minutes. Add remaining ½ cup cream; cook over high heat, stirring constantly until cream is reduced by half, about 4 minutes.

Combine cheeses. Over each cutlet, spoon equal amounts of creamed mushrooms; top with a slice of proscuitto or ham; sprinkle generously with cheeses. Broil 2 to 3 minutes until cheese is melted and browned. Transfer cutlets to warmed plates, top with cream sauce, and serve immediately.

STUFFED VEAL POCKET

Serves 10 to 12

Prepare stuffing a day ahead

Stuffing

1	stick butter	2	tablespoons finely
3	cups finely chopped green		chopped fresh parsley
	pepper	1½	cups dry bread crumbs
2½	cups finely chopped celery	1	egg, slightly beaten
2	cups finely chopped green	1	pound ham
	onions	1	teaspoon salt
1½	cups finely chopped	1	teaspoon pepper
	yellow onion		
2	cloves garlic, finely		
	chopped		

In a Dutch oven, heat butter; sauté green pepper, celery, onions, garlic, and parsley, stirring 7 minutes. Add bread crumbs, egg, ham, salt, and pepper. Reduce heat, cover, and cook 20 minutes. Transfer to a bowl and cool. Cover with foil and refrigerate overnight.

1	5-pound veal shoulder	1	yellow onion, quartered
	roast, boned, slit with a	1	tomato, quartered
	pocket, well trimmed	2	ribs celery, halved
½	teaspoon salt	2	carrots, sliced lengthwise
¼	teaspoon pepper	2	slices rye bread, cubed

Preheat oven to 350°. Dry meat thoroughly with paper towels. Sprinkle inside of pocket with salt and pepper. Place half the stuffing inside pocket, close with toothpicks, allowing stuffing to spill out. Place remaining stuffing in a buttered casserole. Place meat in a shallow roasting pan and surround with onion, tomato, celery, carrots, and bread. Pour 1 inch of water around roast. Roast meat 3 hours, basting occasionally with pan juices. When cooked, transfer meat to a carving board, cover loosely with foil and let rest 20 minutes. Place stuffing casserole in oven and heat 20 to 30 minutes. Prepare gravy. Carve meat in thin slices and arrange on a heated serving platter.

Gravy

½	cup red wine	4	tablespoons butter
1	teaspoon salt	½	pound mushrooms, thinly
½	teaspoon pepper		sliced

Strain pan juices and pour into a large, deep skillet. Add wine, bring to a boil, stirring 2 minutes. Add salt and pepper. Keep warm. In a separate skillet, heat butter and sauté mushrooms, stirring 3 minutes. Add to gravy and serve in a heated sauceboat.

BRAISED VEAL ROAST WITH TARRAGON

Best made ahead   **Serves 6**

1	5-pound veal rump roast, bone-in
1	teaspoon tarragon
4	tablespoons butter
2	tablespoons oil
1½	teaspoons salt
1	teaspoon pepper
2½	cups coarsely chopped green onions
2	carrots, peeled and sliced in ¼-inch rounds
1	bay leaf
¾	cup white wine
1	egg yolk
1	cup heavy cream
½	pound mushrooms, thinly sliced

Dry roast with paper towels. Sprinkle roast with ½ teaspoon tarragon. In a Dutch oven, heat butter and oil and, when very hot, brown roast on all sides. Sprinkle with 1 teaspoon salt and ½ teaspoon pepper. Reduce heat, cover, and cook 30 minutes, turning roast once. Add onions, carrots, bay leaf, wine, ½ teaspoon tarragon, ½ teaspoon salt, and ½ teaspoon pepper. Stir, cover, and simmer 1½ hours. Transfer roast to a heated serving platter, cover loosely with foil, and let rest 15 minutes. Over high heat, bring juices to a boil. Remove pot from heat. In a bowl, whisk yolk and cream; gradually stir into pot. Over low heat, add mushrooms. Continue cooking, stirring occasionally, 10 minutes, but do not simmer. Carve roast into thin slices. Serve sauce in a heated sauceboat.

BREADED VEAL CUTLETS

Serves 4

1½	pounds veal cutlets, 12 slices, ⅜-inch thick	1	egg
1	teaspoon salt	2	tablespoons water
1	teaspoon white pepper	4	tablespoons butter
¼	cup flour	2	tablespoons olive oil
1½	cups dry bread crumbs	½	cup dry white wine
½	cup finely grated Parmesan cheese	2	tablespoons finely chopped fresh parsley
		4	lemon wedges

Between 2 sheets of waxed paper, lightly pound cutlets with smooth meat mallet to ¼-inch thickness. Dry with paper towels. Combine salt, pepper, and flour; dredge cutlets and shake off excess. Combine bread crumbs and cheese. Lightly beat egg with water. Dip cutlets in egg; coat with bread crumb mixture. Let coating dry 10 minutes. In a large, heavy skillet, heat butter and oil, and when very hot, sauté cutlets 2 minutes on each side. Remove cutlets and drain on paper towels. After all cutlets have browned, transfer to a heated serving platter and keep warm. Remove pan from heat; add wine and deglaze pan, scraping brown bits from bottom and sides of pan, until liquid is reduced by half, about 3 minutes. Pour sauce over cutlets. Sprinkle with parsley, arrange lemon wedges, and serve.

VEAL MARSALA

Serves 4 to 6

1½	pounds veal cutlets, 12 slices, ⅜-inch thick	1	tablespoon olive oil
1	teaspoon salt	2	teaspoons lemon juice
1	teaspoon white pepper	½	cup dry Marsala
½	teaspoon paprika	2	tablespoons finely chopped fresh parsley
¼	cup flour	2	tablespoons grated Parmesan cheese
6	tablespoons butter		

Between two sheets of waxed paper, lightly pound cutlets with a smooth meat mallet to ¼-inch thickness. Pat dry with paper towels. Combine salt, pepper, paprika, and flour; dredge cutlets on both sides. Shake off excess. In a large, heavy skillet, heat 3 tablespoons butter and oil and, when very hot, sauté cutlets 1 minute on each side. As cutlets brown, remove to a warm platter. After all cutlets have browned, sprinkle with lemon juice. Pour off fat from skillet. Add Marsala and boil 1 minute, scraping brown bits from bottom of pan. Reduce and melt remaining 3 tablespoons butter. Return veal to pan; add parsley and cook 2 minutes, turning cutlets several times. Transfer to a heated serving platter, top with sauce, and sprinkle with cheese.

VEAL WITH MUSHROOMS IN CREAM SAUCE

Serves 4

1	pound veal cutlets, 8 slices, ⅜ inch thick	1	cup heavy cream
1	teaspoon salt	½	pound mushrooms, thinly sliced
1	teaspoon white pepper	2	tablespoons lemon juice
3	tablespoons flour	2	tablespoons finely chopped fresh parsley
2	tablespoons butter		
1	tablespoon olive oil		
½	cup Calvados or dry white wine		

Between 2 sheets of waxed paper, lightly pound cutlets with a smooth meat mallet or rolling pin to ¼-inch thickness. Dry cutlets with paper towels. Combine salt, pepper and flour, and dredge veal on both sides. Shake off excess. In a large heavy skillet, heat butter and oil and when very hot, sauté veal 2 minutes on each side. As veal is sautéed, transfer to a heated serving platter. Keep warm. Remove skillet from heat. Add wine and over high heat, deglaze pan, scraping brown bits from bottom, reducing liquid slightly, about 1½ minutes. Reduce heat, add cream and mushrooms; continue cooking, stirring constantly, until sauce is reduced by half and lightly browned, about 5 to 6 minutes. Add lemon juice and parsley; cook, stirring 2 minutes. Pour over veal and serve.

VEAL PICCATA

1	pound veal cutlets, 8 slices, ⅜-inch thick		3	tablespoons flour
½	cup white wine		2	tablespoons butter
1	egg yolk, slightly beaten		1	tablespoon olive oil
⅓	cup beef broth		2	tablespoons lemon juice
1	teaspoon salt		2	tablespoons finely chopped fresh parsley
1	teaspoon white pepper		1	lemon, sliced and seeded
⅛	teaspoon oregano		1	tablespoon capers
3	tablespoons grated Parmesan cheese			

Between 2 sheets of waxed paper, lightly pound veal with a smooth meat mallet to ¼-inch thickness. In a cup, combine ¼ cup wine, egg yolk, and broth; blend well. Set aside. Dry cutlets with paper towels. Combine salt, pepper, oregano, cheese and flour; dredge cutlets on both sides. Shake off excess. In a large heavy skillet, heat butter and oil, and when very hot, sauté cutlets 2 minutes on each side. Sprinkle with lemon juice while sautéing. As veal browns, transfer to a heated serving platter. Keep warm. Remove skillet from heat. Add remaining ¼ cup wine and, over high heat, deglaze pan, scraping brown bits from bottom, until liquid is reduced by half, about 2 minutes. Reduce heat; stir in broth mixture. Add parsley and cook, stirring 1 minute. Pour over cutlets and garnish with lemon and capers.

VEAL WITH SHRIMP AND CRABMEAT   Serves 6

Preheat oven to 140°

1½ pounds veal cutlets, 12
     slices, ⅜-inch thick
1   teaspoon salt
1   teaspoon white pepper
3   tablespoons flour
6   tablespoons butter
1   tablespoon olive oil
2   tablespoons finely
     chopped green onions
½   cup dry white wine

1   cup heavy cream
½   pound mushrooms, thinly
     sliced
1   tablespoon lemon juice
2   tablespoons finely
     chopped fresh parsley
¼   pound cooked shrimp,
     peeled and deveined
½   pound fresh lump
     crabmeat

Between 2 sheets of waxed paper, lightly pound veal with a smooth meat mallet to ¼-inch thickness. Dry cutlets with paper towels. Combine salt, pepper, and flour; dredge cutlets on both sides. Shake off excess. In a large, heavy skillet, heat 3 tablespoons butter with oil and, when very hot, sauté cutlets 2 minutes on each side. As veal is browned, transfer to a heated serving platter, and keep warm. Reduce heat, and cook green onions, stirring constantly 1 minute. Remove from heat; add wine, and over high heat, deglaze pan, scraping brown bits from bottom, until liquid is reduced by half, about 2 minutes. Reduce heat, add cream, and simmer 4 minutes until sauce has slightly thickened. Add mushrooms and cook, stirring 3 minutes. Add lemon juice and 1 tablespoon parsley and cook, stirring 1 minute more. Pour over veal, and keep warm. In a separate skillet, melt remaining 3 tablespoons butter, and heat shrimp and crabmeat. Spoon over sauce and sprinkle with remaining tablespoon parsley.

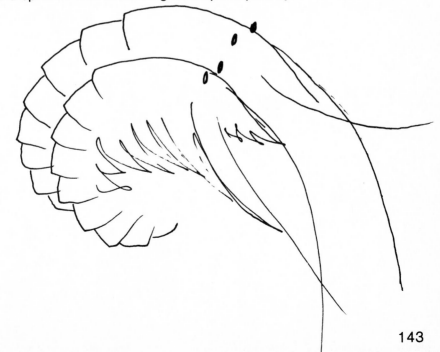

CREOLE VEAL CHOPS

Serves 10

Preheat oven to 350°

6	tablespoons butter	2	bay leaves
⅔	cup finely chopped yellow onion	½	teaspoon sugar
¾	cup finely chopped green pepper	4½	cups veal or beef stock
¾	cup finely chopped celery	3	teaspoons salt
2	cloves garlic, finely chopped	2	teaspoons pepper
½	pound mushrooms, thinly sliced	10	shoulder veal chops, well trimmed, ½-inch thick
1	16-ounce can whole tomatoes, undrained	1	tablespoon rosemary
¾	cup tomato paste	½	cup flour
		1	tablespoon oil
		2	tablespoons finely chopped fresh parsley

In a Dutch oven, heat 4 tablespoons butter; sauté onion, green pepper, and celery, stirring 5 minutes. Add garlic and sauté 2 minutes. Add mushrooms, tomatoes, tomato paste, bay leaves, and sugar. Reduce heat and simmer 15 minutes. Gradually stir in stock and simmer 15 minutes. Season with 1 teaspoon salt and 1 teaspoon pepper. Dry chops with paper towels. Combine remaining 2 teaspoons salt, 1 teaspoon pepper, rosemary, and flour; dredge chops on both sides. Shake off excess. In a large, heavy skillet, heat remaining 2 tablespoons butter with oil and when very hot, brown chops 3 minutes on each side. As chops brown, transfer to a large oven-proof dish. After all chops have browned, top with sauce. Cover with foil and cook 1½ hours. Remove bay leaf. Sprinkle with parsley and serve.

COLD VEAL TONGUE
WITH HORSERADISH SAUCE

Serves 4

Begin a day ahead

Horseradish Sauce

½	cup mayonnaise
½	cup sour cream
2	tablespoons finely chopped parsley
3	tablespoons horseradish
½	teaspoon prepared yellow mustard

½	teaspoon Worcestershire sauce
½	teaspoon lemon juice
¼	teaspoon salt
¼	teaspoon pepper

In a large bowl, combine all ingredients and mix well. Cover and refrigerate overnight.

1½	pounds fresh veal tongue Water to cover tongue by 6 inches
1½	teaspoons salt per quart of water
1	large yellow onion, unpeeled, and studded with 8 cloves

3	ribs celery with leaves, halved
1	carrot, sliced lengthwise
1	clove garlic, halved
2	bay leaves
8	peppercorns

Scrub tongue under warm running water. Soak in cold water 1 hour.

In a Dutch oven, cover tongue with water. Add remaining ingredients. Bring just to a boil. Reduce heat, cover, and simmer 2 hours until tender. Remove tongue and plunge into cold water for less than 1 minute. Skin immediately. Remove roots and gristle. Return to pot to cool completely in liquid. Transfer to a serving platter, slice, and serve with horseradish sauce.

To carve: Slice in ¼-inch thick slices. Cut nearly through to hump parallel to base. Toward tip, slice on diagonal.

GRILLADES

Better made a day ahead

Freezes well

2	pounds boneless veal rounds, ⅜-inch thick, well trimmed, cut into bite-size pieces	1	clove garlic, finely chopped
2	teaspoons salt	½	pound mushrooms, thinly sliced
1	teaspoon white pepper	3	cups tomatoes, peeled and chopped
⅓	cup flour	2	tablespoons tomato paste
1	stick butter	½	cup red wine
2	tablespoons oil	1½	cups water
1	cup finely chopped green onions	2	tablespoons finely chopped fresh parsley
½	cup finely chopped green pepper	1	bay leaf
		½	teaspoon thyme

Between 2 sheets of waxed paper, lightly pound veal with a smooth meat mallet to ¼-inch thickness. Dry with paper towels. Combine 1 teaspoon salt, pepper, and flour; dredge veal on both sides. Shake off excess. In a large, deep, heavy skillet, heat 4 tablespoons butter and oil, and brown veal on both sides. As veal is browned, remove from skillet. Reduce heat; melt 2 tablespoons butter; sauté onions and green pepper, stirring 3 minutes. Add garlic and sauté, 2 minutes. Remove from heat. In a separate skillet, melt remaining 2 tablespoons butter and sauté mushrooms, 3 minutes. To first skillet, add mushrooms, tomatoes, tomato paste, wine, water, parsley, bay leaf, thyme, and remaining teaspoon of salt. Return veal to pan, and stir. Bring just to a boiling point, reduce heat, cover, and simmer 40 minutes. Uncover, remove bay leaf, and cook 20 minutes.

PORCUPINE PORK ROAST

Serves 6

Begin a day ahead

1	7-pound pork loin roast, ribs cracked, untrimmed	½	teaspoon thyme
¼	cup olive oil	⅓	cup flour
1½	teaspoons salt	2	yellow onions, sliced
1	teaspoon pepper	2	tablespoons cornstarch
1½	teaspoons oregano	¾	cup water

With a knife, score fat in a diamond pattern. Rub roast with oil. Sprinkle with salt, pepper, oregano, and thyme. Coat with flour. Arrange onions on scored surface and secure with toothpicks. Place in a shallow roasting pan, cover tightly, and refrigerate overnight.

On day of serving, remove from refrigerator at least 1 hour prior to cooking. Preheat oven to 375° and cook 30 minutes.

Basting Sauce

2¼	cups water	2	cloves garlic, pressed
3	beef bouillon cubes	¾	cup sour cream, room temperature
2	chicken bouillon cubes		
1¼	cups white wine		

In a saucepan, bring water to a boil and dissolve bouillon cubes. Reduce to low heat; add wine and garlic; simmer 5 minutes. Remove from heat and stir in sour cream. Reduce oven temperature to 325° and pour sauce over roast. Cook 4 hours, basting every 30 minutes. Transfer to a heated serving platter, cover loosely with foil, and let rest 15 minutes.

In a cup, stir cornstarch in water. Place roasting pan on stove top; stir in cornstarch; simmer 10 minutes, scraping brown bits on bottom of pan. Serve in a heated sauceboat.

ROAST TENDERLOIN OF PORK Serves 8 to 10

Begin a day ahead

1   **4 to 5 pound pork tenderloin**

Marinade

6   **cloves garlic, pressed**
6   **ounces frozen limeade, undiluted, thoroughly defrosted**

3   **tablespoons soy sauce**
1   **tablespoon pepper**
1   **teaspoon salt**

Place tenderloin in a shallow roasting pan. In a bowl, combine marinade ingredients, mix well, and pour over pork. Cover with foil and refrigerate 24 hours, turning several times.

On day of serving, remove meat from refrigerator 1 hour prior to cooking. Reserve marinade. Preheat oven to 400° and roast pork 20 minutes; reduce heat to 325° and roast 30 minutes, basting every 10 minutes with marinade. Transfer pork to a carving board, cover loosely with foil, and let rest 15 minutes. Carve into thin slices.

Sauce

3   **tablespoons butter**
2   **tablespoons finely chopped green onions**
½   **cup dry red wine**
1   **tablespoon cornstarch**

3   **tablespoons water**
1   **cup heavy cream**
¼   **teaspoon salt**
¼   **teaspoon pepper**

Discard all fat from roasting pan. Place pan on stove top, melt butter and onions and sauté 2 minutes. Add wine and bring to a boil, constantly stirring and scraping bottom of pan. In a cup, blend cornstarch and water. Reduce heat, stir in cornstarch, cream, and pepper; simmer 5 minutes. Serve in a heated sauceboat.

PORK LOIN ROAST WITH CREAM SAUCE

Begin a day ahead   **Serves 8 to 10**

1	**4-pound pork loin roast, untrimmed, boned, tied**

Marinade

½	**cup fresh lime juice**	2	**tablespoons Worcestershire sauce**
¼	**cup soy sauce**		
½	**cup olive oil**	½	**teaspoon salt**
½	**cup finely chopped green onions**	½	**teaspoon pepper**

Place meat in a shallow roasting pan. In a bowl, combine marinade ingredients, and pour over roast. Cover and refrigerate 24 hours, turning several times.

Remove from refrigerator at least 1 hour prior to cooking. Preheat oven to 350°. Strain marinade and reserve. Dry meat with paper towels. Return roast to pan, fat side up, and insert a meat thermometer. Cook roast 1¾ hours, or until thermometer registers 160°, basting every 20 minutes with marinade. Transfer roast to a carving board, cover loosely with foil, and let rest 15 minutes. Carve in thin slices and arrange on a heated serving platter.

Cream Sauce

2	**tablespoons butter**	1	**cup heavy cream**
¼	**cup finely chopped yellow onion**	¼	**cup brandy**
		1	**teaspoon salt**
½	**cup white wine**	½	**teaspoon pepper**

In a heavy skillet, melt butter; sauté onion, stirring 3 minutes. Reduce heat, add wine, and simmer 15 minutes. Gradually stir in cream. Add brandy, salt, and pepper. Over moderately high heat, cook, stirring, to reduce liquid by one-third, about 3 to 4 minutes. Serve in a heated sauceboat.

PORK CROWN ROAST WITH PRUNE AND APRICOT STUFFING

Begin a day ahead   **Serves 10 to 12**

Stuffing

1 pound hot sausage, ground	½ teaspoon sage
1 pound mild sausage, ground	½ teaspoon cinnamon
½ cup finely chopped yellow onion	1½ teaspoons salt
	1 teaspoon pepper
½ cup finely chopped celery	2 eggs, slightly beaten
½ cup finely chopped fresh parsley	1½ cups chopped prunes
	1½ cups chopped dried apricots
2 tablespoons butter	
1 cup dry bread crumbs	
2 tablespoons light brown sugar	

In a heavy Dutch oven, cook sausages, 10 minutes, or until brown. Remove and drain on paper towels. Pour off excess. In drippings. sauté onion, celery, and parsley, stirring 5 minutes. In a separate skillet, melt butter and sauté bread crumbs, tossing frequently until lightly browned, about 8 minutes. In a large bowl, mix sausage, onion mixture, bread crumbs, sugar, sage, cinnamon, salt, pepper, eggs, prunes, and apricots. Cover and refrigerate overnight.

1 12-pound crown pork roast (approximately 20 ribs), ribs cracked, laced in a circle, trimmed	1 teaspoon freshly ground pepper
	2 9-ounce jars kumquats, optional
2 teaspoons salt	1 16-ounce can apricot halves, optional

Preheat oven to 350°. Sprinkle roast with salt and pepper. Place a piece of heavy-duty foil around bottom of roast (so that stuffing will be easily transferred from roasting pan to serving platter). Cover rib tips with foil. Place roast in a large, shallow roasting pan. Insert a meat thermometer. Cook, uncovered, 1 hour. Fill center cavity of roast with stuffing and continue cooking 1 hour or until thermometer registers 165°. Transfer roast to a heated serving platter and let rest 15 to 20 minutes. Remove foil. Optional: Slit kumquats on one end, and garnish rib tips. Place apricot halves, hollow side down, in center of stuffing.

Sauce

1 tablespoon cornstarch	¼ cup finely chopped fresh parsley
½ cup water	
1 cup Madeira	½ teaspoon lime juice
1 clove garlic, pressed	

In a cup, blend cornstarch and water. Skim pan drippings, reserve 3 tablespoons, and pour off excess. Place roasting pan on stove top; add reserved drippings and Madeira. Over high heat, reduce liquid by half, stirring to disslove brown bits on bottom of pan, about 3 minutes. Remove from heat and stir in cornstarch. Return to heat and add garlic, parsley, and lime juice; simmer 10 minutes. Serve in a heated sauceboat.

PORK TENDERLOIN MEDALLIONS — Serves 6

2	pounds pork tenderloin, well trimmed, cut crosswise into 1-inch thick medallions	1	cup dry bread crumbs
		6	tablespoons butter
		2	tablespoons olive oil
		½	cup dry white wine
1	teaspoon salt	½	pound mushrooms, thinly sliced
½	teaspoon pepper		
½	cup flour	1	tablespoon lemon juice
2	eggs	2	tablespoons finely chopped fresh parsley
¼	cup water		

Dry meat with paper towels. Combine salt, pepper and flour; dredge medallions. Shake off excess. Beat eggs with water. Dip medallions in egg and coat with bread crumbs. Press meat with heel of palm to adhere bread crumbs; dry 10 minutes. In a Dutch oven, heat butter and oil; sauté medallions 8 minutes on each side. As meat browns, remove and drain on paper towels. After all medallions have been cooked and drained, transfer to a heated platter, and keep warm. Remove pan from heat. Add wine and, over high heat, deglaze pan, scraping brown bits on bottom and sides of pan, until liquid is reduced by half, about 3 minutes. Add mushrooms and cook, stirring 2 minutes. Add lemon juice and cook, stirring 1 minute. Pour sauce over meat, sprinkle with parsley, and serve immediately.

ROAST SUCKLING PIG   Serves 10 to 12

1	10 to 12 pound suckling pig, cleaned of hair and eyes removed	2½	cups finely chopped yellow onions
1	tablespoon salt	2	cups finely chopped celery
1	teaspoon pepper	1	clove garlic, finely chopped
6	cloves	8	skewers
½	teaspoon sage	½	cup oil
½	teaspoon oregano	1	lime
4	tablespoons butter	2	cherries or cranberries

Wash pig, inside and out, under cold running water. Dry thoroughly with paper towels. Sprinkle inside of cavity with salt, pepper, cloves, sage, and oregano. In a large, heavy skillet, melt butter; sauté onions and celery, stirring 3 minutes. Add garlic and sauté, stirring 2 minutes. Cool. Spread mixture in cavity. Run 4 skewers through both sides of cavity. Skewer front and back legs in place: back legs folded under rump; front legs extended with head resting in between. Place a 2 inch ball of foil in pig's mouth. Cover ears and tail with foil; place a ball of foil in each eye socket. *(To this point, recipe may be prepared in advance. Pig may be covered and refrigerated.)*

Remove from refrigerator 3 hours prior to cooking. Preheat oven to 450°. Cross 2 large sheets of heavy foil (1½ times length of pig) on a rack which has been set diagonally in a shallow roasting pan. Place pig on rack, and turn foil up loosely around pig to allow for drippings. Rub surface of pig with 3 tablespoons oil. Insert meat thermometer in thickest part of thigh. Roast pig 15 minutes, baste with oil; roast 15 minutes more, baste with oil; reduce heat to 350°. Continue basting every 20 minutes until oil is gone, then continue basting with pan drippings. Total roasting time is 3 hours, or until thermometer registers 165°. Turn oven off, and let pig rest in oven 30 minutes before carving. Remove pig from roasting rack, drain, and place on a heated platter. Remove skewers and foil. Place a lime in pig's mouth and cherries or cranberries in eye sockets. At intervals around pig's neck, place toothpicks; attach clusters of frosted grapes to the toothpicks. Garnish platter with clusters of frosted grapes. *Note:* If grapes are not available, string uncooked green peas onto heavy thread for a double-strand necklace. Use ribbon, fresh mint leaves, parsley or celery leaves, flowers, or any combination of these to garnish pig and platter.

Frosted Grapes

2	pounds red or green grapes	2	tablespoons water
2	egg whites	1	cup sugar

Cut grapes into small clusters. In a bowl, beat egg whites and water until frothy. Place sugar in a large shallow bowl. Dip grapes into egg whites; shake off excess. Roll grapes in sugar; shake off excess. Refrigerate until dry and ready to use.

CREOLE PORK CHOPS
Serves 6

8   loin pork chops, ¾-inch thick, well trimmed
3   tablespoons oil
1   cup finely chopped yellow onion
1   cup finely chopped green pepper
1   cup finely chopped celery
2   cloves garlic, finely chopped
1   28-ounce can whole, peeled tomatoes, undrained

3   tablespoons tomato paste
3   cups beef stock
1   teaspoon sugar
1   bay leaf
1   teaspoon oregano
1½   teaspoons salt
1   teaspoon pepper
2   tablespoons finely chopped fresh parsley

Dry pork chops with paper towels. In a Dutch oven, heat oil and, when very hot, brown chops 3 minutes on each side. Remove chops as they brown and keep warm. Reserve 3 tablespoons pan drippings and pour off excess. In drippings, sauté onion, green pepper, celery, and garlic, stirring 5 minutes. Add tomatoes, tomato paste, beef stock, sugar, bay leaf, oregano, salt, and pepper; stir. Reduce heat, cover, and simmer 30 minutes, stirring occasionally. Return chops to Dutch oven, and cook 30 minutes more, turning chops once. Transfer chops to a large, deep, heated platter; pour sauce over chops, sprinkle with parsley; serve.

PORK CHOPS PROVENCALE
Serves 8

Preheat oven to 350°

¼   cup chopped garlic cloves
¼   cup basil
1   tablespoon coarse salt
1   tablespoon crushed pepper
12   pork chops, ½-inch thick, well trimmed

3   tablespoons oil
1   cup white wine
2   tablespoons butter
½   pound mushrooms, thinly sliced
1   tablespoon finely chopped fresh parlsey

In a bowl, mash garlic with a fork. Add basil, salt, and pepper; mix well. Coat both sides of chops with mixture and let stand at room temperature at least 1 hour. In a large heavy skillet, heat oil, and when hot, brown chops 2 minutes on each side. As chops brown, transfer to a shallow roasting pan, overlapping slightly. Pour off excess fat. Add wine and, over high heat, deglaze pan, scraping brown bits on bottom and sides, until liquid is reduced by half, about 3 minutes. Remove from heat. In a separate skillet, melt butter and sauté mushrooms, stirring 3 minutes. Combine mushrooms with wine sauce. Set aside. Place chops in a 350° oven and cook 35 minutes. Remove from oven and drain of all pan drippings. Pour wine sauce into roasting pan. Return chops to oven and continue cooking 15 minutes. Arrange chops on a heated platter, pour sauce over, and sprinkle with parsley.

PORK CHOPS WITH APPLE STUFFING

Serves 4

¾ cup dry bread crumbs
1 cup finely chopped tart apple
1 tablespoon finely chopped yellow onion
½ teaspoon salt
¼ teaspoon freshly ground pepper
1 teaspoon poultry seasoning
2 tablespoons butter, melted
4 double center-cut pork chops, 1¾-inch thick, slit with pockets, well trimmed
¼ cup flour
3 tablespoons oil
¾ cup white wine
¾ cup chicken broth
1 tablespoon cornstarch (optional)
3 tablespoons water (optional)
¼ pound mushrooms, thinly sliced

In a large bowl, combine bread crumbs, apple, onion, salt, pepper, poultry seasoning, and butter; mix well. Fill pockets with equal amounts of stuffing and secure each with a toothpick. Reserve extra stuffing. In 3 tablespoons flour, dredge chops on both sides. Shake off excess. In a Dutch oven, heat oil, and when very hot, brown chops 3 minutes on each side. Pour wine and broth over chops, reduce heat, cover, and simmer 1½ hours. After 1 hour, add reserved stuffing. If sauce needs thickening, blend cornstarch in water, and gradually stir into Dutch oven. Add mushrooms and cook, stirring 3 minutes. Arrange chops on a deep, heated platter. Place extra stuffing on chops and top with sauce.

PORK CHOPS WITH MUSHROOM STUFFING

Preheat oven to 325°　　　　　　　　　　**Serves 4**

2 tablespoons butter
⅓ cup coarsely chopped mushrooms
⅔ cup finely chopped yellow onion
½ cup dry bread crumbs
2 tablespoons finely chopped fresh parsley
⅛ teaspoon thyme
½ teaspoon salt
¼ teaspoon pepper
1 egg, slightly beaten
4 double center cut pork chops, 1¾-inch thick, slit with pockets, well trimmed
2 tablespoons oil

In a skillet, heat butter; sauté mushrooms, onion, bread crumbs, parsley, thyme, salt, and pepper, stirring 5 minutes. Remove from heat and stir in egg. Fill pockets with equal amounts of stuffing. Dry chops with paper towels. In a skillet, heat oil, and when very hot, fry chops 3 minutes on each side. Transfer to a shallow roasting pan and cover with foil. Continue cooking in oven 1 hour.

PORK CHOPS WITH WILD RICE

Serves 4 to 6

Preheat oven to 350°

6	rib pork chops, ¾ to 1-inch thick, well trimmed	¼	cup finely chopped green pepper
3	tablespoons bacon grease or oil	½	pound mushrooms, thinly sliced
1	teaspoon salt	2	beef bouillon cubes
½	teaspoon pepper	2	cups cooked wild rice
¾	cup finely chopped celery	⅓	cup heavy cream
½	cup finely chopped yellow onion	1	tablespoon finely chopped fresh parsley

Dry pork chops with paper towels. In a large, heavy skillet, heat grease and when very hot, brown chops 3 minutes on each side. Remove chops and sprinkle with salt and pepper. Reserve 2 tablespoons pan drippings and pour off excess. Reduce heat and with reserved pan drippings, sauté celery, onion, green pepper, and mushrooms, stirring 3 minutes. Add bouillon cubes, crush, and stir to dissolve. Grease a 12 x 8 oven-proof dish. Spread rice on bottom of dish, place pork chops, slightly overlapping, on bed of rice, and cover with vegetables. Pour cream around edges. Cover with foil. Cook 30 minutes, uncover, and cook 30 minutes. Sprinkle with parsley and serve.

GLAZED PARTY HAM

Serves 20 to 30

Prepare a day ahead

Preheat oven to 350°

1	10-14 pound whole cooked ham, bone-in Whole cloves	2	cups Burgundy
		1	bay leaf
1½	cups peach preserves	½	cup light brown sugar

Place ham, fat side up, in a deep roasting pan with a cover. With a sharp knife, cutting ¼ inch deep, score outside fat in diamond pattern. Spoon preserves over surface. Stud with cloves. Pour wine into bottom of pan; add bay leaf. In a 350° oven, cover and bake 30 minutes. Uncover and coat with brown sugar. Continue to bake, uncovered, basting once or twice, 30 minutes. Transfer ham to a large platter. Cool and refrigerate 24 hours.

BAKED HAM WITH GUAVA JELLY GLAZE

Serves 12 to 14

Preheat oven to 350°

2	cups guava jelly	1	5-7 pound cooked ham, boned, cut in ¼-inch thick slices, loosely tied
½	cup Dijon mustard		

Place ham, fat side up, in a shallow roasting pan. In a saucepan, over low heat, heat jelly and mustard to a liquid consistency. Pour half over ham, letting mixture run between slices. Bake 1 hour, basting every 20 minutes with reserved mixture. Transfer ham to a heated platter and let rest 15 minutes. Discard string. Pour pan juices, and any remaining mixture into a heated sauceboat and serve with ham.

SPICED HAM LOAF WITH CREAMY HORSERADISH SAUCE

Serves 8 to 10

1	tablespoon gelatin	1	tablespoon chopped pimiento
1¼	cups water		
½	cup lemon juice	¼	teaspoon Dijon mustard
2	tablespoons Worcestershire sauce	⅛	teaspoon ground cloves
		⅛	teaspoon ground nutmeg
2	cups ground ham	1	teaspoon seasoned salt
2	tablespoons mayonnaise	⅛	teaspoon cayenne pepper
1	tablespoon horseradish		

In a bowl, sprinkle gelatin over ¼ cup water. DO NOT STIR. Let soak 5 minutes or until all water is absorbed. In a saucepan, combine remaining cup water with lemon juice and heat just to boiling point. Stir into gelatin until thoroughly mixed. Add Worcestershire sauce. Chill until slightly thickened. Stir in remaining ingredients and mix well. Pour mixture into a small greased loaf pan and chill until firm. Unmold and cut in thin slices.

Creamy Horseradish Sauce

½	cup heavy cream, whipped	1	tablespoon lemon juice
1½	tablespoons horseradish	¼	teaspoon salt

Into whipped cream, gently fold horseradish, lemon juice, and salt.

156

RED BEANS AND RICE

Serves 6

Best made ahead

1	pound red beans	⅔	cup chopped green pepper
2	quarts water	1	bay leaf
1	ham bone	1	teaspoon Worcestershire
2	pounds smoked sausage,		sauce
	cut in 1-inch pieces	¼	teaspoon Tabasco
3	cloves garlic, pressed	1	tablespoon minced fresh
1½	cups chopped yellow		parsley
	onions	1½	teaspoons salt
¾	cup chopped green onions	3	cups steamed rice
1½	cups chopped celery		

Rinse and drain beans. In a large pot with a lid, place beans and cover with water. Add ham bone and bring to a boil. Reduce heat and simmer 40 minutes. Add sausage, cover, and cook, 1 hour, stirring occasionally. Add garlic, onions, celery, green pepper, and bay leaf. Continue cooking, covered, 1½ hours, or until soft. Add Worcestershire sauce, Tabasco, parsley, and salt. Simmer 5 minutes. Remove bay leaf; serve over rice.

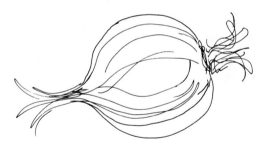

RACK OF LAMB

Serves 8

Preheat oven to 450°

2	8-rib racks of lamb, ribs cracked, bones shortened and cleaned, well trimmed	½	teaspoon powdered thyme
		½	teaspoon salt
		½	teaspoon pepper
2	tablespoons olive oil	2	watercress or fresh parsley bouquets
3	tablespoons Dijon mustard		
2	cloves garlic, pressed		
½	teaspoon powdered rosemary		

Place lamb in a large, shallow roasting pan, meat side up. Cover rib tips with foil to prevent burning. With a sharp knife, cutting ¼-inch deep, score thin layer of fat in a diamond pattern. In a bowl, combine oil, mustard, garlic, rosemary, thyme, salt, and pepper. Brush over lamb. Insert meat thermometer. Roast 35 minutes for rare, or until internal temperature is 150°; 40 to 45 minutes for medium rare, or until internal temperature is 160°; 45 to 50 minutes for medium, or until temperature is 170°. Transfer to a heated serving platter, remove foil; arrange racks facing each other with ribs interlaced. Let rest 8 to 10 minutes. Garnish between racks with watercress or parsley bouquets.

ROAST LEG OF LAMB WITH CHUTNEY SAUCE

Preheat oven to 325°

Serves 6

1	4-pound leg of lamb, boned, rolled and tied	½	teaspoon pepper
		½	teaspoon powdered rosemary
1	teaspoon salt		

Chutney Sauce

1	stick butter	½	teaspoon powdered rosemary
1½	cups Indian chutney, puréed		
		2	cloves garlic, pressed
¼	cup soy sauce		

Sprinkle lamb with salt, pepper, and rosemary; place, fat side up, in a shallow roasting pan. In a saucepan, melt butter; add chutney, soy sauce, rosemary, and garlic; stir and simmer 3 minutes. Brush meat with small amount of sauce. Roast 1¾ hours; remove from oven and pour remaining sauce over lamb. Increase temperature to 400° and cook 10 minutes. Transfer to a carving board, cover with foil, and let rest 10 minutes before carving into thin slices. Arrange slices on a heated serving platter. Pour sauce over lamb, or serve in a heated sauceboat.

BUTTERFLIED LEG OF LAMB

Serves 8 to 10

Begin a day ahead

1 6-pound leg of lamb,
   boned and butterflied

Marinade

1	cup olive oil	1	tablespoon Dijon mustard
½	cup red wine vinegar	1	tablespoon rosemary
2	tablespoons lemon juice	1	tablespoon marjoram
⅔	cup coarsely chopped yellow onion	½	teaspoon basil
		½	teaspoon thyme
2	cloves garlic, pressed	1	teaspoon salt
1	bay leaf, crumbled	1	teaspoon pepper

Make a series of small incisions in lamb so that meat will lie as flat as possible. Place lamb in a large shallow pan. In a bowl, combine marinade, mix well, and pour over lamb. Cover tightly with foil and refrigerate at least 12 hours, turning lamb several times.

Remove lamb from refrigerator at least 1 hour prior to cooking. Preheat broiler. Dry lamb thoroughly with paper towels. In a saucepan, bring marinade to a boil. Reduce to low heat and keep warm. Place lamb in pan, fat side down; broil 4 to 5 inches from heat 15 minutes; turn, baste with marinade, and broil 20 minutes. Transfer to a carving board, cover loosely with foil, and let rest 15 minutes.

Carve in thin slices diagonally across grain.

SAG GOSHT

Serves 6

2	pounds boneless lamb, shoulder or leg, well trimmed, cut in 1-inch cubes	2	10-ounce packages frozen chopped spinach, cooked and drained
¼	cup flour	2	cups sliced artichoke bottoms
3	tablespoons oil	1	teaspoon ground ginger
1	cup finely chopped yellow onion	½	teaspoon turmeric
		1½	teaspoons salt
3	large cloves garlic, finely chopped	1	teaspoon pepper

Dry lamb with paper towels. Dredge in flour; shake off excess. In a Dutch oven, heat oil and brown lamb on all sides in small batches. As lamb browns, remove with a slotted spoon. In same pot, sauté onion, stirring 3 minutes; add garlic and sauté 2 minutes. Return lamb to pot. Add spinach, artichoke bottoms, ginger, turmeric, salt, and pepper, and mix well. Reduce heat, cover, and cook 30 minutes.

LAMB CURRY

4	pounds boneless lamb, shoulder or leg, well trimmed, cut in 1-inch cubes	1¼	cups chicken stock
1	cup golden raisins	⅔	cup Indian chutney
1	cup shredded coconut	4	tablespoons curry powder
2	cups water	2	tablespoons coriander seeds
5	tablespoons oil	¼	teaspoon mace
1	teaspoon salt	¼	teaspoon cayenne pepper
1	cup coarsely chopped yellow onion	¼	teaspoon ground cloves
5	cloves garlic, coarsely chopped	¼	teaspoon ground cinnamon
		4	chicken bouillon cubes
		4	cups steamed rice

Condiments (boys)

1	cup Indian chutney	1	cup mashed bananas
1	cup finely chopped peanuts	1	cup chopped apple (sprinkled with lemon juice)
1	cup finely chopped red onion	1	cup unsweetened pineapple chucks
1	cup finely chopped green onions, tops only	1	cup mandarin oranges
1	cup finely chopped cucumber	1	finely grated hard-boiled egg
1	cup finely chopped tomato	1	cup bacon, cooked and crumbled
1	cup finely chopped green pepper		Optional: (Poppadums, plain Indian curry biscuits)
1	cup finely chopped canned beets		

Dry lamb with paper towels. In separate bowls, soak raisins and coconut in 1 cup water each 1 hour. Drain each, reserving liquid. Blot coconut with paper towels. In a skillet, heat 1 tablespoon oil and cook coconut, tossing frequently until golden brown.

In a Dutch oven, heat 3 tablespoons oil; brown lamb on all sides in small batches. With a slotted spoon, remove lamb as it browns; salt. Reduce heat, add remaining tablespoon oil, sauté onion, stirring 5 minutes. Add garlic and sauté 3 minutes. Remove from heat. Stir in stock; add chutney, curry powder, coriander seeds, mace, cayenne, cloves, and cinnamon. In a saucepan, bring reserved raisin/coconut liquid just to boiling point. Remove from heat, add bouillon cubes, and stir to dissolve. Stir in curry. Return lamb to pot, cover and simmer 1 hour, or until lamb is tender. Serve with rice and condiments of your choice. The reserved raisins and coconut may be served as condiments. If serving poppadums, heat in a preheated 350° oven 7 minutes and crumble on top of curry.

LAMB ROLL WITH CURRANT SAUCE   Serves 10

Preheat oven to 325°

1	5-pound leg of lamb, boned, rolled, and tied	½	teaspoon powdered thyme
1	teaspoon coarse salt	½	teaspoon sage
½	teaspoon crushed pepper	2	cloves garlic, cut in lengthwise slices
½	teaspoon powdered rosemary	10	celery leaves
		1	tablespoon flour

Remove strings and unroll lamb. Sprinkle with salt, pepper, rosemary, thyme, and sage. Add garlic and celery. Re-roll meat, jelly-roll fashion, and tie tightly at 1 to 2 inch intervals. Sprinkle with flour. Place lamb, fat side up, in a shallow roasting pan. Roast 2½ hours. Transfer to a carving board, cover with foil, and let rest 10 minutes.

Currant Sauce

1	stick butter	¼	cup mint leaves
¾	cup currant jelly	1	tablespoon finely chopped orange rind
¼	cup brandy		
¼	cup catsup		

In a small saucepan, melt butter. Add remaining ingredients. Stir and simmer 10 minutes. Slice lamb and arrange on a heated serving platter. Pour sauce over lamb, or serve in a heated sauceboat.

LAMB CHOPS WITH HERBS   Serves 4

1	egg, slightly beaten	½	teaspoon powdered thyme
1	teaspoon salt	8	loin lamb chops, 1 to 1½ inch thick, well trimmed
½	teaspoon pepper		
2	teaspoons finely chopped fresh parsley	4	tablespoons butter
		½	cup heavy cream
½	teaspoon powdered rosemary	⅛	teaspoon sage
		1	tablespoon mint sauce

In a bowl, combine egg, salt, pepper, parsley, rosemary, and thyme; mix well; brush both sides of chops. Cover and let stand 1 hour at room temperature. In a large, heavy skillet, melt butter and cook chops 8 minutes on each side. As chops cook, transfer to a heated platter and keep warm. To skillet, add cream, sage, and mint sauce; cook 3 to 4 minutes, stirring until sauce thickens. Pour over chops and serve immediately.

MOUSSAKA

Serves 6

Can be made ahead

Preheat oven to 350°

1	large eggplant (2 to 2½ pounds), unpeeled and sliced lengthwise in ¼-inch thick slices	½	teaspoon oregano
		½	teaspoon powdered thyme
		½	cup red wine
4	teaspoons salt	1	tomato, peeled, seeded, and chopped
1½	cups olive oil		
2	cups finely chopped yellow onions	⅔	cup tomato sauce
		2	egg whites, room temperature
3	cloves garlic, finely chopped	½	cup dry bread crumbs Béchamel Sauce
1	pound ground lamb		

Sprinkle eggplant with 3 teaspoons salt; drain on paper towels 30 minutes. Pat dry with paper towels. In a large, heavy skillet, heat 3 tablespoons oil and brown eggplant on both sides, adding oil as needed. Drain on paper towels. In a separate skillet with a lid, heat 2 tablespoons oil; add onions and sauté, stirring 4 minutes. Add garlic and sauté, stirring 2 minutes. Add lamb, remaining teaspoon salt, oregano, thyme, wine, tomato, and tomato sauce; stir; cover and simmer 30 minutes. Remove from heat; cool slightly; whisk in egg whites. Add ¼ cup bread crumbs and mix well. Place remaining ¼ cup bread crumbs on bottom of a 2-quart rectangular casserole. Alternate layers of eggplant and lamb mixture, ending with eggplant. Top with Béchamel Sauce. *(Recipe can be prepared several days ahead up to this point.)* Bake 1 hour, or until top is puffed and golden. Cool 20 minutes before cutting into squares.

Béchamel Sauce

2	tablespoons butter	1½	cups milk, warmed
2	tablespoons flour	2	egg yolks, beaten
½	teaspoon salt	½	teaspoon nutmeg

In a saucepan, heat butter, and stir in flour until smooth. Add salt. Gradually stir in milk. Continue to cook until sauce is thick and smooth. Reduce to very low heat. Add a little sauce to yolks in a thin stream. When milk mixture has become warm and thick, return to saucepan. Add nutmeg, blend well and pour over eggplant.

Vegetables, Rice, Pasta & Grits

JAMBALAYA GRITS

Serves 6

2   tablespoons bacon grease
2   tablespoons flour
½   cup chopped onion
1   green pepper, chopped
½   cup chopped celery
1   cup quick grits

3   fresh tomatoes, peeled
     and chopped
     (approximately 1 cup)
1   cup ground ham
     Bacon, cooked and
     crumbled

In a heavy skillet, heat bacon grease and gradually add flour, stirring constantly, until roux becomes light brown. Add onion, green pepper, and celery; cook 5 minutes. Cook grits according to package directions and add to roux. Add tomatoes and ham. Sprinkle with bacon and serve immediately.

ANCHOVIED ARTICHOKES

Serves 4

½   cup sour cream
1½ teaspoons anchovy paste
½   teaspoon salt
½   teaspoon white pepper
⅛   teaspoon garlic salt
⅛   teaspoon Tabasco

½ teaspoon paprika
1 teaspoon lemon juice
1 8-ounce can artichoke
   hearts, drained and cut in
   small pieces

In a saucepan, combine all ingredients except artichoke hearts. Cook over low heat 5 minutes, stirring occasionally until well blended. Gently fold in artichoke hearts. Heat 5 to 10 minutes.

ARTICHOKE MUSHROOM CASSEROLE

Preheat oven to 350°

Serves 6

Cream Sauce

4   tablespoons butter
4   tablespoons flour
1¼ teaspoons salt

¼ teaspoon white pepper
2 cups milk

In a saucepan, over low heat, melt butter. Stir in flour, salt, and pepper. Remove from heat and gradually stir in milk. Return to low heat and stir constantly until thick, about 5 minutes.

6   boiled artichokes
8   tablespoons butter
¼   cup finely chopped green
    onions
1   pound mushrooms, halved

2 teaspoons Worcestershire
   sauce
½ teaspoon Tabasco
¾ cup seasoned bread
   crumbs

Scrape artichoke leaves and quarter bottoms.

In a large skillet, melt 6 tablespoons butter; sauté onions until limp, but not brown. Add mushrooms and sauté 2 to 3 minutes. Reduce heat and stir in cream sauce, Worcestershire sauce, and Tabasco. Add atrichoke scrapings and bottoms. Pour into a 1½-quart casserole. Sprinkle with bread crumbs, dot with remaining 2 tablespoons butter, and bake 25 minutes.

BROCCOLI AMANDINE CASSEROLE

Preheat oven to 350°   Serves 6 to 8

1	bunch fresh broccoli, trimmed, *or* 2 10-ounce packages frozen broccoli florets	2	tablespoons dry sherry
		2	tablespoons lemon juice
		½	teaspoon salt
		¼	teaspoon white pepper
1	beef bouillon cube	½	cup grated Parmesan cheese
¾	cup hot water		
4	tablespoons butter	¼	cup grated Gouda cheese
4	tablespoons flour	¼	cup sliced almonds, toasted
1	cup light cream		

Cook broccoli in rapidly boiling water until just tender, about 6 minutes. Drain and place in a buttered 2-quart casserole. Dissolve bouillon cube in water. In a 1-quart saucepan, melt butter. Add flour and cook, stirring constantly 1 to 2 minutes. Pour in cream and bouillon, beating vigorously with a wire whisk. Bring sauce to a boil and stir until thick and smooth, about 3 to 5 minutes. Remove from heat and add sherry, lemon juice, salt, and pepper. Pour sauce over broccoli. Sprinkle with cheeses and almonds. Bake 20 minutes.

BROCCOLI ONION AU GRATIN   Serves 12

Preheat oven to 350°

3	pounds pearl onions, peeled	1	quart milk
		1	pint light cream
2	bunches fresh broccoli, trimmed	1	tablespoon salt
		¼	teaspoon white pepper
6	tablespoons butter	½	cup grated Parmesan cheese
¾	cup flour		

Boil onions in salted water until tender. Drain.

Cut broccoli into serving-size pieces. Boil until tender, but still crisp. Drain and place in a 2-quart shallow baking dish.

In a large saucepan, over low heat, melt butter. Slowly blend in flour; add milk and cream, stirring constantly, until sauce thickens. Season with salt and pepper. Add the cooked onions and mix well. Pour sauce over broccoli and sprinkle with cheese. Bake 30 to 45 minutes, or until bubbly and brown.

COLD BROCCOLI RING
WITH MARINATED CARROTS

Make ahead   **Serves 12**

1   pound carrots, peeled and
    sliced
1   cup oil and vinegar salad
    dressing
1   package gelatin
1   10¾-ounce can
    consommé mixed with 1
    can water
2   teaspoons lemon juice
5   teaspoons Worcestershire
    sauce
½   teaspoon Tabasco
1½ teaspoons salt
1   teaspoon white pepper
1   bunch broccoli, cooked,
    drained, and chopped
5   eggs, hard-boiled and
    chopped
¾   cup mayonnaise

Cook carrots until slightly tender. Drain and cover with salad dressing; refrigerate. In a large mixing bowl, dissolve gelatin in ¼ cup consommé/water mixture. Heat remaining mixture and add to gelatin, stirring until gelatin dissolves. Stir in lemon juice, Worcestershire sauce, Tabasco, salt, pepper, and broccoli. Cool; add eggs and mayonnaise. Grease an 8-cup ring mold and pour in broccoli mixture. Chill at least 6 hours. Unmold and place marinated carrots in center of ring.

GARDEN CASSEROLE   **Serves 6**

Preheat oven to 375°

2   cups cooked brown rice
2   cups broccoli, cut into ½-
    inch strips, from flower
    through stalk
2   cups carrots, cut into
    julienne strips
1   cup zucchini, sliced
    diagonally
1   cup green beans
1   teaspoon soy sauce
1   16-ounce jar Marinara
    sauce
1   cup shredded Longhorn
    cheese
1   cup shredded Monterey
    Jack cheese

Grease a 10 x 6 x 2 baking dish; place rice in bottom. Cook broccoli, carrots, zucchini, and beans in boiling salted water until tender, 5 to 7 minutes; drain. Reserve 4 zucchini slices for garnish. Spoon vegetables over rice. Combine soy sauce and Marinara sauce; pour over vegetables. Cover dish with foil and bake 30 minutes. Combine cheeses; sprinkle over casserole, and continue baking until cheeses melt, approximately 5 minutes. Garnish with zucchini slices and serve.

CARROT RING WITH WHITE WINE   Serves 8 to 10

Preheat oven to 350°

2	tablespoons butter	2	tablespoons chopped
2	tablespoons flour		fresh parsley
¾	cup milk	½	teaspoon sugar
¼	cup dry white wine	⅛	teaspoon nutmeg
2½	cups cooked, mashed	2	teaspoons salt
	carrots	1	teaspoon white pepper
1½	tablespoons minced	3	eggs, beaten
	yellow onion		

In a large skillet, melt butter and stir in flour. Add milk, stirring constantly until mixture is thick and smooth. Blend in wine, carrots, onions, parsley, sugar, nutmeg, salt, and pepper. Remove from heat and cool 10 minutes; stir in eggs.

Pour mixture into a greased 1-quart ring mold and set in a shallow pan of hot water. Bake 40 to 50 minutes, or until firm. Remove from oven and let stand out of water 5 minutes. Turn out onto a heated serving platter.

Fill center with green peas, mushrooms, broccoli florets, or spinach.

MASHED TURNIPS AND CARROTS   Serves 12

6	cups diced carrots	1	teaspoon salt
6	cups diced white turnips	1	teaspoon white pepper
1	pint water	½	cup light brown sugar
4	tablespoons butter		

In a Dutch oven, combine all ingredients; cover and bring to a boil. Reduce heat and simmer 30 minutes. Remove from heat and mash. Mixture should be moist, but not watery. If necessary, remove excess liquid. Reheat and serve.

VEGETABLE LASAGNA

Serves 10

Preheat oven to 350°

½	pound lasagna noodles
2	tablespoons olive oil
4	cloves garlic, minced
2	cups peeled and chopped tomatoes
2	medium eggplants, peeled and cut in ⅛-inch slices
2	10-ounce boxes frozen chopped spinach, cooked and drained

½ pound fresh ricotta cheese, grated
Salt to taste
Pepper to taste
¼ pound Parmesan cheese, grated

In a large pot, boil noodles in salted water al dente. Drain and place in ice water. In a saucepan, place 2 tablespoons oil and sauté garlic 3 minutes. Add tomatoes and simmer 15 minutes. Deep fry eggplant in oil until golden brown. Drain on paper towel. Salt. Combine spinach and cheese; season with salt and pepper. In a greased, 2-quart rectangular baking dish, alternate layers of noodles, eggplant, spinach, and tomatoes. Top with Parmesan cheese. Bake 30 minutes.

ZUCCHINI LASAGNA

Serves 6

Preheat oven to 350°

6	cups sliced zucchini
½	pound ground beef
1	clove garlic, minced
1	8-ounce can tomato sauce
1	teaspoon salt
¼	teaspoon oregano
¼	teaspoon basil leaves
1	cup small-curd cottage cheese

1 egg, beaten
1 tablespoon chopped fresh parsley
¼ cup dry bread crumbs
1 cup mozzarella cheese (4 ounces)

Boil zucchini 5 minutes. Drain. In a skillet cook beef and garlic 5 minutes. Stir in tomato sauce, salt, oregano, and basil. In a small bowl, combine cottage cheese, egg, and parsley. In a greased, 8-inch square baking dish, layer half zucchini, bread crumbs, cottage cheese, beef, and mozzarella cheese. Repeat layers, except mozzarella cheese. Bake 25 minutes. Sprinkle with remaining cheese. Return to oven just long enough to melt cheese, about 3 minutes.

CREOLE SQUASH

Serves 8

Preheat oven to 350°

4 pounds white squash
2 eggs
1 cup milk
1½ teaspoons salt
¼ teaspoon white pepper
1 cup peeled and chopped tomatoes
2 pieces white bread, diced

4 tablespoons butter, cut into small pieces
2 teaspoons chopped fresh parsley
1 teaspoon paprika
¼ cup grated Romano cheese

Peel squash; cut into small pieces, and parboil until tender, about 6 minutes. Drain and mash.

In a large bowl, mix eggs, milk, salt, and pepper. Add squash and tomatoes and mix gently. Fold in bread and butter; blend well. Pour into a 2-quart casserole and bake 45 minutes. Sprinkle top with parsley, paprika, and cheese.

YELLOW SQUASH AND TOMATOES

Preheat broiler

Serves 6 to 8

2 tablespoons butter
½ cup yellow onion, chopped
2 large tomatoes, peeled, chopped, and drained (about 2 cups)
1 teaspoon sugar
2¼ pounds yellow squash, sliced

1 teaspoon salt
½ teaspoon black pepper
⅛ teaspoon Tabasco
½ cup grated Parmesan cheese
4 strips uncooked bacon, cut into small pieces

In a large skillet, melt butter; sauté onion until limp, about 5 minutes. Add tomatoes and sugar and cook, 10 minutes. Reduce heat; add squash and salt. Cover and cook until tender. Season with pepper and Tabasco. Pour into a 1½-quart shallow baking dish; top with cheese and bacon. Broil until brown, about 10 minutes.

DEVILED CORN

Serves 8 to 10

Preheat oven to 350°

3	slices bacon, cooked and crumbled	1	16-ounce can whole kernel yellow corn, drained
5	tablespoons butter	1	16-ounce can cream-style yellow corn
2	tablespoons flour	½	cup grated Parmesan cheese
1	teaspoon Dijon mustard		
½	teaspoon Worcestershire sauce	½	cup seasoned bread crumbs
1	tablespoon lemon juice		
½	teaspoon salt	3	hard-boiled eggs, cut in wedges
½	teaspoon pepper		
½	cup milk	8	green olives, sliced

In a large saucepan, melt 4 tablespoons butter. Stir in flour, mustard, Worcestershire sauce, lemon juice, salt, pepper, and milk. Cook until mixture thickens, about 8 minutes. Remove from heat and stir in bacon and corn. Pour into a 1½-quart casserole. Sprinkle with cheese.

In a small saucepan, melt remaining tablespoon butter; mix in bread crumbs. Sprinkle over corn. Bake 45 minutes. Garnish with egg wedges and olive slices.

FRIED EGGPLANT

Serves 6

1	large eggplant (about 1 pound), peeled	2	eggs, beaten
		¾	cup Italian bread crumbs
1	tablespoon salt	3	tablespoons powdered sugar, optional
	Oil for deep frying		

Cut eggplant in round slices, ¼ inch thick, or into large strips. Place in a bowl and sprinkle with salt. After 30 minutes, rinse with cool water, drain, and dry with paper towels.

In a large frying pan, heat oil. Dig eggplant in eggs, and then in bread crumbs. Fry in hot oil until golden brown, about 5 minutes. Drain and sprinkle with sugar.

STUFFED EGGPLANT

Serves 6

Preheat oven to 350°

3	eggplants	½	cup chopped fresh parsley
6	strips bacon	1	teaspoon Worcestershire sauce
2½	cups chopped yellow onions	½	teaspoon salt
¾	cup chopped celery	½	teaspoon pepper
¾	cup chopped green pepper	¼	cup seasoned bread crumbs
1	cup chopped green onions	4	tablespoons butter
1	pound ham, chopped		
3	cloves garlic, crushed		

Cut eggplants in half lengthwise. Place in a large pot and cover with cold water. Cook until tender, about ½ hour. Do not let eggplant break. Drain and cool. Scoop out meat of eggplant and drain. Place shells on a baking sheet. Chop bacon in small pieces and fry. Add yellow onions and cook until light brown. Add celery and green pepper and sauté until tender. Add green onions and ham; cook 5 minutes. Add eggplant, garlic, parsley, Worcestershire sauce, salt, and pepper. Cook, over low heat, 10 minutes. Fold in bread crumbs. Remove from heat; add butter and mix well. Fill each shell and bake 30 minutes.

RATATOUILLE NIÇOISE

Serves 8 to 10

4	tablespoons butter	2	tablespoons flour
2	cloves garlic, minced	2	green peppers, cut in strips
1¾	cups thinly sliced yellow onions	½	pound cherry tomatoes
1	pound zucchini, cubed	1	tablespoon salt
1	pound eggplant, peeled and cubed	¼	teaspoon pepper
		1	teaspoon sugar

In a Dutch oven, melt butter and sauté garlic and onions 5 minutes.

Sprinkle zucchini and eggplant with flour. Place half the zucchini, eggplant, and green peppers into Dutch oven. Cover and cook 10 minutes, stirring occasionally. As mixture softens, add remaining zucchini, eggplant, green peppers, and tomatoes. Season with salt, pepper, and sugar. Cook 10 minutes.

EGGPLANT AND TOMATOES

Serves 6 to 8

Preheat oven to 350°

2	large eggplants (about 2 pounds)	¼	teaspoon thyme
4	tablespoons butter	⅛	teaspoon garlic powder
1½	teaspoons salt	¼	cup chopped fresh parsley
¾	teaspoon white pepper	2	slices white bread, cubed
¾	cup chopped yellow onion	1	cup grated Swiss cheese
2	cups peeled and chopped tomatoes		

Peel and cut eggplant into 1-inch thick circles. Boil 10 minutes; drain. Cube enough eggplant to measure ¾ cup. Place circles in a 9 x 12 greased, shallow baking dish. Brush with 2 tablespoons melted butter. Season with ½ teaspoon salt and ½ teaspoon pepper.

In a large skillet, sauté onions in remaining 2 tablespoons butter. Add tomatoes, cubed eggplant; cook over low heat 15 to 20 minutes, until thickened. Stir in 1 teaspoon salt, ¼ teaspoon pepper, thyme, garlic powder, parsley, and bread. Cook and stir 2 minutes.

Place a generous amount (about 2 tablespoons) of eggplant mixture on top of each eggplant circle. Sprinkle with cheese and bake 20 minutes.

PISTO

Serves 8

1	medium eggplant, unpeeled (about 1 pound)	2	cloves garlic, minced
2	tablespoons butter	1	10-ounce package frozen artichokes, thawed
¼	cup diced lean ham	2	teaspoons salt
2	cups thinly sliced red onions	1	cup peeled and chopped tomatoes
1	sweet red pepper, seeded and diced		

Cut eggplant into bite-size pieces.

In a Dutch oven, melt butter and sauté ham 10 minutes. Add onions, pepper, and garlic; cook 10 minutes. Add artichokes, salt, and tomatoes. Reduce heat, cover, and cook until artichokes are tender and tomatoes have cooked to a soft consistency, about 20 minutes. Serve hot or cold.

BAKED TOMATOES

Serves 6

Preheat oven to 325°

6	small tomatoes	1	teaspoon pepper
1	cup seasoned bread crumbs	¾	cup very thinly sliced yellow onion
1	stick butter, melted	6	teaspoons butter
1½	teaspoons salt		

Slice off tomato tops and scoop out 1 tablespoon tomato pulp. Invert and drain 10 minutes. In a small mixing bowl, combine bread crumbs and butter; mix thoroughly. Salt and pepper inside each tomato. Fill with bread crumb mixture; top each with onion and 1 teaspoon butter. Place in 1½-quart shallow baking dish. Bake 35 minutes.

TOMATOES PROVENCALE

Serves 6

Preheat oven to 325°

6	large tomatoes	3	tablespoons minced fresh parsley
1	tablespoon salt	½	cup grated Romano, *or* Swiss cheese
¾	teaspoon pepper		
¾	cup seasoned bread crumbs	¼	teaspoon oregano
3	cloves garlic, minced	4	tablespoons butter, melted

Slice off tomato tops and scoop out 2 tablespoons pulp. Season with salt and pepper.

In a medium bowl, combine bread crumbs, garlic, parsley, cheese, and oregano. Mix thoroughly. Place a generous amount into each tomato. Transfer to a 2-quart baking dish and pour butter on top of each. Bake 1 hour, basting twice.

SPINACH TIMBALES

Serves 6

Preheat oven to 325°

2	10-ounce packages frozen chopped spinach	2	eggs, beaten
2	tablespoons butter	1	teaspoon salt
½	cup chopped yellow onion	½	teaspoon pepper
1	3-ounce package cream cheese, softened	½	teaspoon nutmeg
½	cup sour cream	1½	cups hollandaise sauce (page 46)

Cook spinach and drain very well.

In a large skillet, melt butter and sauté onion 5 minutes. Remove from heat; stir in cream cheese, sour cream, eggs, salt, pepper, nutmeg and spinach. Pour into 6 buttered custard cups, and bake 30 minutes. To serve, invert onto a serving platter and top with hollandaise sauce.

SPINACH AND ARTICHOKE HOLLANDAISE

Preheat oven to 350°

Serves 8

8	cooked artichoke bottoms	2	teaspoons salt
2	10-ounce packages frozen chopped spinach	1	teaspoon white pepper
½	cup water	1½	cups hollandaise sauce (page 46)
1	cup sour cream		

Place artichokes in a 1½-quart baking dish.

Cook spinach and drain very well. In a bowl, combine spinach, sour cream, salt, and pepper. Heap spinach on top of each artichoke, cover with foil, and bake 15 minutes. Before serving, top each artichoke with hollandaise sauce.

GREEK SPINACH PIE

Serves 12

Preheat oven to 350°

White sauce

2 tablespoons butter	⅛ teaspoon white pepper
2 tablespoons flour	1 cup milk
½ teaspoon salt	

In a small saucepan, melt butter. Add flour, salt, and pepper; stir until well-blended. Remove from heat and gradually stir in milk. Return to heat, stirring constantly until thick and smooth.

1½ sticks butter	6 eggs, beaten
1 cup chopped yellow onion	1½ cups crumbled Feta cheese
2 pounds fresh spinach	1 cup white sauce
½ teaspoon salt	6 layers filo pastry dough
¼ teaspoon pepper	

In a Dutch oven, melt 6 tablespoons butter and sauté onions and spinach 20 minutes. Season with salt and pepper; cool.

In a bowl, mix eggs, cheese, and white sauce. Pour into spinach and stir until blended.

Melt remaining 6 tablespoons butter. In a 9 x 12 baking dish, place a layer of filo dough. Brush with some butter, top with some spinach. Repeat layers, ending with filo on top. Bake 30 minutes.

ONION AND BACON GRITS

Serves 6

Preheat oven to 400°

8 strips bacon	1 cup quick grits, uncooked
1 tablespoon bacon grease	1 teaspoon salt
⅔ cup finely chopped onion	½ teaspoon pepper
1 quart milk	1 cup Parmesan cheese
1 stick butter	

Cook bacon, drain well, and crumble. Reserve 1 tablespoon grease. Sauté onion in bacon grease. In heavy saucepan, bring milk and 6 tablespoons butter to a boil; add grits, stir, cover, and reduce heat. Simmer 5 minutes. Remove from heat, add salt, pepper, and onion. Beat until creamy, about 5 minutes. Add half bacon; mix well. Pour mixture into a buttered 13 x 9 x 2 casserole dish and refrigerate until firm. Cut into 6 rectangular bars and place on a baking sheet 2 inches apart. Sprinkle tops with remaining bacon and cheese. Melt remaining 2 tablespoons butter and drizzle some over each bar. Bake 25 minutes.

MIRLITON CASSEROLE

Serves 6 to 8

4	mirlitons
1	stick butter
2	pounds small raw shrimp, peeled
1	cup finely chopped yellow onion
2	cloves garlic, pressed
2	bay leaves
1	tablespoon chopped fresh parsley
¾	cup Italian bread crumbs
1	teaspoon salt
¼	teaspoon pepper
1	tablespoon Worcestershire sauce
¼	teaspoon Tabasco
4	teaspoons butter

Boil whole mirlitons until tender, about 45 minutes. Peel, remove seed and center strings, and mash pulp. In a large skillet, melt butter and add pulp. Stir in shrimp, onion, garlic, bay leaves, and parsley. Simmer, 20 minutes, stirring occasionally. Gradually add ½ cup bread crumbs. Add salt, pepper, Worcestershire sauce, and Tabasco. Simmer 5 minutes, stirring constantly. Remove bay leaves and pour into a 2-quart casserole. Sprinkle with remaining ¼ cup bread crumbs, and dot with butter. Bake 20 to 25 minutes.

BAKED BANANAS

Serves 8

Preheat oven to 350°

8	ripe bananas
¼	cup lemon juice
1	stick butter
½	cup sugar
3	tablespoons cinnamon
8	lemon wedges

Peel and slice bananas lengthwise and place in a shallow baking dish. Sprinkle each with lemon juice. Dot with butter. Sprinkle with sugar and cinnamon. Bake 25 minutes. Garnish with lemon wedges.

HOT CURRIED FRUIT

Serves 10 to 12

Preheat oven to 350°

1	8¾-ounce can apricot halves	1	17-ounce jar dark pitted cherries
1	8½-ounce can sliced pears	2	tablespoons cornstarch
1	8½-ounce can sliced peaches	1	tablespoon curry powder
1	8-ounce can sliced grapefruit	1	tablespoon cinnamon
		1	cup brown sugar
		1	stick butter, melted
1½	cups sliced banana	¼	cup brandy, *or* sherry

Drain fruits and place in a 2-quart buttered baking dish. Combine cornstarch, curry powder, cinnamon, and sugar. Sprinkle over fruit. Combine melted butter and brandy; pour over fruit and gently toss. Bake 30 minutes.

STUFFED BAKED APPLES

Serves 12

Preheat oven to 300°

12 Rome apples

Filling

½	pound brown sugar	½	cup currants, *or* raisins
1	stick butter, melted	6	cinnamon sticks, halved
½	cup chopped pecans		

Slice a piece from the bottom of each apple. Core each apple, being careful not to pierce the bottom. Scoop out 2 or 3 tablespoons pulp.

In a bowl, combine sugar, butter, pecans, and currants; blend well. Fill each apple with a generous amount and place in a 2½-quart shallow buttered baking dish. Place a cinnamon stick in center of each apple and bake 30 to 35 minutes.

FRIED MUSHROOMS

Serves 4

1	pound mushrooms	1½	teaspoons salt
1	cup flour	1	teaspoon baking powder
¾	cup beer	1	teaspoon white pepper
½	teaspoon garlic salt		Oil for frying

Wash mushrooms, trim ends, and dry.

In a bowl, combine flour, beer, garlic salt, salt, baking powder, and pepper. Dip mushrooms in batter and fry in oil, until golden brown. Drain well.

MUSHROOM PIE

Serves 8 to 10

Preheat oven to 350°

3	tablespoons butter	1	teaspoon salt
¼	cup chopped yellow onion	¼	teaspoon white pepper
1	pound mushrooms, sliced	1	egg white, beaten
1	tablespoon flour		Basic Pie Crust (page 229)
½	cup light cream		
1	tablespoon brandy, *or* sherry		

In a large skillet, melt butter and sauté onions 10 minutes. Add mushrooms and cook 4 to 5 minutes. Blend in flour and cream, stirring constantly. Bring to a boil. Stir in brandy, salt, and pepper. Remove from heat and cool. Glaze pie shell with egg white; pour in cooled mushroom mixture. Bake 20 minutes. Serve hot or cold.

ALMOND FRIED RICE

Serves 4

4	tablespoons butter	⅛	teaspoon pepper
½	cup chopped onion	¼	cup soy sauce
¼	cup chopped green pepper	¼	cup slivered almonds, toasted
¼	pound ham, finely chopped	3	cups steamed, cooled rice
¼	teaspoon salt		

In a large skillet, melt butter. Sauté onion and green pepper until tender. Add ham, salt, pepper, soy sauce, almonds, and rice. Simmer 5 minutes.

MUSHROOMS STUFFED WITH EGGPLANT

Preheat oven to 350°   **Serves 8**

2	medium eggplants (about 2 pounds), peeled and diced	¼	teaspoon pepper
		½	teaspoon chili powder
1	tablespoon salt	¼	teaspoon Tabasco
1½	sticks butter	½	cup Italian bread crumbs
½	cup chopped yellow onion	24	large mushrooms
¼	cup chopped green pepper	½	cup dry sherry
2	cloves garlic, minced	1	cup grated Muenster cheese
2	teaspoons salt		

Soak eggplant 30 minutes in salted water to cover. Drain.

In a large skillet, melt butter and sauté onion, green pepper, and garlic 10 minutes. Add eggplant and cook over low heat 25 minutes. Add salt, pepper, chili powder, Tabasco, and bread crumbs; cook 5 minutes.

Wash mushrooms, remove stems, and dry. Fill each with eggplant mixture and place in a greased 2-quart baking dish. Pour a little sherry over each. Bake 15 minutes. Sprinkle with cheese and bake another 15 minutes.

OKRA JAMBALAYA   **Serves 6 to 8**

4	dozen okra, trimmed	3	cups chopped tomatoes
3	tablespoons butter	1	teaspoon minced fresh parsley
½	cup finely chopped yellow onion	1½	teaspoons salt
2	cloves garlic, minced	¼	teaspoon black pepper
½	cup minced green pepper	⅛	teaspoon cayenne pepper

In a Dutch oven, melt butter; sauté onion, garlic, and green pepper 6 to 8 minutes. Add tomatoes, parsley, salt, pepper, cayenne, and okra; cook 20 minutes, until tender.

POTATO SOUFFLE

Serves 8

Preheat oven to 425°

3	cups mashed potatoes	⅛	teaspoon cayenne pepper
4	tablespoons butter, softened	½	cup finely chopped green onions
16	ounces small curd cottage cheese	¼	cup grated Parmesan cheese
½	cup sour cream		Chopped fresh parsley, *or*
2	eggs, beaten		chopped chives, *or* paprika
2	teaspoons salt		

In a large bowl, blend potatoes and butter. Beat in cottage cheese, sour cream, eggs, salt, cayenne, and onions. Pour into a 2-quart soufflé dish. Sprinkle with cheese and bake 50 minutes. Garnish with parsley, chives, or paprika.

SWEET POTATO RING

Serves 10 to 12

Preheat oven to 350°

8	sweet potatoes, peeled	1	teaspoon nutmeg
1½	sticks butter, softened	1	egg, lightly beaten
½	cup light brown sugar	¾	cup raisins
1	5.3-ounce can evaporated milk	¾	cup dark brown sugar
		1	cup pecan halves

Parboil sweet potatoes 25 minutes or until tender. In a large bowl, mash potatoes; add 1 stick butter, light brown sugar, milk, nutmeg, and egg. Mix well. Gently fold in raisins. Grease a 9-cup ring mold with remaining 4 tablespoons butter. Sprinkle dark brown sugar inside ring mold. Place pecans in bottom. Gently spoon in sweet potato mixture. Bake 45 to 60 minutes. Cool 5 minutes and turn onto a warm serving platter.

SWEET POTATO SOUFFLÉ

Serves 8

Preheat oven to 300°

Potatoes

1	pound fresh sweet potatoes or yams, cooked, *or* 1-pound 13-ounce can sweet potatoes, drained	1	teaspoon vanilla
		¼	cup sugar
		2	eggs
¾	cup milk	6	tablespoons butter, melted

Beat potatoes, milk, vanilla, sugar, eggs, and butter. Bake in ungreased 1½-quart baking dish until edges leave side of pan, approximately 45 minutes.

Topping

6	tablespoons butter, softened	½	cup dark brown sugar
½	cup chopped pecans	¾	cup crushed corn flakes

In a bowl, mix all topping ingredients until smooth. Spread on top of baked soufflé. Brown topping under broiler about 1 minute.

SPAGHETTI PIERRO

Serves 4 to 6

6	strips bacon, cut in 1-inch pieces	½	teaspoon salt
		⅛	teaspoon cayenne pepper
⅓	cup chopped onion	½	pound spaghetti
1	10-ounce can tomato purée	¾	cup freshly grated Parmesan cheese
⅓	cup water	½	cup heavy cream

Brown bacon, but not too crisp. Add onions and cook until limp. Add tomato purée, water, salt, and cayenne. Cook 20 minutes.

In boiling, salted water, cook spaghetti al dente. Drain. In a large bowl, combine spaghetti, sauce, and cheese. Add cream and toss well.

SPAGHETTI PRIMAVERA   Serves 8

½	pound cauliflower	6	tablespoons olive oil
½	pound broccoli	1	teaspoon minced garlic
½	pound zucchini	3	cups cubed tomatoes
4	asparagus	1	teaspoon salt
½	pound green beans	½	teaspoon pepper
⅔	cup green peas	6	fresh basil leaves, *or* 1
5	tablespoons butter		teaspoon dried basil
½	cup chopped green onions	2	ounces ham, chopped
½	pound mushrooms, thinly sliced	1	pound spaghetti
1	teaspoon finely chopped red or green chilies, *or* ½ teaspoon dried red pepper flakes	¼	cup chicken broth
		¾	cup heavy cream
		⅔	cup grated Parmesan cheese
¼	cup chopped fresh parsley	⅓	cup pine nuts, toasted

Trim cauliflower and broccoli and break into bite-size pieces. Trim ends of zucchini, cut in 1-inch pieces. Cut each asparagus into thirds. Cut green beans into 1-inch lengths. In a large pot, cook vegetables in boiling, salted water until crisp. Drain. Rinse with cold water and drain. Add peas. Heat 1 tablespoon butter in skillet; add onions and mushrooms. Cook 3 minutes. Add chilies and parsley. Place in a bowl. Heat 3 tablespoons oil in saucepan; add garlic, tomato, salt, and pepper. Cook 4 minutes, stirring gently. Stir in basil and ham.

Cook spaghetti in boiling water, al dente. Drain and return to pot.

Heat 3 tablespoons oil in large skillet and add vegetable mixture. Heat thoroughly, stirring gently.

In a large pot, melt 4 tablespoons butter. Add broth, cream, and cheese, stirring constantly. Cook over very low heat until smooth. Add spaghetti and toss. Add half vegetables and pour in liquid from tomato mixture, tossing and stirring. Add remaining vegetables and if sauce seems dry, add more cream. Sauce should not be soupy. Add nuts and toss. Serve in soup or spaghetti bowls and spoon tomato mixture over each.

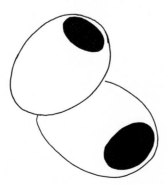

LINGUINI MOLLUSCA

Serves 6

¼	cup olive oil	1	pint oysters
2	tablespoons flour	½	cup oyster liquid
½	cup chopped green onions	1	teaspoon salt
5	tomatoes, peeled and chopped (approximately 4 cups)	¼	teaspoon pepper
		12	ounces linguini, boiled in salted water and drained
2	cloves garlic, minced	2	ounces freshly grated Parmesan cheese
½	teaspoon oregano leaves		
2	bay leaves		

In pan, heat oil. Stir in flour. Add onions, tomatoes, garlic, oregano, and bay leaves. Simmer 20 minutes. Add oysters and liquid; simmer 15 minutes. Add salt and pepper. Remove bay leaves. Fold linguini into sauce. Sprinkle with cheese and serve.

NOODLES CAESAR

Serves 4 to 6

8	ounces noodles	½	pound mushrooms, chopped
1	stick butter		
¼	cup olive oil	¼	cup half and half cream
2	green onions, minced	1	cup grated Parmesan cheese
3	cloves garlic, minced		

In a large pot, boil noodles in salted water. In a pan, heat butter and oil; add onions and garlic and cook 3 minutes. Add mushrooms and cook 3 minutes. Drain noodles and return to pot. Pour butter mixture over noodles, tossing lightly. Add half and half and sprinkle with cheese. Serve immediately.

NOODLES AND ZUCCHINI

Serve 6 to 8

½	pound mushrooms, trimmed and sliced	12	ounces noodles
		2	tablespoons salt
1½	sticks butter	1	tablespoon oil
1½	pounds zucchini, cut in julienne strips	¾	cup grated Parmesan cheese
1	cup heavy cream	½	cup chopped fresh parsley

In a very large skillet, sauté mushrooms in ½ stick butter 2 minutes. Add zucchini, cream, and remaining 1 stick butter, cut in pieces. Bring liquid to a boil and simmer 3 minutes.

In a large pot, cook noodles, adding salt and oil to water. Drain noodles and add to skillet. Mix well; add cheese and parsley. Toss.

BROCCOLI RICE CASSEROLE   Serves 8 to 10

Preheat oven to 350°

1¼	cups rice	¾	cup chopped mushrooms
6	cups chicken stock	½	cup flour
2	10-ounce packages	1	cup evaporated milk
	frozen broccoli	1	teaspoon salt
1	stick plus 2 tablespoons	¼	teaspoon pepper
	butter	½	cup dry bread crumbs
¾	cup finely chopped onion		

Cook rice, substituting 3 cups stock for water. Fluff with fork. Parboil broccoli; drain thoroughly. In a 12-inch skillet, melt butter. Sauté onion and mushrooms until soft. Blend in flour and cook 2 to 3 minutes, stirring constantly. Add remaining 3 cups stock and milk and continue stirring. Cook until mixture comes to a boil. Add salt and pepper.

Place rice in a buttered 2½ to 3-quart casserole. Spread broccoli on top; cover with sauce. In a small skillet, melt remaining 2 tablespoons butter. Add bread crumbs, stirring until lightly browned. Sprinkle over casserole. Bake until sauce bubbles, 30 minutes.

CORN AND RICE STUFFED TOMATOES

Preheat oven to 375°   Serves 8

8	tomatoes	½	pound mushrooms, sliced
	Salt to taste	½	cup corn
	Pepper to taste	2	cups steamed rice
	Oregano to taste	1	teaspoon salt
½	cup chopped onion	¼	teaspoon pepper
½	cup chopped green pepper	½	cup sharp grated cheddar
2	tablespoons butter		cheese

Slice tops off tomatoes; scoop out pulp and reserve. Sprinkle salt, pepper, and oregano into shells. In a skillet, cook onion and green pepper in butter until tender. Add mushrooms and sauté. Add corn, rice, tomato pulp, salt, and pepper. Heat. Add ¼ cup grated cheese and stuff shells. Sprinkle with remaining ¼ cup cheese. Put ½ inch water in a rectangular baking dish; place tomatoes in water and bake 25 minutes.

WILD RICE WITH WATER CHESTNUTS   Serves 4

¾	cup wild rice	½	cup sliced water chestnuts
3	cups stock (chicken or beef)	2	tablespoons minced fresh parsley
6	tablespoons butter	¼	teaspoon sage
¼	cup minced onion	1	teaspoon salt
1	cup chopped mushrooms	¼	teaspoon pepper

Wash rice in cold water 3 or 4 times. In a saucepan, bring stock to a boil and slowly add rice. Reduce heat, cover, and simmer 50 to 60 minutes.

In a skillet, melt butter; sauté onions and mushrooms 5 minutes. Add water chestnuts, parsley, sage, salt, pepper, and rice. Fluff with fork and serve immediately.

Good for stuffing Cornish game hens.

FRUIT SPICED RICE   Serves 8 to 10

5	cups water	½	cup dried apricots, chopped
2	cups brown rice		
¾	teaspoon cinnamon	4	tablespoons butter
¾	teaspoon nutmeg	½	cup blanched almonds
½	teaspoon salt	2	tablespoons sugar
½	cup raisins		

Combine water, rice, cinnamon, nutmeg, salt, raisins, and apricots; bring to a boil. Reduce heat, stirring once; cover and simmer 45 minutes. Melt butter; sauté almonds until golden; sprinkle with sugar. Pour over rice and serve. Good with ham or pork.

EVANGELINE RICE WITH PEAS   Serves 4 to 6

4	tablespoons butter	1	cup rice
¼	cup chopped onion	2¼	cups chicken stock
¼	cup chopped celery	1	teaspoon salt
1	slice bacon, diced	¼	teaspoon pepper
2	cups fresh green peas*	2	tablespoons grated Parmesan cheese
½	cup diced cooked ham		

In a large pot, heat butter; add onion, celery, and bacon; sauté 5 minutes. Add peas and ham and cook 5 minutes. Add rice, cook 3 minutes, stirring constantly. Add stock, salt, and pepper; bring to a boil. Cover and cook over low heat 25 minutes. Stir in cheese.

*If using frozen peas, thaw and add 5 minutes before rice finishes cooking.

SPINACH DRESSING

Serves 6 to 8

Preheat oven to 350°

2	10-ounce packages frozen chopped spinach	2	ribs celery, finely chopped
1	loaf stale French bread, cubed (should equal approximately 10 cups)	1	tablespoon chopped fresh parsley
2	cups chicken stock	2	eggs, beaten
4	tablespoons butter	2	tablespoons grated Parmesan cheese
1	tablespoon oil	1	tablespoon thyme
½	pound pork sausage	1	tablespoon beau monde seasoning
½	pound ground beef	1	teaspoon salt
½	cup finely chopped onion	¼	teaspoon pepper
3	green onions, finely chopped		Cayenne pepper to taste

In a saucepan, cook spinach; drain very well. Soak bread in stock; squeeze dry. In a large skillet, heat butter and oil. Sauté sausage and meat; add onions, celery, and parsley. Mix spinach, bread, eggs, cheese, and spices with meat mixture. Bake in 2-quart casserole 20 minutes, or use as stuffing for chicken, turkey, or Cornish game hens.

WALNUT STUFFING

Serves 12

1	cup rice	1	teaspoon salt
3½	cups beef stock	½	teaspoon pepper
1	bay leaf	1½	teaspoons thyme
1	cup chopped green onions	1	teaspoon sage
2	cloves garlic, pressed	2	tablespoons chopped fresh parsley
1	cup chopped celery	½	cup water
3	tablespoons bacon grease	¾	cup chopped walnuts
1	pound pork sausage		
¼	cup chopped ham		
2	cups stale French bread crumbs		

Cook rice in 2 cups stock with bay leaf 20 minutes. Remove bay leaf. In a large skillet, sauté onions, garlic, and celery in bacon grease. Cook sausage in a separate pan and drain. Add sausage and ham to onion mixture. Add bread crumbs and rice. Add spices; moisten with remaining 1½ cups stock and water. Add walnuts. Stuff loosely in bird. Can also be baked in a 3-quart casserole 25 to 30 minutes at 350°.

LOUISIANA OYSTER AND PECAN STUFFING

Serves 4

1½	cups stale French bread cubes
¼	cup chopped white onion
2	small minced green onions
¼	teaspoon minced garlic
½	cup chopped celery
¼	cup minced green pepper
¼	teaspoon thyme
1	teaspoon poultry seasoning

1	bay leaf
½	teaspoon salt
¼	teaspoon pepper
1½	cups coarsely chopped pecans
1	pint large oysters, reserving liquid
1	stick butter, melted
1	egg, slightly beaten

Mix all ingredients with butter and small amount of oyster water; add egg. Will stuff a 4 to 5 pound bird.

SAUSAGE DRESSING

Serves 4

Begin a day ahead

5-6	**slices bread**	**2**	**tablespoons butter**

Place bread on center rack in oven to dry overnight. Butter slices and crumble, to equal 2 cups.

½	cup pork sausage
½	cup chopped celery
¼	cup chopped onion
¼	cup chopped tart apple
¼	teaspoon salt

1	tablespoon poultry seasoning
¼-½	cup chicken broth
½	cup raisins, optional
⅓	cup sherry, optional

In a skillet, heat sausage. Drain. Add celery, onion, apple, salt, poulty seasoning, and bread crumbs. Moisten with broth. Add raisins plumped in sherry. Good with ham.

Breads &
Cookies

MUFFINS JAMBALAYA

Makes 24 muffins

Freezes well

Preheat oven to 400°

3	tablespoons butter	2	teaspoons baking soda
½	cup finely chopped green pepper	1	teaspoon salt
½	cup finely chopped green onions	2	eggs
1	cup yellow corn meal	2	cups buttermilk
1¼	cups flour	1	cup finely chopped ham
		1	cup finely chopped cooked sausage

In a skillet, melt butter and sauté green pepper and onions until soft, but not brown. In a large bowl, sift cornmeal, flour, soda, and salt. In a smaller bowl, beat eggs and stir in buttermilk. Add egg mixture to flour mixture all at once, stirring only until blended. Carefully fold in ham, sausage, green pepper, and onions (with any butter not absorbed). Spoon into well-greased muffin tins, filling ⅔ full. Bake 30 minutes, or until nicely browned.

To freeze: Seal cooled muffins in plastic bags. Before serving, thaw in bags 15 minutes, remove, wrap tightly in foil, and place in 400° oven 15 minutes.

FRENCH BREAD

Makes 4 loaves

Freezes well

Preparation time-3 hours

2	cups warm water	5-6	cups flour
2	packages dry yeast	2	tablespoons margarine
3	tablespoons oil	2	tablespoons cornmeal
1	tablespoon sugar	½	cup water
1	tablespoon salt		

In a large bowl, place water and yeast. In a small bowl, combine 2 tablespoons oil, sugar, and salt. Add to yeast water. Stir in 4 cups flour. When it becomes difficult to stir, put some of remaining flour on a smooth surface, turn dough out and knead 10 to 12 minutes, until smooth and pliable, adding more flour as needed.

Grease a large bowl with 1 tablespoon oil and place dough in it, turning once to grease top. Cover with a damp cloth and let rise in a warm place until doubled, about 1 hour.

Turn dough out onto a floured surface, divide into fourths. Roll each section into rectangle about 6 x 12. Roll up like a jelly roll, pulling long side toward you, keeping it as tight as possible. Pinch and shape ends.

Grease 2 15-inch baking sheets with margarine and sprinkle with cornmeal. Place loaves, seam-side down on sheets, stretching if necessary to make each loaf 15 inches long. Brush tops with water; make a ¼ inch slash in top the length of each loaf. Allow to rise uncovered, until doubled, about 1 hour.

Preheat oven to 400°. Place pan of hot water in bottom of oven. Brush loaves with water; bake 10 minutes; brush with water again and bake 20 minutes longer. Bread should be a deep golden brown on top and is done if it sounds hollow when thumped.

To freeze: Wrap cool loaves tightly in plastic. Reheat bare loaves in 400° oven 10 to 15 minues to restore crispness.

191

GARLIC BREAD

Serves 8

Preheat oven to 400°

1½ sticks butter
1   tablespoon minced garlic
¹⁄₁₆ teaspoon thyme
2   15-inch loaves French
    bread

⅔   cup grated fresh Parmesan
    cheese

In small skillet, melt butter. Sauté garlic until soft, but not brown. Add thyme. Remove from heat. Slice bread in half lengthwise. Place cut side up on baking sheet. Sprinkle cheese on bread, pour butter and garlic over all, spreading evenly.

Bake until brown, about 10 minutes. Remove from oven, cut into 1½-inch slices and serve hot.

FRENCH PEASANT BREAD

Makes 2 loaves

Freezes well

Preparation time-2½ hours

2   cups warm water
1   tablespoon sugar
2   teaspoons salt
1   package dry yeast
4   cups unsifted, unbleached
    flour

2   tablespoons oil
2   tablespoons cornmeal
2   tablespoons butter, melted

In a large warm bowl, place water, sugar, salt, and yeast. Stir until dissolved. Stir in flour. Dough will be stickly. Scrape into a greased bowl, cover with towel and let rise 45 minutes in warm place. Stir dough down. Grease 2 baking sheets with 1 tablespoon oil each and sprinkle each with 1 tablespoon cornmeal. Mound half dough onto each sheet. Let rise, uncovered, 45 minutes.

Preheat oven to 425°. Brush with butter and bake 10 minutes. Reduce heat to 375° and bake 20 minutes. Loaf will be flat and crusty.

To freeze: Wrap cooled loaves tightly in plastic. Before serving, thaw in plastic 30 minutes; remove plastic; wrap in foil and place in 400° oven 15 minutes.

HERBED DILL BREAD

Makes 2 loaves

Freezes well

Preparation time-4½ hours

1	cup milk	½	cup warm water
½	cup sour cream	2	eggs
1	tablespoon salt	2	tablespoons dill seed
2	tablespoons sugar	1	cup chopped green onions
3	tablespoons butter	½	cup chopped fresh parsley
2	packages dry yeast	5-6	cups flour

In a saucepan, heat milk and sour cream. Stir in salt, sugar, and butter. Cool 30 minutes. In a small bowl, dissolve yeast in warm water. In a large mixing bowl, beat eggs; stir in cooled milk mixture, yeast water, dill seed, onions and parsley. Stir in 2 cups flour and beat vigorously. Stir in 2 more cups flour until it becomes difficult to stir. Flour a smooth surface with 1 cup flour; turn dough out and knead until it becomes elastic and is no longer sticky, adding remaining 1 cup flour as necessary. Place in a well-greased bowl, turning once to coat top. Cover and let rise in a warm place until doubled, 1 to 1½ hours.

Turn out on a floured surface and knead 2 to 3 minutes. Return to bowl, cover and let rise again until almost doubled, about 45 minutes. Turn out on lightly floured surface, divide into 2 balls, kneading to remove air bubbles.

Preheat oven to 375°. Place each ball in a greased 1½-quart round casserole. Cover and let rise until dough comes to top, 30 to 45 minutes. Bake 40 minutes. Bread should be brown all over and is done if it sounds hollow when thumped.

To freeze: Wrap cooled loaves tightly in plastic. Before serving, thaw in plastic 30 minutes; remove plastic; wrap in foil and place in 400° oven 15 to 20 minutes.

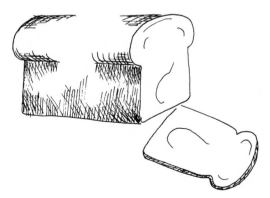

WINE AND CHEESE BREAD

Makes 1 loaf

Freezes well

Preparation time-3½ hours

3	cups flour	1	teaspoon salt
1	package dry yeast	3	eggs
½	cup dry white wine	4	ounces Monterey Jack, *or*
1	stick butter		Jarlsburg, *or* cheddar
2	teaspoons sugar		cheese, cubed

In a large mixing bowl, combine 1½ cups flour and yeast. In a saucepan, heat wine, butter, sugar, and salt until warm (115° to 120°), stirring, until butter is just melted. Add this to flour mixture. Add eggs. Beat at low speed of mixer 30 seconds, scraping constantly. Beat 3 minutes at high speed. Stir in cheese. Add enough flour to make a soft dough (1 to 1½ cups). Turn out on lightly floured board. Knead 3 to 5 minutes, until dough is smooth. Place in a well-greased bowl, cover, and let rise in a warm place until doubled, about 1½ hours. Punch down. Let rest 10 minutes. Shape into an 8-inch round loaf. Place in a greased 9-inch pie pan. Cover and let rise until doubled, about 40 minutes. Preheat oven to 375°; bake 20 minutes. Cover loosely with foil and bake 20 minutes.

SOUR CREAM BREAD

Makes 2 loaves

Preparation time-4½ hours

1½	cups sour cream	⅓	cup warm water
½	cup butter	2	packages dry yeast
½	cup sugar	3	eggs
½	teaspoon salt	4½	cups flour

In a small saucepan, heat sour cream until warm. In a large bowl, mix butter, sugar, and salt. Add sour cream and stir until butter melts. Dissolve yeast in warm water. Add to cream mixture. Add eggs and flour alternately, beating well. Let rise in a warm place until doubled, about 2 hours. Stir dough down and beat. Spoon into 2 greased loaf pans, 9 x 5 x 3. Let rise until doubled, about 1 hour. Preheat oven to 350°; bake 35 minutes. Remove from pans to cool.

ONION CHEESE BREAD

Makes 2 loaves

Freezes well

Preparation time-4½ hours

1½	cups milk	½	cup warm water
2	tablespoons sugar	3	cups chopped onion
3	tablespoons butter	6	ounces sharp cheddar
2	teaspoons salt		cheese, grated
2	packages dry yeast	6-7	cups flour

In a saucepan, scald milk and add sugar, butter and salt, stirring to dissolve. Let cool 30 to 40 minutes. Dissolve yeast in warm water. In a large bowl, combine milk mixture, yeast water, onions, and cheese. Stir in 4 cups flour. When it becomes difficult to stir, turn out on a surface floured with remaining 1 cup flour. Knead until dough is pliable and no longer sticky, about 10 minutes, adding remaining 1 to 2 cups flour as necessary. Place in well-greased bowl, turning once to grease top. Cover and let rise in a warm place until doubled, about 1 hour. Turn out on a floured surface and knead 2 to 3 minutes. Return to bowl to rise again until almost doubled, about 45 minutes. Remove to lightly floured surface, form into 2 loaves, tuck ends under, and place in 2 greased 9 x 5 x 3 loaf pans. Cover and let rise to top of pan, about 45 minutes.

Preheat oven to 400° and bake 15 minutes. Reduce to 375° and bake 15 to 20 minutes or until bottom of loaf sounds hollow when thumped. Remove from pan to cool.

Onion Cheese Buns: (Makes 3 dozen.) When dough is divided in half after second rising, roll to less than ½-inch thickness. With a 4-inch cutter, cut out and place on greased baking sheets, leaving room for rising. Let rise 1 to 1½ hours, until about double. Bake at 375° 20 minutes or until tops are golden brown. To freeze: Seal cool buns in plastic bags. Before serving, bring to room temperature in bags.

Onion Cheese Rolls: (Makes 6 dozen.) After first rising, roll dough to about ¼-inch thickness. Cut with 3-inch biscuit cutter. Let rise 1 hour. Bake at 400° 12 to 15 minutes or until brown.

To freeze: Bake until rolls just begin to brown, remove from oven, cool, and freeze in plastic bags. Before serving, thaw in bags 30 minutes, place on baking sheet, and bake at 400° 10 to 12 minutes, or until brown.

SOURDOUGH FRENCH BREAD   Makes 2 loaves

Freezes well

Preparation time-3 hours

1 package dry yeast	6-8 cups unbleached flour
1½ cups warm water	1 teaspoon cornstarch
1½ cups sourdough starter	1 cup water
2 teaspoons salt	¼ cup cornmeal
2 tablespoons oil	
4 teaspoons sugar	

In a large bowl, sprinkle yeast over warm water. Add starter, salt, 1 tablespoon oil, sugar, and 3 cups flour. Mix well. Add remaining flour, 1 cup at a time up to about 6 cups. Put 1 cup flour on a smooth surface, turn dough out and knead until smooth, adding one more cup flour if needed.

Grease a large bowl with 1 tablespoon oil, put dough in bowl and turn to coat top. Cover with a towel and let rise in a warm place until doubled, about 1 hour. Turn out onto a floured surface and knead 8 to 10 minutes until smooth, adding flour if needed.

Preheat oven to 375°. In a small bowl, dissolve cornstarch in 1 teaspoon water; stir in remaining water. Grease 2 baking sheets and sprinkle with cornmeal. Shape dough into 2 oblong loaves and place each on a baking sheet, painting top with cornstarch glaze. Slash top with a sharp knife ¼-inch deep.

Allow dough to rise until doubled, about 45 minutes. Glaze again. Place a large pan of boiling water in bottom of oven. Place in center of oven. Bake 20 minutes; glaze; bake 20 minutes.

To freeze: Wrap cooled loaves tightly in plastic. Before serving, thaw and reheat bare loaves in 400° oven 10 to 15 minutes.

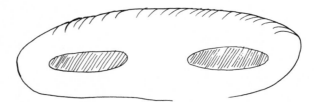

SOURDOUGH STARTER

Makes 3½ cups

Begin 4 days ahead

1½   cups unbleached flour
2   tablespoons sugar
1   tablespoon salt

1   package dry yeast
2   cups warm liquid (milk, water, *or* potato water)

In a large crock or glass bowl, mix flour, sugar, and salt. Sprinkle yeast over liquid. Add liquid to dry ingredients and stir with a wooden spoon. Mixture will be very thick and sticky, but not stiff. Keep in a warm place. Allow to sour 3 to 4 days.

Stir in 2 cups flour, 1 cup warm liquid, 1 tablespoon salt, and 2 tablespoons sugar. Let stand overnight (it will rise and bubble) and it will be ready to use.

SOURDOUGH ORANGE MUFFINS

Preheat oven to 375°

Makes 18 to 22 muffins

¼   cup sugar
½   cup dark brown sugar, firmly packed
1½   cups sifted flour
½   cup sifted whole wheat flour
1   teaspoon salt
1   teaspoon baking soda

4½   teaspoons dried orange rind
1   egg, beaten
½   cup oil
¾   cup sourdough starter
½   cup buttermilk
2   teaspoons orange extract
1   cup coarsely chopped nuts

In a large bowl, mix sugars, flours, salt, soda, and rind. Make a well in center. In a separate bowl, mix egg, oil, starter, buttermilk, and extract. Pour wet mixture into center of dry mixture. Mix only until all ingredients are blended. Batter will be slightly lumpy. Fold in nuts. Spoon into greased or paper-lined muffin tins, filling ⅔ full. Bake 20 minutes, until brown.

ONION RYE BREAD

Makes 1 large loaf

Freezes well

Preparation time-4½ hours

1	cup milk	½	cup finely chopped onion
1	tablespoon sugar	1	tablespoon caraway seeds
1½	teaspoons salt	2	cups flour
2	tablespoons butter	2	cups rye flour
2	tablespoons molasses		Cornmeal
1	package dry yeast		Cream
¼	cup warm water		Salt

In a saucepan, scald milk; stir in sugar, salt, butter, and molasses. Cool 20 to 30 minutes. Dissolve yeast in water. In a large bowl, combine milk mixture, yeast, water, onion, and caraway seeds. Stir in flours. Turn out on floured board to knead when it becomes too difficult to stir. (Use rye flour to flour board.) Knead to incorporate flour, 5 to 10 minutes.

Place in a greased bowl, cover, and let rise in a warm place until doubled, 1½ hours. Turn out on floured board (use rye flour) and knead 3 to 5 minutes. Return to greased bowl, cover, let rise again until doubled, 1 hour.

Remove from bowl; shape into loaf. Place in a 9 x 5 x 3 loaf pan which has been greased and dusted with corn meal. Brush top of loaf with cream and sprinkle with salt.

Let rise a third time, almost to top of pan, about 45 minutes. Preheat oven to 400° and bake 40 minutes. Cool on wire rack. This recipe doubles easily.

NO KNEAD BREAD

Freezes well

Preparation time-4 hours

2	cups milk	3	eggs
2	sticks butter	4	teaspoons vanilla
¾	cup sugar	2	teaspoons salt
3	packages dry yeast	8-9	cups flour
½	cup warm water	1½	tablespoons oil

In a saucepan, scald milk. Add butter and sugar; cool. In a small bowl, dissolve yeast in water. In an extra large bowl, beat eggs, add vanilla, and salt. Add milk and yeast water. Add flour, 1 cup at a time, until dough is soft and still sticky, mixing well. Cover and let rise in a warm place until doubled, about 1 hour. Punch down and transfer to another large bowl greased with 1 tablespoon oil. Oil top of dough with remaining ½ tablespoon oil. Cover and let rise again until doubled, about 45 minutes. Punch down and scrape dough into 3 greased 9 x 5 x 3 loaf pans. Cover and let rise until dough reaches top of pan, about 1 hour.

Preheat oven to 400°. Place pans in center and bake 10 minutes. Reduce heat to 350° and bake 25 minutes. Loaf is done if it sounds hollow when thumped. Remove from pans to cool. For a softer crust, brush tops of loaves with melted butter and cover with a cloth while cooling.

CREAM CHEESE BISCUITS

Preheat oven to 375°

4	ounces cream cheese, softened	1	stick butter, softened
		1	cup flour

In a mixing bowl, cream cheese and butter; add flour and continue beating until mixed well. Roll dough out on floured waxed paper to ¼-inch thickness; cut with 2-inch biscuit cutter. Place biscuits on ungreased baking sheet and bake 15 minutes, or until golden brown.

Food Processor Method: Place cold cream cheese, cold butter, and flour in bowl of food processor, fitted with steel blade. Process until dough forms a ball, about 1 minute. Roll out and cut.

WHITE BREAD

Freezes well

Preparation time-3 hours

1	cup milk	1½	teaspoons sugar
1½	teaspoons salt	3	cups flour
¼	cup warm water	1	tablespoon oil
1	package dry yeast		

In a small saucepan, heat milk and add salt. Cool to lukewarm. In a large bowl, mix water, yeast, and sugar; let it start to bubble. Add milk to yeast mixture. Stir in 2½ cups flour, reserving ½ cup to flour board for kneading. Turn dough out onto floured board and knead about 5 minutes, until smooth. Place in a bowl greased with oil, turning once to coat top. Let rise until doubled, about 45 minutes. Turn dough out onto lightly floured board and knead to remove air bubbles. Place in greased 9 x 5 x 3 loaf pan and let rise until doubled, about 45 minutes. Preheat oven to 350°. Bake 35 minutes. Bread is done if it sounds hollow when thumped.

Pizza Crust: Mix all ingredients as above and knead until smooth. Divide in half and roll out to fit 2 large 14 to 16-inch pizza pans. Do not bake before adding sauce and pizza toppings.

BISCUITS

Makes 1½ dozen

Freezes well

Preheat oven to 450°

2	cups flour	½	cup shortening
3	teaspoons baking powder	1	cup milk
1	teaspoon salt		

In a large bowl, sift flour, baking powder, and salt. Cut in shortening until mixture resembles coarse crumbs. Add milk and stir just until moistened. Place on floured board, knead if necessary to get dough to hold together, and roll out to ¼-inch thickness. Cut with 2-inch biscuit cutter and place on ungreased baking sheet. Bake 20 minutes, or until brown.

To freeze, bake about 15 minutes, but do not allow to brown. Wrap cooled biscuits tightly in plastic. Before serving, thaw completely, bake at 450° 10 to 15 minutes, or until brown.

WHOLE WHEAT BRAN ROLLS

Freezes well   **Makes 2½ to 3 dozen**

Preparation time-3½ hours

1	cup milk	2	tabelspoons molasses
1	cup bran cereal	1½	teaspoons salt
½	cup warm water	¾	cup plus 1 tablespoon oil
2	packages dry yeast	3	cups whole wheat flour
3	eggs, beaten	2	cups white flour
2	tablespoons dark brown sugar		

In a saucepan, scald milk; add cereal and cool to lukewarm. In a small bowl, dissolve yeast in water. In a large bowl, mix eggs, sugar, molasses, salt, and ¾ cup oil. Beat. Add milk and yeast water. Add 2 cups whole wheat flour and stir vigorously. Stir in white flour. Flour a smooth surface with remaining 1 cup flour; turn dough out and knead until smooth, 5 to 10 minutes. Place dough in large bowl greased with remaining 1 tablespoon oil, turning once to coat top. Cover and let rise in a warm place until doubled, about 1½ hours. On a lightly floured surface, roll out to about ½-inch thickness. Cut with a 3-inch biscuit cutter. Fold and place on a greased baking sheet. Let rise until puffy, about 1 hour. Preheat oven to 350°. Bake 15 to 20 minutes, or until browned.

To Freeze: Bake until rolls just begin to brown, about 13 to 15 minutes. Wrap cooled rolls in plastic bags. Before serving, allow to thaw in plastic, 30 minutes. Remove from plastic, bake at 350° 10 to 15 minutes, until brown.

BRAN MUFFINS   **Makes 3 dozen**

Freezes well

Preheat oven to 425°

3	cups bran flakes	1¼	cups sugar
1	cup boiling water	2½	cups flour
2	cups raisins	1	teaspoon salt
2	eggs	2½	teaspoons baking soda
2	cups buttermilk	½	teaspoon cinnamon
½	cup oil		

In a bowl, place bran flakes; pour boiling water over; stir in raisins. In a large mixing bowl, beat eggs; add buttermilk; beat in oil, sugar, flour, salt, soda, and cinnamon. Add bran and raisins and spoon into paper-lined muffin tins, filling each ⅔ full. Bake 20 to 25 minutes, until brown.

BRAIDED BREAD WITH FRUIT

Makes 3 loaves

Freezes well

Preparation time-3 hours

2	packages dry yeast	4-6	cups flour
1¼	cups warm water	3	tablespoons butter, melted
3	tablespoons sugar	1	tablespoon vegetable oil
1	tablespoon salt		
2	tablespoons butter, softened		

In a large bowl, dissolve yeast in water. Add sugar, salt, and butter, stirring until sugar and salt are dissolved. Stir in 3 cups flour.

Flour a smooth surface with 1 cup flour. Turn dough out and knead until smooth, adding remaining flour as necessary. Place in a large bowl greased with oil, cover with a towel, let rise in a warm place until doubled, about 1 hour.

Punch down and divide dough into thirds. Roll each section into a rectangle about 6 x 12. Prepare fillings. Amounts are for 1 loaf. Make diagonal cuts in outside portions of dough about 1-inch apart from filling to edge.

Fold strips, alternating sides (lattice-like) over filing, stretching to form a compact loaf and to be sure all filling is enclosed. Lift loaves carefully onto greased baking sheets and brush each loaf with 1 tablespoon butter.

Let rise in a warm place 20 to 30 minutes. Preheat oven to 350° and bake 40 minutes, or until brown. To freeze: Wrap cooled loaves in plastic. Before serving, thaw in plastic 30 minutes. Heat 15 to 20 minutes.

Filling #1

½	cup raisins	½	cup brown sugar
¼	cup orange juice	2	teaspoons cinnamon
1	large apple, unpeeled	½	teaspoon nutmeg

Soak raisins in orange juice 20 to 30 minutes. Drain. Slice apple into thin wedges. Place in center of prepared dough; sprinkle raisins on top. Combine sugar, cinnamon, and nutmeg and sprinkle on top of fruit.

Filling #2

1	large banana, sliced
⅓	cup orange marmalade

Place sliced bananas in center of prepared dough. Heat marmalade and pour over bananas.

Filling #3

1	large pear, or 2 peaches, underripe	2	teaspoons cinnamon
½	cup brown sugar	½	teaspoon nutmeg

Peel and slice fruit. Place slices in center of prepared dough. Combine sugar, cinnamon, and nutmeg and sprinkle on top of fruit.

BUTTERFLAKE ROLLS
Makes 2½ dozen

Refrigerate overnight

2	packages dry yeast	1	cup warm water
¼	cup warm water	4½	cups flour
½	cup sugar	2	teaspoons salt
2	sticks butter, softened	4	tablespoons butter, melted
3	eggs, beaten		

Dissolve yeast in water. Cream sugar and 1 stick butter; add eggs, 1 cup water, and yeast water. Stir in flour and salt. Dough will be very moist and sticky. Refrigerate overnight or at least 6 hours. Preparation time from this point is 3½ hours. On a well-floured cloth or board, roll dough out until it is a thin rectangle about 10 x 22 inches . Dough will be sticky. Spread with remaining 1 stick butter. Roll up along long side. Stretch to an equal thickness before cutting. Cut dough in ¾ to 1-inch slices with floured knife; dip slices in melted butter. Place in greased muffin tins, buttered side up. Let rise until doubled, about 3 hours. Preheat oven to 400°. Bake 10 minutes, or until light brown.

POTATO ROLLS

Makes 3 dozen

Freezes well

Preparation time-3½ hours

1	medium potato (⅔ cup mashed)	¼	cup sugar
¼	cup potato water	1½	teaspoons salt
1	package dry yeast	4-5	cups flour
2	tablespoons shortening	2	eggs, lightly beaten
1	cup milk (can use evaporated)		Melted butter

Boil peeled potato in water to cover. When tender, measure ¼ cup potato water, adding water if needed. Cool to lukewarm, 20 to 30 minutes; add yeast. In a large bowl, mix shortening and potato until smooth. In a small saucepan, warm milk and stir in sugar and salt. Add to potato mixture and stir until smooth. Add 2 cups flour, one at a time, mixing well. Add eggs, mixing well again. Add yeast water and ½ to 1 cup more flour if needed to make a stiff dough. Let rise 2 hours. Punch down; add about 2 cups flour to make a workable dough. Turn out on floured board and knead 8 to 10 minutes, using up to 5 cups flour as necessary. Dough will be sticky, but less flour makes a lighter final result. Roll out on a floured surface to ½-inch thickness. Cut with 3 inch biscuit cutter; brush each with butter and fold in half, pressing edges together. Place rolls, touching each other, on a greased baking sheet. Let rise about 1 hour. Preheat oven to 350°. Bake 12 to 15 minutes, or until brown.

To freeze, bake only until very lightly brown, about 10 to 12 minutes; remove from oven, cool, and freeze in plastic bags. To use, let thaw in bags 30 minutes, place on baking sheet and bake at 350° 10 to 12 minutes or until brown.

ROLLS

Freezes well

Preparation time-2½ hours

1	cup milk	½	cup sugar
½	cup warm water	1½	teaspoons salt
2	packages dry yeast	6	cups flour
3	eggs, well beaten	1	stick butter, melted
½	cup oil		

In a small saucepan, scald milk; allow to cool to lukewarm. Dissolve yeast in warm water. Mix eggs, oil, sugar, and salt. Add milk and yeast to egg mixture. Add 3 cups flour and stir vigorously 2 to 3 minutes. Stir in 2 more cups flour. Flour board with remaining cup. Turn dough out and knead well, incorporating flour as needed. Place in greased bowl, cover with towel, and let rise 2 hours in a warm place. Turn out on lightly floured board. Roll out for Crescent or Parker House rolls. Let rise until doubled, about 30 minutes. Preheat oven to 400°. Bake 12 to 15 minutes, or until brown.

Crescent Rolls: Divide in half. Refrigerate half you are not working with. Roll dough in a circle to ⅛-inch thickness. Brush with melted butter. Cut in 16 wedges. Roll each from wide end, place on baking sheet, point down. Let rise, until doubled, about 30 minutes. Preheat oven to 400°. Bake 10 to 15 minutes until brown.

Parker House Rolls: Roll dough to ¼-inch thickness. Cut with 3-inch biscuit cutter; brush with melted butter; fold in half and place on baking sheet. Let rise, until doubled, about 30 minutes. Preheat oven to 400°. Bake 10 to 15 minutes until brown.

Freezing: Cook rolls until they just begin to brown, about 10 minutes. Remove from oven. Cool thoroughly. Place in plastic bags, close tightly and freeze. When ready to use, let thaw in bags about 30 minutes. Cook on baking sheet in preheated 400° oven until brown, about 10 minutes.

KING CAKE

Makes 2-9 x 12 inch cakes

Freezes well

Preparation time-5½ hours

Cake

1	stick plus 1 tablespoon butter	⅓	cup warm water
⅔	cup 99% fat free skim evaporated milk	4	eggs
½	cup sugar	1	tablespoon grated lemon rind
2	teaspoons salt	2	tablespoons grated orange rind
2	packages dry yeast	6	cups flour

In a saucepan, melt 1 stick butter, milk, ⅓ cup sugar, and salt. Cool to lukewarm. In a large mixing bowl, combine 2 tablespoons sugar, yeast, and water. Let stand until foaming, about 5 to 10 minutes. Beat eggs into yeast; then milk mixture and rinds. Stir in flour, ½ cup at a time, reserving 1 cup to flour kneading surface. Knead dough until smooth, about 5 to 10 minutes. Place in large mixing bowl greased with 1 table-spoon butter; turning dough once to grease top; cover and let rise in a warm place until doubled, about 1½ to 2 hours.

Filling

½	cup dark brown sugar, packed
¾	cup granulated sugar
1	tablespoon cinnamon
1	stick butter, melted

Topping

1	egg, beaten
1	cup sugar, colored (⅓ cup each of yellow, purple, and green)
2	plastic babies (¾-inch) or 2 beans

For filling, mix sugars and cinnamon. Set aside.

For topping, tint sugar by mixing food coloring until desired color is reached. For purple, use equal amounts of blue and red. A food pro-cessor aids in mixing and keeps the sugar from being too moist.

When dough has doubled, punch down and divide in half. On a floured surface, roll half into a rectangle 30 x 15. Brush with half of melted butter and cut into 3 lengthwise strips. Sprinkle half of sugar mixture on strips, leaving a 1-inch lengthwise strip free for sealing. Fold each strip lengthwise toward the center, sealing the seam. You will now have 3   30-inch strips with sugar mixture enclosed in each. Braid the 3 strips and make a circle by joining ends. Repeat with other half of dough. Place each cake on a 10 x 15 baking sheet, cover with a damp cloth, and let rise until doubled, about 1 hour. Brush each with egg and sprinkle top with colored sugars, alternating colors. Preheat oven to 350°. Bake 20 minutes. Remove from pan immediately so sugar will not harden; while still warm, place 1 plastic baby* in each from underneath.

To freeze: Wrap cooled cake tightly in plastic. Before serving, remove plastic and thaw.

*In New Orleans, this cake is served during Carnival season from the Feast of Epiphany (January 6) until Mardi Gras (the day before Ash Wednesday). The person receiving the baby (or the bean) is considered lucky; by custom that person must also supply the next King Cake.

RAISIN CINNAMON BREAD

Makes 2 loaves

Freezes well

Preparation time-3 hours

2	packages dry yeast	7-9	cups unbleached flour
2¼	cups warm water	1½	cups raisins
1	cup sugar, *or* ¼ cup honey*	½	cup brown sugar
1	tablespoon salt	4	teaspoons cinnamon
2	tablespoons butter, softened	2	tablespoons water
		3	tablespoons butter, melted

In a large mixing bowl, dissolve yeast in ½ cup water. Stir in remaining 1¾ cups warm water, sugar, or honey, salt, and butter. Add 3½ cups flour and stir vigorously. Add raisins and enough flour to make dough easy to handle, about 3 cups. Turn dough onto lightly floured surface and knead until smooth and elastic, adding remaining ½ cup flour as needed. Place in a greased bowl, turing to coat top, cover and let rise in a warm place until doubled, about 1 hour.

Punch dough and divide in half. Roll each half into a rectangle about 9 x 18 inches. In each of 2 small bowls, mix ¼ cup brown sugar and 2 teaspoons cinnamon. Sprinkle each dough half with 1 tablespoon water and sugar-cinnamon mixture. Roll each up, starting on short side. Pinch seams and each end to seal. Place each loaf seam side down in greased 9 x 5 x 3 loaf pan. Brush with melted butter and let rise until dough reaches tops of pans, about 45 minutes.

Preheat oven to 425°. Bake 30 to 40 minutes. Loaves are done when light brown and bottom sounds hollow when thumped. Remove bread from pans to cool on racks. Serve hot with butter or freeze for later use. Wrap tightly in plastic.

*If you use honey, dough will absorb more flour than if you use sugar.

BUTTERY BREAD

Makes 2 loaves

Freezes well

Preparation time-4½ hours

1	cup milk	1	cup warm water
½	cup sugar	2	packages dry yeast
1	tablespoon salt	2	eggs, beaten
1	stick butter	6-7	cups flour

In a saucepan, scald milk; add sugar, salt, and butter; stir until butter melts. Cool to lukewarm. In a large bowl, dissolve yeast in water. Combine milk mixture with yeast water. Add eggs. Add 3 cups flour and beat vigorously. Add 3 more cups flour and mix well. Turn out on smooth surface floured with some of remaining flour. Knead until smooth, adding rest of flour as needed. Dough will be soft. Place in a greased bowl, turning once to coat top. Cover with a towel and let rise in a warm place until doubled, about 1½ hours. Turn out on a floured surface and knead again 2 to 3 minutes. Return to bowl; let rise until almost doubled, about 1 hour. Turn out onto lightly floured board and form into 2 loaves, kneading to remove air bubbles. Place each loaf in greased loaf pan, 9 x 5 x 3. Let rise almost to top of pan, about 45 minutes. Preheat oven to 400°. Bake 30 minutes. Bread is done when bottom sounds hollow when thumped. Remove from pan. Cool on racks.

Variations: 1. Use half white and half whole wheat flour.
2. Use only whole wheat flour. Loaf will be heavier and more compact.

CARROT BREAD

Makes 2 loaves

Freezes well

Preheat oven to 350°

1	cup oil	1	teaspoon cinnamon
1½	cups sugar	½	teaspoon salt
3	eggs	½	teaspoon nutmeg
1	teaspoon vanilla	2	cups grated carrots
1½	cups sifted flour	1	cup chopped pecans
1½	teaspoons baking soda		

In a large mixing bowl, beat oil, sugar, eggs, and vanilla. Sift flour, soda, cinnamon, salt, and nutmeg; add to oil mixture. Blend well. Fold in carrots and pecans. Pour into 2 greased and floured 9 x 5 x 3 loaf pans. Bake 40 minutes or until a toothpick inserted in the center comes out clean.

STRAWBERRY BREAD

Makes 2 loaves

Preheat oven to 350°

2 cups flour
1 teaspoon baking soda
1 teaspoon salt
1 tablespoon cinnamon
4 eggs
1¼ cups oil

2 cups sugar
2 10-ounce packages frozen strawberries, with juice (thawed)
1¼ cups chopped pecans

In a bowl, sift flour, soda, salt, and cinnamon. In a large mixing bowl, beat eggs; add oil and sugar. Gradually add flour mixture, strawberries, and pecans. Pour into 2 greased and floured 9 x 5 x 3 loaf pans; bake 1 hour or until a toothpick inserted in center comes out clean.

CRANBERRY BREAD

Makes 2 loaves

Preheat oven to 325°

4 cups flour
2 cups sugar
3 teaspoons baking powder
1 teaspoon salt
1 teaspoon baking soda
2 eggs
1 cup orange juice

4 tablespoons butter, melted
¾ cup water
2 cups raw cranberries, coarsely chopped
2 tablespoons grated orange rind
1 cup chopped pecans

In a bowl, combine flour, sugar, baking powder, salt, and soda. In a large mixing bowl, beat eggs; add juice, butter, water, cranberries, rind, and pecans. Add flour mixture to egg mixture and mix well. Pour into 2 greased and floured 9 x 5 x 3 loaf pans. Bake 1 hour or until toothpick inserted in center comes out clean. Remove from pan and cool on wire rack.

ZUCCHINI PINEAPPLE BREAD   Makes 2 loaves

Freezes well

Preheat oven to 350°

3	eggs	1	teaspoon nutmeg
2	cups sugar	1½	cups grated, unpeeled zucchini
1	cup oil		
2	teaspoons vanilla	1	8-ounce can crushed pineapple, drained
3	cups flour		
2	teaspoons baking soda	½	cup raisins
1	teaspoon salt	1	cup chopped pecans
½	teaspoon baking powder	1	4-ounce package instant vanilla pudding
1½	teaspoons cinnamon		

In a large bowl, beat eggs, sugar, oil, and vanilla until foamy. In a separate bowl, sift flour, soda, salt, baking powder, cinnamon, and nutmeg. Combine with egg mixture; stir in zucchini, pineapple, raisins, pecans, and pudding. Pour into 2 greased and floured 9 x 5 x 3 loaf pans. Bake 1 hour or until a toothpick inserted in center comes out clean.

BEIGNETS   Makes 4 dozen

½	cup warm water	¼	cup sugar
1	package dry yeast	1	teaspoon salt
½	cup evaporated milk	3	cups flour
1	egg, beaten		Oil for deep frying
1	teaspoon vanilla		Powdered sugar
2	tablespoons oil		

In a large mixing bowl, dissolve yeast in water. Add milk, egg, vanilla, oil, sugar, and salt. Add flour, beating vigorously. Dough will be very sticky.

On a heavily-floured surface, place a fourth of dough, and roll out with a well-floured rolling pin to about ⅛-inch thickness. Cut into 2-inch squares. Heat oil to 370°, or until 2 matches floating in oil ignite.

Drop beignets a few at a time into oil. They will rise to surface and puff up. As they puff up, turn over to brown other side. Remove and drain on paper towels; dust with powdered sugar. Serve warm. Unused dough can be refrigerated up to 1 week.

WHOLE WHEAT ORANGE MUFFINS   Makes 12

Freezes well

Preheat oven to 400°

2	eggs	1	cup flour
½	cup sugar	1½	cups whole wheat flour
⅓	cup oil	1	teaspoon baking powder
1	cup orange juice	1	teaspoon baking soda
2	tablespoons grated orange rind	½	teaspoon salt
		½	cup chopped pecans

In a large bowl, beat eggs; add sugar and oil, beating continuously. Stir in juice and rind. Sift flours, baking powder, soda, and salt. With swift strokes, stir flour mixture into egg/orange juice mixture. Do not over mix. Stir in pecans. Fill greased or paper-lined muffin tins ⅔ full. Bake 15 to 20 minutes, until light brown.

CARROT MUFFINS   Makes 18 to 20

Freezes well

Preheat oven to 350°

2	eggs	2	cups flour
1	cup sugar	1	teaspoon cinnamon
1	cup oil	1	teaspoon salt
½	teaspoon vanilla	2	teaspoons baking powder
2	cups grated carrots		

In a bowl, beat eggs; continue to beat while adding sugar, oil, and vanilla. Stir in carrots. Into a large mixing bowl, sift flour, cinnamon, salt, and baking powder. Add liquid mixture to dry mixture. Stir just until well-moistened. Spoon into paper-lined muffin tins, filling each ⅔ full. Bake 30 minutes, until light brown. Serve hot or let cool and freeze for later use.

To freeze: Wrap cooled muffins tightly in plastic. To use, thaw in plastic 15 minutes, then wrap tightly in foil and place in 400° oven 15 minutes.

APPLE COFFEE CAKE

Serves 10 to 12

Preheat oven to 350°

4 cups diced apples	2½ cups flour
2 cups sugar	2 teaspoons soda
2 egg whites	1 teaspoon salt
2 egg yolks	1 teaspoon cinnamon
1 cup oil	1 cup chopped pecans

In a large bowl, mix apples and sugar. In a separate bowl, beat egg whites until stiff. In a third bowl, beat yolks until light; gradually beat in oil. Add yolks and oil to whites; mix. Add this to apples and sugar; mix well. In another bowl, sift flour, soda, salt, and cinnamon; and add with pecans to apple mixture. Blend well and pour into greased and floured bundt pan. Bake 1 hour, or until toothpick inserted in the center comes out clean.

BROWN SUGAR COFFEE CAKE

Serves 12 to 15

Preheat oven to 350°

2 cups flour	½ cup butter
1 cup sugar	3 eggs
½ teaspoon nutmeg	1 cup milk
1 teaspoon cinnamon	1 cup grated apple
1 teaspoon salt	½ cup brown sugar
4 teaspoons baking powder	1 cup broken pecans

In a large bowl, sift flour, sugar, nutmeg, cinnamon, salt, and baking powder. Cut in butter until mixture resembles coarse crumbs.

In a separate bowl, beat eggs; add milk. Add flour, stirring until smooth. Pour into greased 8 x 10 baking pan. Sprinkle apples into batter and top with brown sugar and pecans. Bake 30 to 40 minutes, until toothpick inserted in center comes out clean.

CAJUN COWBOY COOKIES

Makes 6 dozen

Freezes well

Preheat oven to 350°

1	cup sugar	1	teaspoon baking powder
1	cup brown sugar, packed	2	cups rolled oats
2	sticks butter	1	6-ounce package semi-sweet chocolate chips
1½	teaspoons vanilla		
2	eggs	½	6-ounce package butterscotch chips
2	cups flour		
1	teaspoon baking soda	2	cups finely chopped nuts
½	teaspoon salt		

In a large bowl, mix sugars, butter, vanilla, and eggs until mixture is fluffy. In another bowl, sift flour, baking soda, salt, and baking powder. Add to sugar and blend well. Stir in oats, chocolate chips, and butterscotch chips. Place nuts in a small bowl. Shape a rounded teaspoon of dough into a ball, roll it in nuts, and place on ungreased cookie sheet. Bake 18 to 20 minutes, or until light brown.

CRUNCHY NUT COOKIES

Makes 5 dozen

Freezes well

Preheat oven to 375°

1	cup sugar	3	cups flour
1	cup brown sugar, packed	1	teaspoon soda
1	stick butter, softened	½	teaspoon salt
2	eggs	1½	cups chopped pecans
1	teaspoon vanilla		Powdered sugar

Thoroughly mix sugars, butter, eggs, and vanilla. Sift flour, soda, and salt; stir into egg mixture. Add nuts. Shape a level tablespoon into a ball. Place on ungreased baking sheet. Flatten with bottom of a greased glass, dipped in powdered sugar. Bake 10 to 12 minutes, until brown.

ORANGE MERINGUE KISSES

Makes 3 dozen

Preheat oven to 250°

4	egg whites	1	teaspoon orange juice
½	teaspoon cream of tartar	1	cup finely chopped pecans
1	cup sugar		
½	teaspoon grated orange rind		

Beat egg whites and cream of tartar until foamy. Gradually add sugar. Beat until stiff. Fold in rind, juice, and pecans. Drop by heaping teaspoons onto cookie sheets lined with heavy brown paper. Bake 45 minutes.

PRALINE MERINGUE KISSES

Makes 4 dozen

Preheat oven to 250°

½	cup sugar	½	teaspoon cream of tartar
½	cup dark brown sugar, packed	¼	teaspoon lemon juice
3	egg whites	¼	teaspoon vanilla
		1	cup finely chopped pecans

In a small bowl, combine sugars. In a large bowl, beat egg whites and cream of tartar until stiff. Beat in 1 tablespoon sugar at a time, alternating with drops of lemon juice and vanilla. Beat until stiff and glossy. Fold in pecans. Drop by well-rounded teaspoons onto cookie sheets lined with heavy brown paper, and bake 45 minutes.

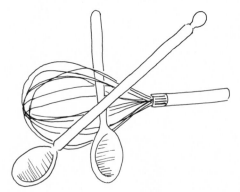

FUDGE BROWNIES

Makes 16

Preheat oven to 350°

2	1-ounce squares semi-sweet chocolate	1	cup sugar
½	cup butter	½	cup finely chopped nuts
½	cup flour	2	eggs, beaten

In a small saucepan, melt chocolate and butter. In a large bowl, sift flour and sugar. To flour mixture, add nuts, eggs, chocolate, and butter; mix well. Pour into 8 x 8 greased pan and bake 20 to 25 minutes. (These should be very moist.) Cool, frost, cut in squares.

Frosting

1	1-ounce square unsweetened chocolate	2	cups powdered sugar
1	tablespoon butter	2	teaspoons vanilla
		2-3	tablespoons boiling water

In a saucepan, melt chocolate and butter; stir in sugar and vanilla. Add water. Beat vigorously 3 to 5 minutes.

CHOCOLATE CHIP KISSES

Makes 4 dozen

Preheat oven to 250°

4	egg whites	1	6-ounce package semi-sweet chocolate chips
½	teaspoon cream of tartar	1	cup finely chopped pecans
1	cup sugar		
1	teaspoon vanilla		

In a large bowl, beat egg whites with cream of tartar until stiff; gradually add sugar and vanilla. Fold in chocolate chips and pecans. Spoon by heaping teaspoons onto cookie sheet lined with heavy brown paper. Bake 45 minutes.

Chocolate Mint Kisses: With vanilla, add 1 teaspoon peppermint extract. Delete pecans and add 2 to 3 drops green food coloring.

PECAN COOKIES

Makes 3 dozen

Freezes well

Preheat oven to 350°

1	stick butter, softened	1	cup flour
1	cup dark brown sugar, packed	½	teaspoon baking powder
1	teaspoon vanilla	1	cup pecans, coarsely chopped
1	egg		

In a large bowl, cream butter and sugar. Add vanilla and egg, mixing well. In a medium bowl, sift flour with baking powder. Add gradually to butter mixture, and stir in pecans. Drop by well-rounded teaspoons onto ungreased cookie sheet. Bake 12 to 15 minutes. Remove from sheet immediately and cool on rack.

SUGAR COOKIES

Makes 5 to 6 dozen

Preheat oven to 350°

3	cups flour	1	egg
1¾	cups sugar	3	teaspoons vanilla
1	teaspoon baking powder	2	tablespoons milk
2	sticks butter, softened	½	cup colored sugar crystals

Sift flour, sugar, and baking powder. In a large bowl, cream butter; gradually add half the flour mixture, until dough is stiff. In a small bowl, beat egg; add vanilla and milk. Add to dough; mix in remaining flour mixture. Refrigerate at least 1 hour.

On lightly floured waxed paper, roll out dough to ⅛-inch thickness; cut with a 2½-inch round cookie cutter. Place on ungreased cookie sheet 2 inches apart. Sprinkle each cookie with sugar crystals. Bake 12 to 15 minutes, or until lightly brown.

GINGER COOKIES

Makes 4 dozen

Freezes well

Preheat oven to 350°

⅔   cup oil
1   cup sugar
1   egg
1   tablespoon molasses
2   cups flour

2   teaspoons baking soda
1   teaspoon ginger
1   teaspoon cinnamon
   Dash of salt

In a large bowl, mix oil, sugar, egg, and molasses. In a separate bowl, sift flour, baking soda, ginger, cinnamon, and salt. Add to egg-molasses mixture and mix well. Roll into quarter-sized balls and place on ungreased cookie sheet. Bake 10 to 12 minutes, or until lightly browned.

ORANGE COOKIES

Makes 3 dozen

Freezes well

Preheat oven to 350°

1   stick butter, softened
1   cup sugar
1   large egg
1   teaspoon orange extract
1½ cups flour

1   teaspoon baking powder
½   teaspoon salt
2   teaspoons grated orange
   rind
   Sugar

In a large bowl, cream butter and sugar. Add egg and extract, mixing well. In a separate bowl, sift flour, baking powder, and salt and stir into butter mixture. Add rind. Drop by teaspoons onto greased cookie sheet, leaving room to spread. Bake 10 to 12 minutes, or until edges are golden brown. Transfer to a rack and while still warm, sprinkle with sugar.

Lemon Cookies: Substitute 1 teaspoon lemon extract and 2 teaspoons lemon rind for orange extract and orange rind.

GINGERBREAD MEN

Makes 3 dozen

Preheat oven to 350°

4	cups flour	½	cup butter, softened
1	tablespoon cinnamon	½	cup brown sugar, packed
1	teaspoon salt	1	cup molasses
1	teaspoon baking soda	2	teaspoons cider vinegar
1	teaspoon ginger		Raisins
½	teaspoon ground cloves		Candies

In a bowl, sift flour, cinnamon, salt, soda, ginger, and cloves. In another bowl, cream butter, sugar, molasses, and vinegar. In a large bowl, mix dry and creamed ingredients. Knead dough if necessary. Dough will be very stiff. Roll out on floured waxed paper with a floured rolling pin. Cut out gingerbread men with a 3½-inch cutter. Lift carefully to a greased baking sheet. Use raisins and candies for eyes, nose, and buttons. Bake 15 minutes, or until lightly browned. Cool on rack.

Note: This recipe is also suitable for use as a Gingerbread House.

JELLY ROLL

Makes 15-inch roll

Preheat oven to 375°

4	egg yolks	½	teaspoon salt
¾	cup sugar	¼	cup powdered sugar
½	teaspoon vanilla	1	12 to 15 ounce jar
4	egg whites		blackberry jelly or any tart
¾	cup sifted cake flour		preserves
1	teaspoon baking powder		

In a bowl, beat yolks until lemon-colored, 3 to 5 minutes. Gradually beat in ¼ cup sugar and vanilla. In a large bowl, beat egg whites to soft peaks, gradually adding sugar; continue beating until it forms stiff peaks. Fold yolks into whites. In another bowl, sift flour, baking powder, and salt; fold into egg mixture.

Turn batter into a greased and lightly floured 12 x 15 jelly roll pan. Bake 12 minutes, or until cake is lightly brown and springs back when touched. Loosen and turn out into a towel sprinkled with powdered sugar. Roll up lengthwise, making a 15-inch roll. Cool; unroll and spread with jelly. Roll up again and slice in 1-inch pieces. Can also be filled with whipped cream and fresh fruit.

CHEESECAKE COOKIES

Makes 4 dozen

Preheat oven to 350°

Crust

1	cup flour	1	cup finely chopped pecans
¼	cup light brown sugar, packed	1	stick butter, melted

In a small bowl, mix flour, brown sugar, pecans, and butter and press into bottom of 13 x 9 glass baking dish. Bake 10 to 15 minutes, or until brown.

Filling

16	ounces cream cheese	1	teaspoon vanilla
1	cup sugar	3	eggs

In a bowl, beat cream cheese, sugar, and vanilla. Add eggs and beat well. Pour over crust. Bake 20 minutes.

Glaze

2	cups sour cream	1	teaspoon vanilla
6	tablespoons sugar		

In a small bowl, mix sour cream, sugar, and vanilla and pour over baked filling. Bake 3 to 5 minutes. Cool and refrigerate before cutting into squares.

ALMOND SQUARES

Makes 4 dozen

Freezes well

Preheat oven to 300°

2	sticks butter, softened	½	teaspoon almond extract
1	cup sugar	2	cups sliced, unblanched almonds
1	egg yolk		
2	cups flour	1	egg white

In a mixing bowl, cream butter and sugar. Add yolk, continuing to cream. Add flour and extract, mixing well. Batter will be very stiff. Spread batter into 10 x 15 jelly roll pan. Sprinkle almonds over all. Press almonds gently into batter. In a small bowl, beat egg white with a fork until foamy. Brush over top of batter and nuts. Bake 50 minutes, or until golden brown. Cut into squares while warm.

DATE STICKS

Freezes well

Preheat oven to 350°

2	eggs	1	cup chopped pecans
1	cup sugar	1	cup chopped dates
1	cup flour		Powdered sugar

In a large bowl, beat eggs; add sugar, then flour, mixing until smooth. Fold in pecans and dates. Spread in greased 9 x 13 shallow pan. Bake 20 minutes. While warm, cut into 3 x ½-inch sticks; roll in powdered sugar. Sticks will be soft and may not appear to be done.

CHRISTMAS FRUIT COOKIES

Freezes well

Makes 8 to 10 dozen

Preheat oven to 325°

1½	cups raisins	3	eggs, separated
1½	cups currants	½	cup evaporated milk
1½	cups candied pineapple	1½	teaspoons vinegar
1½	cups candied cherries	½	teaspoon soda
½	cup citron, thinly sliced	½	teaspoon salt
1½	cups broken nuts	1	teaspoon cinnamon
2	cups flour	1	teaspoon ground cloves
2	sticks butter, softened	1	teaspoon allspice
1½	cups light brown sugar, packed	½	teaspoon nutmeg

Wash raisins and currants and drain on paper towels. Cut pineapple, cherries, and citron into small pieces. In a bowl, mix all fruits and nuts, and ½ cup flour. In a large bowl, cream butter. Add sugar gradually and cream well. Beat in yolks, one at a time. Mix milk and vinegar in a small bowl; add to butter mixture. In another bowl, sift remaining flour, soda, salt, and spices. Stir dry mixture into butter mixture; add fruit and nuts. In a bowl, beat whites until stiff, but not dry, and fold into batter. Drop by teaspoons onto greased cookie sheet and bake 20 to 25 minutes, until lightly browned. Cool on racks.

Desserts

JAMBALAYA BREAD PUDDING
Serves 12

Preheat oven to 375°

1	loaf French bread (1½ feet long)	2	tablespoons vanilla
1	quart milk	1	teaspoon cinnamon
3	eggs, beaten	1	cup raisins
2	cups sugar	3	tablespoons butter

In a large bowl, break bread into bite-size pieces. Cover with milk and soak 1 hour. Mix well. Add eggs and sugar. Stir in vanilla, cinnamon, and raisins. Melt butter in a 13 x 9 x 2 baking dish, tilting to coat all sides. Pour in pudding and bake 1 hour.

Sauce

1	stick butter	1	egg, beaten
1	cup sugar	¼	cup bourbon

In top of a double boiler, melt butter and sugar. Gradually whisk egg. Cool slightly. Add bourbon. If serving right away, pour warm sauce over pudding. If not, warm sauce slightly before serving and serve in a sauce boat.

ORANGE CREAM CAKE

Serves 14

Preheat oven to 325°

Cake

4	egg whites, room temperature		1	cup flour
¼	teaspoon cream of tartar		¾	cup orange juice
1¼	cups sugar		1	teaspoon baking powder
6	egg yolks		½	teaspoon salt
			⅓	cup water

In a large bowl with mixer at high speed, beat egg whites and cream of tartar until soft peaks form. Gradually sprinkle in ½ cup sugar, 2 tablespoons at a time, beating until each addition is completely dissolved. Do not scrape sides of bowl. Whites should stand in stiff peaks.

In a large bowl with mixer at high speed, beat yolks until thick and lemon colored. Continue beating, gradually sprinkling in ½ cup sugar; beat until pale yellow. Reduce to low speed; add flour, ¼ cup orange juice, baking powder, and salt until well-mixed, occasionally scraping bowl with spatula. Fold egg white mixture into yolk mixture until just blended.

Line 2 9-inch round cake pans with waxed paper. Pour batter into pans and bake 40 minutes, or until cake springs back when lightly touched. Cool in pans on wire racks 10 minutes. Remove from pans and cool completely on racks. With fork, prick holes in cake layers.

In a small saucepan, boil water and remaining ¼ cup sugar 3 minutes. Stir in remaining ½ cup orange juice. Drizzle evenly over layers and let stand 30 minutes.

Icing

2	cups whipping cream	Orange sections or grated orange rind
3	tablespoons powdered sugar	
2	tablespoons grated orange rind	

In a small bowl, with mixer at medium speed, beat cream and sugar until soft peaks form. Fold in rind.

Place one layer on serving platter and spread with icing. Top with second layer. Frost top and sides with remaining icing. Garnish with orange sections or grated rind. Refrigerate.

COLONIAL CHOCOLATE CAKE   Serves 12

Preheat oven to 350°

Filling

1 21-ounce can cherry pie
   filling
2 tablespoons sugar

2 tablespoons Kirsch (cherry
   liqueur)

In a large bowl, combine pie filling, sugar, and liqueur. Chill several hours or place in freezer while proceeding with recipe. Must be very cold to spread.

Cake

1¾ cups flour
2   cups sugar
¾   cup cocoa
2   teaspoons baking soda
1   teaspoon baking powder
1   teaspoon salt
2   eggs
1   cup strong black coffee, *or*
    2 teaspoons instant coffee
    plus 1 cup boiling water

1   cup buttermilk, *or* 1 cup
    milk plus 1 tablespoon
    vinegar
½   cup oil
1   teaspoon vanilla

In a large bowl, combine flour, sugar, cocoa, soda, baking powder, and salt. Add remaining ingredients. Beat at medium speed for 2 minutes. Batter will be thin. Pour into 2 well-greased and floured 9-inch cake pans. Bake 35 to 40 minutes. Remove from pans after 2 minutes and cool completely.

Icing

1½ cups whipping cream   ¼   cup powdered sugar

Beat cream and sugar until stiff. Assemble cake by placing one layer upside down on serving platter. Make a ring of icing ½ inch high and 1 inch wide around outer edge of layer.

Fill center with about 1 cup filling. Carefully place second layer, top side up onto filling. Gently spread icing on entire top of cake. Fill center of top of cake with remaining filling. Chill at least 1 hour before serving. Keep refrigerated.

SOUR CREAM POUND CAKE

Serves 12

Freezes well

Preheat oven to 350°

1½	sticks butter	½	teaspoon salt
1½	cups sugar	1	cup sour cream
2	eggs	1	teaspoon vanilla extract
2¼	cups flour	1	teaspoon almond extract
1	teaspoon baking powder		

In a large bowl, cream butter and sugar; add eggs one at a time. Beat until fluffy. In a separate bowl, sift flour, baking powder, and salt; add alternately with sour cream to butter mixture. Add extracts. Beat at high speed until fluffy, 2 to 3 minutes. Pour into greased and floured tube pan. Bake 45 minutes or until toothpick inserted in center comes out clean.

BROWN SUGAR POUND CAKE

Serves 16

Freezes well

Preheat oven to 325°

½	cup coarsely chopped pecans	5	eggs
3	sticks butter, softened	3	cups flour
2	cups brown sugar, packed	½	teaspoon baking powder
1	cup sugar	1	cup milk
		1	teaspoon vanilla

Grease and flour a bundt pan or 10-inch tube pan. Sprinkle pecan pieces on bottom of pan. In a large bowl, cream butter and sugars. Add eggs one at a time. In a small bowl, combine flour and baking powder. In another small bowl, combine milk and vanilla. Add to butter alternately. Pour into pan and bake 1½ to 2 hours or until toothpick inserted in center comes out clean. Cool in pan 30 minutes.

POUND CAKE

Freezes well

2	sticks butter	3	cups flour
3	cups sugar	1	cup whipping cream
6	eggs	1	teaspoon vanilla

In a large bowl, cream butter and add sugar gradually. Beat in eggs one at a time. Add flour alternately with cream, blending well. Add vanilla. Pour into greased and floured tube pan. Place in cold oven. Turn to 325° and bake 1 hour and 15 minutes, or until a toothpick inserted in center comes out clean. Cool in pan 15 to 20 minutes (do not be concerned that it "shrinks" after it comes out of the oven).

CARROT CAKE

Serves 14

Preheat oven to 350°

4	eggs	2	teaspoons cinnamon
1½	cups oil	1	cup chopped pecans, reserving 12 halves for garnish
2	cups sugar		
2	cups flour	3	cups grated carrots
2	teaspoons baking soda		
½	teaspoon salt		

In a large bowl, beat eggs with mixer until lemon colored and fluffy, about 5 minutes. Blend in oil and slowly beat in sugar. In a bowl, sift flour, soda, salt, and cinnamon; add nuts. Fold dry ingredients and carrots into batter.

Grease and flour 3 8-inch cake pans or 2 9-inch pans; pour in batter. Bake 35 minutes or until layers pull away from sides of pans.

Icing

8	ounces cream cheese, softened	1	16-ounce box powdered sugar
8	tablespoons butter, softened	2	teaspoons vanilla

In a large bowl, blend cream cheese and butter until smooth and free of lumps. Add sugar gradually and blend well. Add vanilla. Spread icing between cooled layers and cover top and sides of cake. Garnish top with pecan halves.

APPLE SPICE CAKE

Preheat oven to 325°

Cake

1	stick butter, softened	2	cups flour
2	cups sugar	2	teaspoons baking soda
2	eggs	½	teaspoon salt
4	cups cooking apples, peeled and diced	2	teaspoons cinnamon
1	cup chopped pecans	½	teaspoon nutmeg
½	cup raisins	½	teaspoon allspice

In a bowl, cream butter and sugar. Beat in eggs until mixture is thick and creamy. Fold in apples, pecans, and raisins.

In a large bowl, mix all dry ingredients. Add butter mixture and blend well. Pour batter into a buttered 9 x 13 baking pan and bake 1 hour.

Caramel Icing

1½	cups light brown sugar	3	tablespoons butter
¼	teaspoon salt	1	teaspoon vanilla
½	cup milk	3	cups powdered sugar

In a saucepan, combine brown sugar, salt, and milk and bring to a boil. Cook slowly 5 minutes, or until slightly thickened. Remove from heat; beat in butter and vanilla. Cool slightly. Add powdered sugar and blend well.

ORANGE FRUIT CAKE

Serves 12

Preheat oven to 300°

1 cup crystallized orange rind	1½ cups sugar
1 cup chopped pitted dates	3 eggs
2½ cups flour	½ teaspoon vanilla
½ teaspoon soda	½ cup orange juice
½ teaspoon cinnamon	1 cup chopped pecans
½ teaspoon ground cloves	1 cup chopped almonds
2 sticks butter	½ cup orange brandy or curaçao

In a bowl, sprinkle rind and dates with ½ cup flour. In a separate bowl, sift remaining 2 cups flour with soda, cinnamon, and cloves. In a large bowl, cream butter and sugar. Add eggs, one at a time; add vanilla. Add flour mixture, alternating with orange juice. Mix well. Add rind and dates. Stir in nuts. Spoon into greased and floured tube pan or 2 9 x 5 x 3 loaf pans. Bake 2 hours or until a toothpick inserted in the center comes out clean. Cool completely in pan. Pour brandy over cake. Store tightly wrapped, in a cool place. (Will keep for several weeks.) If more brandy flavor is desired, every few days, pour 2 ounces more brandy over cake.

MOCHA MACAROON TORTE

Serves 12

Make a day ahead

1 stick butter, softened	2 cups whipping cream
1½ cups powdered sugar	2 3-ounce packages ladyfingers, split
4 egg yolks	
1 ounce rum	2 dozen almond macaroons, crumbled
1 ounce strong black coffee	
1 teaspoon vanilla	
⅓ cup blanched sliced almonds	

In a large bowl, cream butter and sugar until pale yellow. Beat in egg yolks, rum, coffee, vanilla, and almonds. Mix well. Whip 1 cup cream and fold in until just blended.

Line bottom and sides of an 8-inch spring-form pan with ladyfingers. Pour half of mixture over ladyfingers and cover with half of macaroon crumbs. Add remaining mixture and top with remaining macaroon crumbs. Let stand 30 minutes; cover with foil and refrigerate. Chill at least 24 hours. When ready to serve, spread remaining whipped cream on top of torte.

BAVARIAN APPLE TORTE

Serves 10

Preheat oven to 400°

Crust

1	stick butter	½	teaspoon vanilla
⅓	cup sugar	1	cup flour

In a bowl, cream butter, sugar, and vanilla. Blend in flour. Spread dough onto bottom and 1-inch up sides of a 9-inch spring-form pan.

Cream Layer

1	8-ounce package cream cheese, softened
¼	cup sugar
1	egg
½	teaspoon almond extract

Combine cream cheese and sugar; mix well. Blend in egg and extract. Pour into pastry-lined pan and bake 10 minutes.

Spiced Apples

½	cup sugar	1	tablespoon lemon juice
½	teaspoon cinnamon	¼	cup sliced almonds
½	teaspoon allspice	1	tablespoon butter
4	cups peeled and sliced cooking apples		

Combine sugar, cinnamon, allspice, apples, and lemon juice. Spoon apples over cream layer and sprinkle top with almonds. Dot with butter. Bake 25 minutes. After 10 minutes cover torte with foil. Cool before removing rim. Serve with hard sauce or sweetened heavy cream.

BASIC PIE CRUST

Makes 1 9-inch crust

½	cup less 1 tablespoon solid shortening	1	teaspoon milk
3	tablespoons boiling water	1¼	cups sifted flour
		½	teaspoon salt

In a bowl, beat shortening, water, and milk, until smooth and thick. Add flour and salt; blend well. Form into a ball and flatten to a 6-inch circle. Between 2 sheets of lightly floured waxed paper, roll dough to a 12-inch circle. Place in pie plate. For a baked pie crust, bake in preheated 450° oven 15 minutes.

DEEP DISH APPLE PIE

Serves 8

Preheat oven to 350°

8 cups peeled and sliced cooking apples	2 tablespoons water
½ cup light brown sugar	1 teaspoon cinnamon
2 tablespoons flour	½ cup chopped pecans or walnuts

Toss apple slices with brown sugar, flour, water, and cinnamon; place in a round 1½-quart greased casserole. Sprinkle with nuts.

Topping

1 cup flour	1½ cups dark brown sugar
1 stick butter, softened	

In a bowl, blend all ingredients. Knead. Form into a ball and roll out to cover casserole. Place over apples and bake 1 hour, or until lightly browned.

BANANA CREAM PIE

Serves 8

1 9-inch pie shell, baked and cooled	1 tablespoon butter
½ cup sugar	1 teaspoon vanilla
6 tablespoons flour	3 ripe bananas
¼ teaspoon salt	1 cup whipping cream
2¼ cups milk	1 tablespoon powdered sugar
1 egg	

In top of a double boiler, mix sugar, flour, and salt. Gradually stir in milk and cook over boiling water until thickened, about 10 minutes, stirring constantly with wire whisk. Cover and cook 10 minutes, stirring occasionally. In separate bowl, beat egg; add a little custard to blend; add to double boiler and cook 2 minutes. Remove from heat; add butter and vanilla. Cool completely. Slice bananas and line bottom of pie shell. Pour half the custard over bananas, add layer of bananas, and pour remaining custard on top. Refrigerate several hours. When ready to serve, whip cream and sugar until stiff, and spread over pie.

MACAROON GRAHAM PECAN PIE

Serves 10

Preheat oven to 350°

3	eggs, room temperature	½	teaspoon almond extract
½	teaspoon baking powder	¾	teaspoon vanilla
1	cup sugar	1	cup whipping cream
11	graham cracker squares, crushed	3	tablespoons powdered sugar
1	cup chopped pecans		

In a bowl, beat eggs with baking powder until foamy. Slowly add sugar and continue beating until stiff. Carefully fold in graham cracker crumbs and pecans. Add extracts. Spread into a heavily buttered 10 inch pie pan. Bake 30 minutes or until top of pie rises. Cool completely, then chill at least 4 to 5 hours.

Before serving, whip cream and gradually add sugar. Spread over top of pie.

CREOLE PECAN PIE

Serves 8

Preheat oven to 350°

1	9-inch pie shell, unbaked	¹⁄₁₆	teaspoon salt
4	tablespoons butter, softened	1	teaspoon vanilla
½	cup sugar	1	cup chopped pecans
3	eggs	2	teaspoons grated orange rind
½	cup cane syrup (no substitute)	½	cup pecan halves
½	cup light corn syrup	1	cup whipping cream

In a bowl, cream butter and sugar. Add eggs, one at a time, beating until light and fluffy. Add syrups, salt, vanilla, pecans, and rind; blend well. Pour into pie shell. Arrange pecan halves over top of pie. Bake 45 minutes or until firm when gently shaken. Remove and cool on wire rack. Serve with whipped cream.

BLUEBERRY PIE

Serves 8

4 cups fresh blueberries, *or*
1 16-ounce bag frozen
blueberries
½ cup sugar
½ cup brown sugar, firmly
packed
2½ tablespoons flour
1 tablespoon butter

1 tablespoon lemon juice
½ teaspoon cinnamon
⅛ teaspoon nutmeg
¼ teaspoon salt
1 8-inch pie shell, baked
1 cup whipping cream
1 teaspoon vanilla

In a saucepan, combine 2 cups blueberries with sugars, flour, butter, lemon juice, spices, and salt. Cook and stir over low heat until mixture comes to a boil. Simmer 10 minutes until thickened. Cool. Stir in remaining 2 cups blueberries. Pour into pie shell. Chill. Before serving, whip cream and add vanilla. Spread over pie.

CARAMEL NUT ANGEL PIE

Serves 8

Preheat oven to 400°

Meringue Pie Shell

2 egg whites
¼ teaspoon salt
¼ cup sugar
1½ cups finely chopped
almonds, *or* pecans

1 quart coffee ice cream,
slightly softened
1 quart chocolate ice cream,
slightly softened

In a bowl, beat egg whites with salt at high speed until soft peaks form. Gradually add sugar, 1 tablespoon at a time, beating 1 minute after each addition to form a stiff meringue. Fold in nuts. Spread meringue into well-buttered 9-inch pie pan with sides extending over rim. Bake 10 minutes or until lightly browned. Remove and cool. Fill with ice cream; cover tightly; freeze.

Caramel Sauce

2 tablespoons butter
½ cup brown sugar, packed
¼ cup half and half cream

½ teaspoon vanilla
2 tablespoons nuts

In a saucepan, melt butter; stir in sugar and cook until dissolved. Slowly mix in half and half and cook one minute, stirring constantly. Stir in vanilla and nuts; cool slightly. When ready to serve pour over frozen pie.

PRALINE PUMPKIN PIE

Serves 8

Make a day ahead

Preheat oven to 375°

1   9-inch pie crust

Prick pie shell and bake 10 minutes, until lightly browned.

Praline Mix

4 tablespoons butter	1 cup chopped pecans
½ cup sugar	

In a skillet, cook butter, sugar, and pecans, stirring until golden, about 3 minutes. Spread onto foil. Cool; crumble. Sprinkle 1 cup over pie shell.

Filling

1 envelope gelatin	½ teaspoon salt
½ cup cold water	1 teaspoon cinnamon
¾ cup brown sugar, packed	¾ teaspoon nutmeg
1 1-pound can pumpkin	1 cup whipping cream
¼ cup milk	

In a saucepan, mix gelatin with cold water. Cook over low heat until dissolved. Remove from heat and add brown sugar. Blend in pumpkin, milk, salt, cinnamon, and nutmeg. Beat cream until stiff, but not dry; fold into pumpkin mixture. Pour into shell and top with remaining praline pieces.

Topping

½ cup whipping cream	2 tablespoons powdered
½ teaspoon vanilla	sugar

Beat cream until stiff, gradually blending in vanilla and sugar. Place a dollop on each serving.

CHOCOLATE MERINGUE PIE

Serves 8

Preheat oven to 325°

Crust

1¼ cups crushed *buttery* shortbread cookies	1 tablespoon sugar
	6 tablespoons butter, melted

In a small bowl, mix all ingredients. Pat into bottom and up sides of 9-inch pie pan; bake 7 minutes.

Filling

2	cups milk	¼	teaspoon salt
3	tablespoons cocoa	3	egg yolks
1	cup sugar	2	teaspoons vanilla
⅓	cup flour	1	tablespoon butter

In a saucepan, scald milk. In a bowl, combine cocoa, sugar, flour, salt; gradually add to milk, whisking until thick. Do not boil. Beat yolks and add to chocolate mixture, cooking and stirring 3 minutes. Add vanilla and butter and continue to cook another minute. Pour filling into cooled pie shell.

Meringue

3 egg whites	3 tablespoons sugar

Beat whites until soft peaks form; gradually add sugar, 1 tablespoon at a time, beating until stiff. Spread meringue over filling, completely covering crust edges. Bake 10 to 12 minutes, or until lighlty browned.

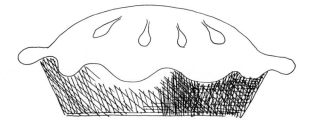

COTTAGE PEACH COBBLER

Serves 14

Preheat oven to 375°

Filling

2½	tablespoons flour	½	stick butter, melted
1⁄16	teaspoon salt	¼	teaspoon almond extract
1½	cups sugar		
1	teaspoon cinnamon		
12	large fresh peaches, sliced, *or* 3 1-pound cans sliced peaches, drained		

In a large bowl, mix flour, salt, sugar, and cinnamon. Add peaches, butter, and extract.

Pastry

2	cups flour	1	tablespoon butter, softened
1	teaspoon salt		
½	teaspoon baking powder	4	tablespoons ice water
⅔	cup solid shortening	4	tablespoons butter, melted

Blend flour, salt, baking powder, shortening, and butter until texture is like coarse meal. Gradually add water and mix until dough stays together in a ball. Divide dough in half. Roll one portion onto floured board or between 2 floured pieces of waxed paper. Lightly grease a 9 x 13 x 2 baking dish. Line sides and 1-inch around bottom with strips of dough. Pour peach mixture into dish. Roll out remaining dough; cut into ¾-inch wide strips. Place in a lattice or criss-cross design over peaches. Pour butter over top. Bake 45 minutes, or until pastry is light brown.

Garnish

1½	pints whipping cream	1	box fresh blueberries

Whip cream. Top each serving with cream and blueberries.

FRESH LEMON PIE

Preheat oven to 300°

Crust

1½ cups graham cracker crumbs	¼ cup sifted powdered sugar
6 tablespoons butter, melted	1 teaspoon cinnamon

In a bowl, mix all ingredients. Pat into a 8-inch pie pan. Bake 15 minutes. Cool.

Filling

1 can condensed milk	¼ teaspoon almond extract
⅓ cup lemon juice	

In a small bowl combine all ingredients. Pour into crust.

Topping

1 cup whipping cream	¼ teaspoon vanilla
⅛ cup sugar	Lemon slices

Whip cream and blend in sugar and vanilla. Spread over pie. Garnish with lemon slices. Serve cold.

GRAND MARNIER CRÊPES

Serves 6

2 sticks butter	2 ounces Grand Marnier, warmed
1 cup powdered sugar	
½ cup fresh orange juice	18 crêpes
⅛ teaspoon cinnamon	

In a skillet, melt butter; add sugar. Stir until sugar dissolves; add juice. Cook over low heat, stirring, until thickened. Add cinnamon. Add Grand Marnier and flame, stirring until flame dies. Place crêpes in skillet one at a time, folding into quarters. Serve with remaining sauce spooned over top.

CRÊPES

Makes 16 to 20 6-inch crêpes

Freezes well

1	cup flour	1½	cups milk
3	eggs	4	tablespoons butter
	Pinch of salt		

In a large bowl, place flour and make a well in center. Add eggs, salt, and ½ cup milk. Beat, starting from center until batter is thick. Gradually beat in remaining cup milk until batter is consistency of light cream; it should just coat a spoon. Refrigerate at least 2 hours, or preferably overnight. Stir well. If needed, add more milk to bring it back to light cream consistency. In a 6-inch skillet, melt butter. Pour butter into batter and stir well. Wipe pan with paper towels and heat until a drop of water bounces. Spoon in 1 tablespoon batter or just enough to cover bottom of skillet. Turn when top looks dry, or cook only on one side. Stir batter frequently. Recipe does not work with a crêpe maker.

To freeze: Stack with waxed paper in between each crêpe, and wrap tightly in plastic. Thaw to room temperature.

CRÊPES SUZETTE

Serves 6

12	crêpes (see above)	¼	cup fresh orange juice
1	8-ounce jar orange	1	ounce brandy, warmed
	marmalade	3	teaspoons sugar
4	tablespoons butter		

In center of each crêpe, place 1 tablespoon marmalade and fold into quarters. In a large skillet or chafing dish, melt butter; add remaining marmalade and juice. Simmer until blended. Place crêpes in sauce, arranging in an overlapping circle around skillet. Can be made several hours ahead up to this point. Before serving, pour in brandy and flame. Spoon sauce over crêpes and sprinkle tops with sugar.

CLASSIC CREAM PUFFS OR PROFITEROLES

Preheat oven to 450° **Makes 12 2-inch cream puffs**

24 1-inch profiteroles

Puff Pastry

1	cup water	2	tablespoons sugar
4	tablespoons butter	½	teaspoon salt
1½	cups sifted flour	4	eggs, room temperature

In a saucepan, boil water; add butter and melt. Combine flour, sugar, and salt; add to water all at once. With a wooden spoon, mix thoroughly and cook over medium heat about 4 minutes until mixture leaves sides of pan to form a soft dough. Cool 5 minutes. Add eggs, one at a time, beating well after each addition until pastry is smooth and shiny. Onto a lightly greased baking sheet, mound puffs with a spoon or a pastry bag to form either 2-inch cream puffs or 1-inch profiteroles, leaving 2 inches between each puff. Bake in a 450P oven 15 minutes; reduce heat to 325° and bake 20 minutes until puffy and browned. Remove and slit each puff horizontally. Turn oven off and return puffs 2 minutes, leaving door ajar to dry out puffs. Cool on rack; store in air-tight container until ready to fill.

Cream Puff Filling

2	cups milk	½	teaspoon salt
3	egg yolks	⅓	cup sifted flour
⅔	cup sugar	2	teaspoons vanilla
1	tablespoon butter, softened	2	teaspoons Grand Marnier

In top of a double boiler, scald milk. In a bowl, beat egg yolks until lemon colored. Add sugar and butter; blend until light and fluffy. Mix in salt and flour. Slowly add milk to egg mixture, blending with a wire whisk. Return to double boiler and cook 6 to 8 minutes until creamy and thick, stirring constantly. Add vanilla and Grand Marnier. Cool. Cover and chill until ready to fill puffs. Fill puffs with fudge sauce. Makes 2 cups.

Profiterole Filling

2	cups whipping cream	1	teaspoon vanilla
2	tablespoons powdered sugar		

In a bowl, whip cream; add sugar and vanilla. Fill puffs and stack in a pyramid on serving platter. Drizzle with sauce and serve remaining sauce in warmed sauceboat.

Fudge Sauce

4	tablespoons butter	6	squares semi-sweet chocolate
2¼	cups powdered sugar		
⅔	cup evaporated milk	½	teaspoon vanilla

In top of double boiler, blend butter and sugar. Add milk and chocolate. Cook 30 minutes. Do not stir while cooking. Remove from heat and beat in vanilla. Thin with milk if necessary, not water. Serve warm. Refrigerate and reheat as needed. Makes 2 cups

CHOCOLATE CHEESECAKE   Serves 12

Preheat oven to 375°

Crust

1	6-ounce box zwieback toast	1½	teaspoons cinnamon
2	tablespoons sugar	1	stick butter, melted

Crush toast to fine crumbs. Add sugar, cinnamon, and butter. Mix well and press into bottom and sides of a 9-inch spring-form pan.

Filling

3	8-ounce packages cream cheese	2	ounces German sweet chocolate, grated finely or chopped fine in food processor
1	cup sugar		
3	eggs		
		½	teaspoon vanilla

Cream cheese until fluffy; gradually add sugar and continue to cream. Add eggs, one at a time, beating after each addition. Add vanilla; stir in chocolate. Spoon into crust. Bake 20 minutes. It will not be firm in center. Cool completely. Reduce temperature to 350°

Topping

2	cups sour cream	1	ounce German chocolate, grated finely
4	tablespoons sugar		
½	teaspoon vanilla		

Beat sour cream, sugar, and vanilla. Spoon over cheesecake and bake 10 minutes. Cool and refrigerate overnight. Before serving, sprinkle chocolate over top.

ORANGE CHEESECAKE

Serves 12 to 16

Preheat oven to 500°

Crust

1¼ cups graham cracker crumbs	¼ cup sugar
	4 tablespoons butter, melted

In a small bowl, mix all ingredients; press into bottom and sides of a 9-inch spring-form pan.

Filling

5 8-ounce packages cream cheese	2 tablespoons grated orange rind
1¾ cups sugar	5 eggs
3 tablespoons flour	2 egg yolks
1 tablespoon grated lemon rind	¼ cup whipping cream

In a large bowl, cream cheese until fluffy. Mix sugar and flour; blend into cheese. Add rinds, then eggs and yolks, one at a time. Stir in cream. Spoon mixture into crust and bake 10 minutes. Reduce temperature to 200° and bake 1 hour. It will be shaky in the middle. Cool.

Glaze

1 tablespoon lemon juice	2 tablespoons cold water
1 tablespoon cornstarch	¾ cup orange juice

In a saucepan, cook all ingredients over low heat, stirring, until thick. Spoon over filling. Refrigerate overnight.

LEMON CHEESECAKE

Serves 12

Make a day ahead

Preheat oven to 350°

Crust

1   tablespoon butter
¼   cup graham cracker
        crumbs

Butter bottom and sides of a 9-inch spring-form pan and sprinkle graham cracker crumbs over all.

Filling

3   8-ounce packages cream   1   egg yolk
        cheese, softened   2   tablespoons lemon juice
1¼   cups sugar   1   tablespoon grated lemon
3   eggs   rind

Cream cheese until fluffy, add sugar and continue to cream. Beat in eggs and yolk, one at a time. Add juice and mix well. Fold in rind. Spoon into pan and bake 20 minutes. Cool.

Topping

2   cups sour cream   1   teaspoon lemon juice
¼   cup sugar

Beat all ingredients until smooth. Spoon over filling and bake 10 minutes. Cool and refrigerate overnight.

FROZEN LEMON CREAM

Serves 6

1   cup milk   3   large lemons, cut in half
1   cup whipping cream   lengthwise and scooped
1   cup sugar   out
2   teaspoons grated lemon   Lemon leaves or mint
        rind   sprigs
3   tablespoons lemon juice

In a bowl, mix milk, cream, and sugar until sugar is dissolved. Pour into shallow bowl and freeze until slightly thickened. Whisk in rind and juice. Refreeze 2 hours. Beat cream again thoroughly. Refreeze until solidly frozen. Fill each lemon half with frozen cream; garnish with leaves or mint sprig.

ORANGE CRÈME BRULÉE

Serves 8

3	cups light cream	12	egg yolks
⅔	cup brown sugar, packed	1	tablespoon orange extract
¼	teaspoon salt		

In top of a double boiler, scald cream with sugar and salt. Whisk yolks and extract until well blended. Gradually stir some cream mixture into yolks, a tablespoon at a time. Add yolks and cream to double boiler and cook over very low heat, stirring constantly. When mixture reaches consistency of a thick cream sauce, place in 8 custard cups or ramekins; chill.

Topping

¾　cup light brown sugar

Preheat oven to 300°. On a buttered piece of foil, form 8 very thin circles of brown sugar the size of the tops of your custard cups. Place in oven 10 minutes. Cool and peel from foil. Place one on top of each custard ½ hour before serving.

CHILLED LEMON SOUFFLÉ

Serves 12

2	envelopes gelatin	1	tablespoon grated lemon rind
½	cup water		
6	eggs	2	cups whipping cream
1½	cups sugar plus 2 teaspoons	1	teaspoon vanilla
⅔	cup fresh lemon juice	1	tablespoon powdered sugar

In a saucepan, sprinkle gelatin over water to soften. Let sit 5 minutes; heat until clear. Cool. In a bowl, beat eggs and sugar until very thick, about 7 minutes. Combine juice, rind, and gelatin; add to egg mixture. Blend thoroughly. Freeze. Stir every 2 minutes until mixture thickens, about 6 to 8 minutes. Whip 1½ cups cream with vanilla. Fold into lemon mixture. Pour into a soufflé dish or individual dessert glasses. Refrigerate 2 to 3 hours. Whip remaining cream with powdered sugar and garnish soufflé before serving.

FRENCH CREAM

Serves 8

1	cup whipping cream	2	pints strawberries, *or* other
⅓	cup sifted powdered sugar		fresh fruit—blueberries,
½	cup sour cream		raspberries, grapes or
½	teaspoon grated fresh		peaches
	lemon rind	1	tablespoon sweet dark
2	ounces Grand Marnier		chocolate, grated

In a bowl, whip cream. Fold in sugar, sour cream, and rind. Add Grand Marnier. Arrange fruit in a serving bowl and top with French Cream. Garnish with chocolate.

CLASSIC CARAMEL CUSTARD

Serves 6

Preheat oven to 325°

3	eggs	½	teaspoon vanilla
1	cup sugar	⅛	teaspoon salt
2	cups half and half cream, scalded	¹⁄₁₆	teaspoon nutmeg, optional

In a bowl, beat eggs and ½ cup sugar. Slowly add half and half, whisking until well blended. Add vanilla and salt. Place six custard cups in 1 inch of warm water in a shallow pan. In a skillet, heat remaining ½ cup sugar until it dissolves and turns caramel color, being careful not to burn, about 10 minutes. Pour a little caramel into each cup and swirl before hardening.

Pour custard over caramel and sprinkle with nutmeg. Bake 1 hour, or until a knife inserted in center comes out clean. Cool and refrigerate. Before serving, loosen edges of custards with a thin knife and reverse onto plates. Drizzle excess caramel over tops.

MOUSSE IN A MINUTE

Serves 10

1	12-ounce bag semi-sweet chocolate chips	4	egg yolks
¼	cup sugar	1½	cups half and half cream
⅛	teaspoon salt	½	cup whipping cream
7	tablespoons strong coffee, *or* 3½ tablespoons coffee and 3½ tablespoons Kahlua		Chocolate shavings

Place chocolate chips, sugar, salt, coffee or Kahlua, and egg yolks into a blender. In saucepan, bring half and half to boiling point; pour immediately into blender. At high speed, blend well for several minutes until dark brown and smooth. Pour into 10 dessert cups (⅓ cup each). Chill several hours before serving.

Before serving, whip cream; place a dollop on each mousse and sprinkle with chocolate.

FRESH FIG MOUSSE

Serves 8

1	cup fresh figs, peeled	½	cup powdered sugar
3	tablespoons fresh lemon juice	1	cup whipping cream
		8	figs, peeled and halved

In a bowl, mash figs with a fork. Add juice and sugar and mix until all sugar is blended. Whip cream. Fold into fig mixture. Freeze in dessert cups until firm, 3 to 4 hours. Serve each topped with fig halves.

CHOCOLATE MOUSSE

Serves 4

4	eggs, separated	1	tablespoon brandy
4	ounces semi-sweet dark chocolate	1	tablespoon water
		½	cup whipping cream

Beat yolks until thick and creamy. In a saucepan, melt chocolate in water and brandy over very low heat. Slowly stir into yolks. Beat egg whites until stiff; fold into chocolate mixture with a metal spoon. Pour into pots de crème and refrigerate at least 4 hours. Whip cream and place dollop on each serving.

DRAMBUIE FLUMMERY

Serves 4

4	egg yolks	1	cup whipping cream
¼	cup sugar	2	egg whites
¼	cup Drambuie		

In a double boiler, beat yolks and sugar until mixture has thickened and increased in volume. Add Drambuie. Mixture will thicken and stand in soft peaks.

In a bowl, whip cream with egg whites until stiff peaks appear, then gently fold into yolk mixture until just blended. Pour into champagne glasses or dessert dishes and refrigerate several hours.

Topping

1	tablespoon slivered almonds	½	cup whipping cream
1	teaspoon butter		

In a small saucepan, sauté almonds in butter until nicely browned. Drain.

Before serving, top each dessert with a spoonful of whipped cream and sprinkle with toasted almonds.

BOURBON ON A CLOUD

Serves 8

Make ahead

1	envelope gelatin	1	cup whipping cream, whipped
12	tablespoons sugar		
3	eggs, separated	2	teaspoons semi-sweet chocolate shavings
¾	cup bourbon		

In a bowl, mix gelatin with 6 tablespoons sugar. In a saucepan, beat yolks slightly and slowly add bourbon. Add gelatin mixture and cook over low heat until sauce coats a spoon, stirring constantly. Cool. In a large bowl, beat egg whites until stiff, but not dry, gradually adding remaining sugar. Fold egg mixture into whites. Whip cream, reserving enough to decorate top of each serving. Fold cream into egg mixture. Spoon into dessert bowls and refrigerate at least 6 hours. Top each serving with a dollop of cream and garnish with chocolate.

PRALINE SAUCE

Makes 2½ cups

¾   cup white corn syrup
1½ cups light brown sugar,
    lightly packed
4   tablespoons butter

1   5.3-ounce can evaporated
    milk
¾   cup chopped pecans

Combine corn syrup, brown sugar, and butter; heat to boiling point. Remove from heat and cool. When lukewarm, add milk and pecans; blend well. Refrigerate.

PRALINE PARFAIT SAUCE

Makes 2 to 2½ cups

1½ cups dark corn syrup
½   cup dark brown sugar,
    packed
4   teaspoons flour
¼   teaspoon salt

2   tablespoons butter
1   cup water
1½ teaspoons vanilla
1   cup chopped pecans

In a saucepan, combine all ingredients except vanilla and pecans and boil 10 minutes. Remove from heat and add vanilla and pecans. Serve warm or cold. Good over ice cream or layered in parfait glasses with ice cream and topped with whipped cream.

YUM YUM CHOCOLATE SAUCE

Makes 3 cups

2   cups sugar
1   cup cocoa
1   cup milk

1   cup white corn syrup
2   tablespoons butter
1   teaspoon vanilla

In a saucepan, boil sugar, cocoa, milk, butter, and corn syrup and cook 5 minutes. Add vanilla. Serve hot on ice cream or cake. Keeps in refrigerator for several weeks.

HOT CHOCOLATE SAUCE

Makes 3 cups

1   8-ounce package
    unsweetened chocolate
2   cups sugar
2   tablespoons corn syrup,
    light or dark

1   13-ounce can evaporated
    milk
2   teaspoons vanilla
½   teaspoon salt

In top of double boiler, melt chocolate. Gradually add sugar until all is well mixed. Stir in corn syrup. Gradually add evaporated milk and mix until sauce is creamy. Remove from heat; stir in vanilla and salt.

HARD SAUCE

Makes 1 pint

2   sticks butter, softened
1   16-ounce box powdered
     sugar

1   egg, separated
¼   cup whiskey, *or* brandy

In a bowl, cream butter and sugar until smooth. In a separate bowl, beat egg yolk and add to butter mixture. In a bowl, beat egg white until stiff and fold into butter mixture. Gradually fold in whiskey, mixing well between additions. Refrigerate.

MERINGUE NESTS WITH RASPBERRY SAUCE

Preheat oven to 250°

Makes 8 3½-inch nests

Freezes well

Nests

4   egg whites, room
     temperature
½   teaspoon cream of tartar
1   cup sugar

1   teaspoon vanilla
1   cup chopped pecans

Beat egg whites until frothy. Add cream of tartar and vanilla; continue beating until doubled. Mix sugar, a tablespoon at a time, until meringue is stiff and glossy. Fold in pecans. Form individual meringues by dropping a spoonful (about 2 tablespoons) onto a cookie sheet lined with brown paper, and hollow center with back of spoon to form a nest. Bake 50 minutes. Turn oven off and leave 10 minutes to dry out. Remove, cool, and store in airtight container.

Raspberry Sauce

2   tablespoons cornstarch
⅔   cup sugar
2   pints fresh raspberries, *or*
     2 10-ounce packages
     frozen raspberries

2   tablespoons lemon juice,
     freshly squeezed

Mix cornstarch with sugar in top of a double boiler. Add raspberries and gradually stir until thickened and shiny. Add lemon juice. Refrigerate.

Serve meringue nest with a scoop of vanilla ice cream topped with raspberry sauce.

TANGERINE ICE

Serves 6

Make a day ahead

¾   cup light corn syrup
⅔   cup sugar
½   cup water
2   cups tangerine, *or* Louisiana Satsuma juice (reserve scraped out shells for serving containers)

3   tablespoons fresh lemon juice
2   egg whites
1   tablespoon chilled vodka, optional
     Satsuma rind, slivered

In a saucepan, combine corn syrup, sugar, and water. Boil 5 minutes. Cool 10 minutes. Add juices. Freeze in a shallow bowl until almost firm. Beat egg whites until soft peaks form. Remove mixture from freezer; transfer to a chilled bowl and beat until smooth. Fold in egg whites. Freeze until firm. If mixture has separated, beat again and return to freezer.

Serve splashed with vodka and garnished with rind.

LOUISIANA PECAN PRALINES

Makes 2 dozen

1   cup light brown sugar, not packed
1   cup sugar
½   cup evaporated milk
2   tablespoons butter

2   tablespoons light corn syrup
⅟₁₆ teaspoon salt
1   teaspoon vanilla
1¾   cups pecan halves

In a saucepan, using a wooden spoon, mix sugars, milk, butter, syrup, and salt. Cook to soft ball stage, about 10 minutes. Test by dropping a drop of mixture into cold water. Drop should be soft when picked up with fingers. Remove from heat; add vanilla and nuts. Beat until mixture begins to thicken, about 1 minute. Drop by teaspoonfuls onto buttered waxed paper.

EQUIVALENTS

Ingredient	Equivalent
3 medium apples	3 cups sliced apples
3 medium bananas	2½ cups sliced, 2 cups mashed banana
1 medium lemon	2 to 3 tablespoons juice and 2 teaspoons grated rind
1 medium lime................	1½ to 2 tablespoons juice
1 medium orange	⅓ cup juice and 2 tablespoons grated rind
4 medium peaches	2 cups sliced peaches
4 medium pears	2 cups sliced pears
1 quart strawberries	4 cups sliced strawberries
1 pound head cabbage	4½ cups shredded cabbage
1 pound carrots...............	3 cups shredded carrots
2 medium corn ears	1 cup whole kernel corn
1 large green pepper	1 cup diced green pepper
1 pound head lettuce	6¼ cups torn lettuce
8 ounces raw mushrooms	1 cup sliced cooked mushrooms
1 medium onion	½ cup chopped onion
3 medium white potatoes	2 cups cubed cooked or 1¾ cups mashed white potatoes
3 medium sweet potatoes......	3 cups sliced sweet potatoes
8 slices cooked bacon	½ cup crumbled bacon
1 pound American or Cheddar cheese	4 to 5 cups shredded cheese
4 ounces cheese..............	1 cup shredded cheese
5 large whole eggs	1 cup eggs
6 to 7 large eggs..............	1 cup egg whites
11 to 12 large eggs............	1 cup egg yolks
1 cup quick-cooking oats	1¾ cups cooked oats
1 cup uncooked long grain rice .	3 to 4 cups cooked rice
1 cup pre-cooked rice.........	2 cups cooked rice
1 pound coffee	40 cups perked coffee
1 pound pitted dates	2 to 3 cups chopped dates
1 pound all-purpose flour	4 cups flour
1 pound granulated sugar......	2 cups sugar
1 pound powdered sugar.......	3½ cups powdered sugar
1 pound brown sugar	2¼ cups firmly packed brown sugar
1 cup (4 ounces) uncooked macaroni	2¼ cups cooked macaroni
4 ounces uncooked noodles	2 cups cooked noodles
7 ounces uncooked spaghetti ..	4 cups cooked spaghetti
1 pound shelled nuts	4 cups chopped nuts

1 cup whipping cream	2 cups whipped cream
1 cup soft bread crumbs	2 slices fresh bread
1 pound crab in shell	¼ to 1 cup flaked crab
1½ pounds fresh, unpeeled shrimp	2 cups cooked, peeled, deveined shrimp
1 pound fresh small shrimp	35 or more shrimp
1 pound fresh medium shrimp	26 to 35 shrimp
1 pound fresh large shrimp	21 to 25 shrimp
1 pound fresh jumbo shrimp	less than 20 shrimp

Crackers

19 chocolate wafers	1 cup crumbs
14 graham cracker squares	1 cup fine crumbs
28 saltines	1 cup finely crushed crumbs
22 vanilla wafers	1 cup finely crushed crumbs

SUBSTITUTIONS

Recipe Ingredients	Substitution
1 cup sour or buttermilk	1 tablespoon vinegar or lemon juice plus sweet milk to make 1 cup
1 cup commercial sour cream	1 tablespoon lemon juice plus evaporated milk to equal 1 cup
1 cup yogurt	1 cup sour or buttermilk
1 whole egg	2 egg yolks plus 1 tablespoon water
1 tablespoon cornstarch	2 tablespoons all-purpose flour
1 teaspoon baking powder	½ teaspoon cream of tartar plus ¼ teaspoon soda
1 cup cake flour	1 cup all-purpose flour minus 2 tablespoons
1 cup self-rising flour	1 cup all-purpose flour plus 1 teaspoon baking powder and ½ teaspoon salt
1 cup honey	1¼ cups sugar plus ¼ cup liquid
1 ounce unsweetened chocolate	3 tablespoons cocoa plus 1 tablespoon butter or margarine
1 pound fresh mushrooms	6 ounces canned mushrooms
1 tablespoon fresh herbs	1 teaspoon ground or crushed dry herbs
1 teaspoon onion powder	2 teaspoons minced onion
1 clove fresh garlic	1 teaspoon garlic salt or ⅛ teaspoon garlic powder

MEASUREMENTS TO REMEMBER

3 teaspoons	=	1 tablespoon
4 tablespoons	=	¼ cup
8 tablespoons	=	½ cup
16 tablespoons	=	1 cup
5 tablespoons plus 1 teaspoon	=	⅓ cup
4 ounces	=	½ cup
8 ounces	=	1 cup
16 ounces	=	1 pound
1 ounce	=	2 tablespoons fat or liquid
2 cups fat	=	1 pound
2 cups	=	1 pint
1 pound butter	=	2 cups or 4 sticks
2 pints	=	1 quart
4 cups	=	1 quart

THE METRIC SYSTEM

2 cups	=	473 milliliters
1 cup	=	237 milliliters
¾ cup	=	177 milliliters
⅔ cup	=	157 milliliters
½ cup	=	118 milliliters
⅓ cup	=	79 milliliters
¼ cup	=	59 milliliters
1 tablespoon	=	15 milliliters
1 teaspoon	=	5 milliliters
1 fluid ounce	=	30 milliliters

How to Convert:

liters	x 2.1	= pints	kilograms	x 2.2	= pounds
liters	x 1.06	= quarts	grams	x .035	= ounces
cups	x .24	= liters	pounds	x .45	= kilograms
gallons	x 3.8	= liters	ounces	x 28	= grams

Temperatures:

250 degrees Fahrenheit = 121 degrees Celsius
300 degrees Fahrenheit = 149 degrees Celsius
350 degrees Fahrenheit = 177 degrees Celsius
400 degrees Fahrenheit = 205 degrees Celsius
450 degrees Fahrenheit = 232 degrees Celsius

INDEX

The Junior League of New Orleans presents

Louisiana Cookery for Modern Kitchens

Two of the most insistent reminders of Louisiana's past are her cuisine and her plantations. Each represents a way of life that time and tragedy have altered, but not destroyed. As this beautiful and unusual book shows, far from being mere poignant memories, Louisiana's great mansions and her food are very much a part of life today.

And, here, in the first book of its kind, the two traditions are brought together. First, the reader is introduced to twenty-nine of Louisiana's extravagant plantations — each accompanied by an evocative line drawing by M. Dell Weller, a brief historical note, and directions for motorists on how to find each one — and then to more than three hundred recipes for creating the kind of meals that were once served in them.

The guidebook section of the book takes you on a sentimental journey of townhouse and plantation mansions of yesteryear in New Orleans' French Quarter and along the peaceful bayous of the Louisiana countryside.

In the recipe section, the Junior League of New Orleans presents a collection of 300 time-honored recipes which are rich in the exciting flavors of Creole cookery, echoing Louisiana's heritage of highly spiced French, Spanish and West Indian cuisine interlaced with the hardy fare of the state's northern settlements. Crawfish Bisque (a rich, thick savory sauce in which spicy stuffed crawfish float), Jambalaya (the original Creole favorite, with ham, sausage, shrimp, oysters and highly flavored rice) and Grillades (pieces of veal or beef simmered to tender perfection in a dark, rich sauce) are just a few of the authentic recipes which the Junior League has adapted for modern kitchens. All the courses are covered, from appetizer and party breads to entrees and triumphant desserts, with recipes which have been prepared in Louisiana kitchens since plantation days.

There is not other book quite like THE PLANTATION COOKBOOK. Whether you are traveling down a backroad to one of Louisiana's stately plantation homes or preparing a famous Creole dish, you are off on an adventure into one of the most unique legacies of America's past.

Junior League of New Orleans Publications
4319 Carondelet Street
New Orleans, Louisiana 70115

Please send _____ copies of **JAMBALAYA**
    @ $11.95 per copy   _____

Please send _____ copies of **THE PLANTATION**
    COOKBOOK @ $17.95 per copy   _____

(Louisiana residents add 3% tax.)   _____

Gift wrap @ 50¢ per book   _____

Shipping and handling @ $2.00 per book   _____

Total enclosed   _____

Visa, Mastercard_____ Expiration Date _____
Make check payable to Junior League of New Orleans Publications. (Sorry, no C.O.D.'s. All orders must be prepaid.)

Name _____

Address _____

City _____ State _____ Zip ___
(No P.O. Box addresses, please)

Junior League of New Orleans Publications
4319 Carondelet Street
New Orleans, Louisiana 70115

Please send _____ copies of **JAMBALAYA**
    @ $11.95 per copy   _____

Please send _____ copies of **THE PLANTATION**
    COOKBOOK @ $17.95 per copy   _____

(Louisiana residents add 3% tax.)   _____

Gift wrap @ 50¢ per book   _____

Shipping and handling @ $2.00 per book   _____

Total enclosed   _____

Visa, Mastercard _____ Expiration Date _____
Make check payable to Junior League of New Orleans Publications. (Sorry, no C.O.D.'s. All orders must be prepaid.)

Name _____

Address _____

City _____ State _____ Zip ___
(No P.O. Box addresses, please)

Names and addresses of bookstores, gift shops, etc. in your area would be appreciated.

Names and addresses of bookstores, gift shops, etc., in your area would be appreciated.

Junior League of New Orleans Publications
4319 Carondelet Street
New Orleans, Louisiana 70115

Please send _____ copies of **JAMBALAYA**
    @ $11.95 per copy   _____

Please send _____ copies of **THE PLANTATION**
    COOKBOOK @ $17.95 per copy   _____

(Louisiana residents add 3% tax.)   _____

Gift wrap @ 50¢ per book   _____

Shipping and handling @ $2.00 per book   _____

Total enclosed   _____

Visa, Mastercard_____ Expiration Date _____
Make check payable to Junior League of New Orleans Publications. (Sorry, no C.O.D.'s. All orders must be prepaid.)

Name _____

Address _____

City _____ State _____ Zip ___
(No P.O. Box addresses, please)

Junior League of New Orleans Publications
4319 Carondelet Street
New Orleans, Louisiana 70115

Please send _____ copies of **JAMBALAYA**
    @ $11.95 per copy   _____

Please send _____ copies of **THE PLANTATION**
    COOKBOOK @ $17.95 per copy   _____

(Louisiana residents add 3% tax.)   _____

Gift wrap @ 50¢ per book   _____

Shipping and handling @ $2.00 per book   _____

Total enclosed   _____

Visa, Mastercard _____ Expiration Date _____
Make check payable to Junior League of New Orleans Publications. (Sorry, no C.O.D.'s. All orders must be prepaid.)

Name _____

Address _____

City _____ State _____ Zip ___
(No P.O. Box addresses, please)

Names and addresses of bookstores, gift shops, etc. in your area would be appreciated.

Names and addresses of bookstores, gift shops, etc., in your area would be appreciated.

**Junior League of New Orleans Publications
4319 Carondelet Street
New Orleans, Louisiana 70115**

Please send _____ copies of **JAMBALAYA**
  @ $11.95 per copy   _____

Please send _____ copies of **THE PLANTATION
  COOKBOOK** @ $17.95 per copy   _____

(Louisiana residents add 3% tax.)   _____

Gift wrap @ 50¢ per book   _____

Shipping and handling @ $2.00 per book   _____

Total enclosed   _____

Visa, Mastercard_____ Expiration Date _____
Make check payable to Junior League of New Orleans Publications. (Sorry, no C.O.D.'s. All orders must be prepaid.)

Name _____

Address _____

City _____ State _____ Zip ___
(No P.O. Box addresses, please)

**Junior League of New Orleans Publications
4319 Carondelet Street
New Orleans, Louisiana 70115**

Please send _____ copies of **JAMBALAYA**
  @ $11.95 per copy   _____

Please send _____ copies of **THE PLANTATION
  COOKBOOK** @ $17.95 per copy   _____

(Louisiana residents add 3% tax.)   _____

Gift wrap @ 50¢ per book   _____

Shipping and handling @ $2.00 per book   _____

Total enclosed   _____

Visa, Mastercard _____ Expiration Date _____
Make check payable to Junior League of New Orleans Publications. (Sorry, no C.O.D.'s. All orders must be prepaid.)

Name _____

Address _____

City _____ State _____ Zip ___
(No P.O. Box addresses, please)